THE REAL WAGNER

THE
REAL
WAGNER

Rudolph Sabor

ANDRE DEUTSCH

The author dedicates this book
with gratitude to the Bayreuth Festival

First published in Great Britain 1987
by André Deutsch Ltd
105–106 Great Russell Street, London WC1B 3LJ
Copyright © 1987 by Rudolph Sabor
All rights reserved

British Library Cataloguing in Publication Data

Sabor, Rudolph
The real Wagner.
1. Wagner, Richard. 1813–1883.   2. Composers
— Germany — Biography
I. Title
782.1'092'4   ML410.W1

ISBN 0–233–97870–4

Printed in Great Britain by
Ebenezer Baylis & Son Limited
Worcester

CONTENTS

ACKNOWLEDGEMENTS

During the preparation of *The Real Wagner* several people have helped me in several different ways. The manuscript has been read by Dr Manfred Eger, curator of the Richard Wagner Museum, Bayreuth; by Dr Oswald Bauer, then director of the press buro at the Bayreuther Festspiele; by Professor Uwe Faerber of the Freie Universität, Berlin; and by Dr Peter Sabor of Queen's University, Kingston, Ontario. I have had the advantage of their erudition, and I have greatly profited from their detailed comments and cautions. It is impossible for me to speak too highly of the active assistance I have received from Dr Maurice Pearton, London, and Lilian Banner, Eltham, whose linguistic competence was frequently called upon and readily put at the author's disposal. Maurice Pearton's translation of Wolfgang Wagner's Foreword is a sample of his skill. Monika Sabor, Cardiff, has been untiring in her painstaking scrutiny of the manuscript; her good counsel illuminates every chapter. I also wish to thank the copyright holders of all the pictorial material for their permission to reproduce the illustrations in this volume and, regarding portions of the text itself, but I would like to express my particular gratitude for permissions granted by V E B Deutscher Verlag für Musik, Leipzig; R. Piper Verlag, Munich; Paul List Verlag, Munich; G. Braun Verlag, Karlsruhe; and the Nationalarchiv der Richard Wagner Stiftung, Bayreuth. To my editor, Esther Whitby, I owe particular thanks for her encouragement of my work and for her adroit steerage of what has become our joint Wagnerian vessel. Steve Cox, in his capacity as copy editor, has been so unfailingly sure-footed that no author could wish for a more punctilious guardian of his manuscript. I offer my warmest thanks to Wolfgang Wagner whose wise productions of his grandfather's works have told me more about Richard Wagner than words can tell. To the members of my Wagner seminars at Crayford Manor I feel a particular obligation for their questing minds which compelled me to reconsider many current opinions, conjectures and doctrines. My greatest debt is to Emmi Sabor who double-checked every line in the manuscript and who with serenity and good humour has endured the rivalry of Richard Wagner for the best part of our lives.

LIST OF ILLUSTRATIONS

Note: NA/RWG refers to the Nationalarchiv der Richard-Wagner Stiftung/ Richard-Wagner-Gedenkstätte Bayreuth

FOREWORD

Wolfgang Wagner

Dear Mr Sabor,
            Your manuscript offers a most unusual Wagner text indeed. The title itself, 'The Real Wagner', can be construed as striking or scandalous, depending on the point of view. But as soon as one gets into the book, it is clear that you do not lay claim to know the real Wagner and then present him to the reader, but that, varying the words of Pilate, you ask 'where is the truth?'; the response, the judgement, rests with the reader himself. I know of no book in the extensive literature on Wagner which attempts to lay hold of his complex personality by such an approach; on the one hand his frequently unconsidered opinions inspired by the spontaneity of the moment and on the other the highest forms of artistic concentration evidenced in his works. In my view, a documentation of this kind is timely, for it is only since the publication of Cosima Wagner's diaries – the last great biographical source, open to research since 1976 – that all significant documents for the biography of Richard Wagner are at hand.

It cannot have been an easy task to grasp the immense documentary material, to sift it and evaluate each item to decide what to include in the text and what to leave out. But an approach to the personality as a whole and its often insoluble contradictions can only be made when one presents the widest possible spectrum of personal statements. In face of the complexity of the facts, scepticism and caution are needed; they do not simplify the range of problems but, on the other hand, they do guard against a precipitate and facile judgement. The procedure of weighing a 'case' was once a sound tradition in our culture but, unfortunately, it has now fallen into disuse in many areas. The Romans expressed it, '*sine ira et studio*', the British use the notion 'fair', and it is not inappropriate to allow Richard Wagner himself to comment, as he lets Hans Sachs say to the narrow-minded and jealous Beckmesser, 'Let neither hatred nor love interfere with your judgement.'

You have dedicated your book 'with gratitude' to the Bayreuth Festival. I sense in that a meaning and a link. It was my brother's and my task – at first together, now mine alone – always to renew the quest for 'the real Wagner' in his work and its interpretation, on the stage. Since the beginning of New Bayreuth in 1951, we too have gone back into the sources, to the documents, and have tried to get at his 'true' intentions, without the interpretative burden of the past hundred years.

1

Doubtless much was achieved then, but misunderstandings and misuse erected barriers behind which the 'real Wagner' as he expressed himself was often hardly to be recognised.

A performance or book can provide the spectator or reader with understanding and insight, but one can expect no ultimate, permanently valid solutions. Everyone must seek for the true Wagner himself. Your book is an outstanding signpost for this quest, suited to the extraordinary character of its subject and as entertaining as it is instructive.

Yours sincerely,
Wolfgang Wagner

CHRONOLOGY

1813 Wilhelm Richard Wagner born in Leipzig (22.5).

Father Friedrich Wagner, police official, dies.

1814 Mother Johanna Rosine marries Ludwig Geyer, poet, painter and actor (28.8).

Family moves to Dresden.

1815 Cäcilie, Wagner's half-sister, is born.

1817 Attends Cantor Schmidt's Infant School in Dresden.

1820 Boards with Pastor Wetzel in Possendorf, near Dresden.

1821 Ludwig Geyer dies. ('He was on his death bed . . . I played a tune on the piano for him. He asked my mother, "Do you think he has a talent for music"?': *Mein Leben*.)

Boards with Geyer's brother Carl, goldsmith in Eisleben.

1822 Attends school (Kreuzschule) in Dresden, as Wilhelm Richard Geyer.

1823 Shows interest for ancient mythology.

1825 Performs Weber's *Freischütz* at home with friends.

1826 Writes and burns his first tragedy.

Translates the first three books of Homer's *Odyssey* into German.

Stays behind in Dresden, as mother and sisters Rosalie, Klara, Ottilie and Cäcilie move to Prague, where Rosalie (1803–37) starts her theatrical career.

1827 Begins his tragedy, *Leubald*.

Confirmed in Dresden.

Drops the name Geyer.

Settles with the rest of the family in Leipzig.

1828 Attends school (Nikolai Gymnasium) in Leipzig, as Richard Wagner.

Leubald completed.

Composition lessons with Gottlieb Müller.

1829 Compositions: Piano Sonata in D minor
String Quartet in D major
Piano Sonata in F minor.

1830 Copies Beethoven's Ninth Symphony and makes piano arrangement.

Leaves Nikolai Gymnasium and attends Thomas-Schule in Leipzig.

Offers piano arrangement of Ninth Symphony to the music publisher Schott in Mainz.

Compositions: Overture in B flat major (*Drum Beat*)
Overture to *The Bride of Messina*
Overture in C major.

Overture in B flat major performed in Leipzig. ('The audience was startled': *Mein Leben*.)

1831 Student of Music at Leipzig University.

Neglects, then terminates his studies.

Composition lessons with Theodor Weinlig, Cantor at Thomas-Schule (Johann Sebastian Bach's former post).

Compositions: Seven *Kompositionen* to Goethe's *Faust*
Piano Sonata in B flat major for 4 hands
Piano Sonata in B flat major
Concert Overture in D minor
Piano Fantasia in F sharp minor.

Concert Overture in D minor performed in Leipzig.

1832 Compositions: Piano Sonata in A major
Overture *King Enzio*
Concert Overture in C major
Symphony in C major
Song: 'Abendglocken' (Evening Bells), to words by his
friend Theodor Apel
Introduction, Chorus and Septet of his first opera, *Die
Hochzeit* (The Wedding), later abandoned.

Piano Sonata in B flat major is published.

Overture *King Enzio* performed in Leipzig. ('The audience was not particularly worried': *Mein Leben*.)

Concert Overture in C major performed in Leipzig.

Travels to Vienna and Pravonin (near Prague). Falls in love with daughter of Count Pachta.

Writes libretto to his opera *Die Hochzeit*. ('Rosalie disliked it, so I destroyed it': *Mein Leben*.)

Symphony in C major performed in Prague.

Returns to Leipzig.

1833 Writes libretto to his first completed opera, *Die Feen* (The Fairies).

Symphony in C major performed in Leipzig. ('Reviewed by all the newspapers, none of them actually malicious': *Mein Leben*.)

Post as chorus master in Würzburg.

Works at composition of *Die Feen*.

1834 *Die Feen* completed, but remains unperformed until 1888.

Leaves his post at Würzburg and returns to Leipzig.

Works at libretto for his next opera, *Das Liebesverbot* (The Ban on Love), after Shakespeare's *Measure for Measure*.

Post as musical director with travelling company in Lauchstädt, where he first meets his future wife, the actress Minna Planer. ('I ran into her by her front door . . . and immediately rented a room in the house': *Mein Leben*.)

Musical director at Magdeburg theatre.

1835 Composes *Columbus* Overture.

On his summer travels he visits Bayreuth, where he is to build his festival theatre, some forty years later.

Begins his diary, the *Rote Brieftasche* (Red Notebook).

1836 *Das Liebesverbot* completed.

First performance at Magdeburg of *Das Liebesverbot*, renamed *The Novice of Palermo*, due to the censor's objections.

Composes *Polonia* Overture.

Travels to Königsberg (Eastern Prussia), hoping to secure a post.

Marries Minna Planer at Königsberg (24.11).

1837 Composes *Rule Britannia* Overture.

Post as musical director at Königsberg theatre.

Minna elopes with Herr Dietrich, but returns after three weeks.

Minna elopes for a second time, again with Dietrich, but resumes married life after three months.

Begins work on libretto to *Rienzi*.

Pursued by creditors, he travels to Riga, where his conducting is well received. Minna joins him and retires as an actress. ('She confessed the error of her ways and begged my forgiveness': *Mein Leben*.)

Rosalie Wagner dies.

Cosima, daughter of Franz Liszt and Countess d'Agoult, is born (25.12).

1838 Libretto to *Rienzi* completed.

Composition of *Rienzi* begun.

Composes song, 'Der Tannenbaum' (Fir Tree).

Conducts a series of successful concerts in Riga in which he includes his own compositions.

1839 He loses his post as conductor at Riga.

To escape his creditors, he crosses the Russian border, with Minna and Robber, their Newfoundland dog.

Perilous sea journey (24 days!) to London. Arrives 12.8.

Lodges at King's Arms, Old Compton Street. He visits both Houses of Parliament. ('With horror did we experience the ghost-like atmosphere of a Sunday in London': *Mein Leben*.)

Travels to Boulogne; first meeting with Meyerbeer.

Travels to Paris and lodges in Rue de la Tonnellerie.

Unsuccessful performance in Paris of his *Columbus* Overture.

1840 *Faust* Overture completed.

Compositions of French poems, including 'Les deux Grenadiers'.

Growing debts force him to do journalistic work and make arrangements of popular music for publisher Maurice Schlesinger.

Moves to Rue de Helder.

Article: 'On German Music' in Schlesinger's *Gazette Musicale de Paris*.

Rienzi completed.

Novella: *A Pilgrimage to Beethoven*.

First meeting with Franz Liszt.

1841 Novella: *An End in Paris* (closes with: 'I believe in God, Mozart and Beethoven').

'Reports from Paris' for a Dresden journal.

Libretto (original version) to *Der fliegende Holländer* completed.

Meyerbeer recommends *Rienzi* to Dresden Opera who accept the work.

Essay: 'The Artist and the Public'.

Moves to Meudon, near Paris ('An escape from the impossible to the inconceivable': *Mein Leben*); returns to Paris six months later.

Der fliegende Holländer completed.

1842 Moves from Paris to Dresden, and visits family in Leipzig. ('I wanted to return to Germany which appeared to me now in a quite different, ideal light': *Mein Leben*.)

Begins work on prose sketch to *Tannhäuser*.

First performance of *Rienzi* in Dresden, with Josef Tichatschek as Rienzi and Wilhelmine Schröder-Devrient as Adriano; immense success.

1843 First performance, under Wagner's direction, of *Der fliegende Holländer* at Dresden, with Schröder-Devrient as Senta.

Autobiographic Sketch published in Leipzig journal.

Appointment as Royal Saxon Court Conductor. ('The audience with the King was the climax of my fortunate career in Dresden; after that, I encountered adversity in its varied guises': *Mein Leben*.)

Composition: *Das Liebesmahl der Apostel* (The Love Feast of the Apostles, an oratorio).

First performance of *Das Liebesmahl der Apostel* in the Frauenkirche, Dresden.

Wagner household established in Ostra Allee, Dresden.

1844 *Der fliegende Holländer* performed in Berlin, attended by royalty, conducted by the composer to public acclaim, but hostile press.

Performance of *Rienzi* in Hamburg, conducted by the composer.

Further work on *Tannhäuser*.

Weber's remains brought from London to Dresden, with Wagner's *Trauermusik* (Funeral Music) at the grave of the composer he revered.

1845 *Tannhäuser* completed.

Writes prose sketch for *Die Meistersinger von Nürnberg*.

Prose sketch for *Lohengrin* completed.

The future King Ludwig II of Bavaria is born (25.8).

First performance of *Tannhäuser* at Dresden Court Theatre, under Wagner, with Tichatschek as Tannhäuser, Schröder-Devrient as Venus, and Wagner's niece Johanna as Elisabeth.

1846 Wagner's performance, in Dresden, of Beethoven's Ninth Symphony. ('The unexpectedly huge success . . . strengthened my conviction that I had the ability and the power to accomplish anything, as long as I put my mind to it': *Mein Leben*.)

First meeting between Wagner and Hans von Bülow (1830–94).

Dresden opera authorities make large grant, repayable over ten years, to enable Wagner to pay off his debts.

1847 Continued work on *Lohengrin*.

In Berlin with Minna, to prepare performance of *Rienzi*.

Rienzi at Berlin Court Opera, conducted by the composer, with two repeat performances. Wagner receives no fee. ('The Berlin critics pitched into me, of course, and tried to destroy my work': *Mein Leben*.)

1848 Wagner's mother dies, aged 74.

First meeting between Wagner and Jessie Laussot, with whom he is to fall in love two years later.

Lohengrin completed.

Essay: 'What is the Relation between Republican Ambitions and the Monarchy?'

Prose sketch for the libretti of his future *Der Ring des Nibelungen*.

Poem of *Siegfried's Tod*, first version (later to be renamed *Götterdämmerung*).

1849 Sketch for projected drama, *Jesus von Nazareth*, which depicts Jesus as a social revolutionary.

Essays: 'Man and Existing Society'
'The Revolution'
'The Art-work of the Future'.

King of Saxony dissolves both chambers of deputies, triggering off Dresden uprising in which Wagner is actively involved.

The uprising is quelled and Wagner escapes a police warrant, first to Liszt in Weimar, then with forged passport, as Prof. Werder from Berlin, into exile in Switzerland.

Minna considers whether to join him. ('What can you offer me now?')

Minna joins him in Rorschach.

Essay: 'Art and Revolution'.

1850 Prose sketch for an opera intended for Paris, *Wieland der Schmied* (Wieland the Blacksmith).

Entanglement with Jessie Laussot in Bordeaux. Plans to elope with her and informs Minna of his intention to leave her. The adventure collapses, and he returns to Minna in Zurich.

Essay: 'Judaism in Music', published anonymously.

First performance of *Lohengrin* at Weimar, under Liszt. As an exile, Wagner is unable to attend.

1851 Extended Essay: *Opera and Drama*.

Poem (first version) of *Der junge Siegfried* completed (later renamed *Siegfried*).

First version of his autobiographical account, *A Communication to my Friends*, is completed.

Water cure in Albisbrunn. ('My faith in this method increased every day': *Mein Leben.*)

Frau Julie Ritter, his Swiss patron, grants a substantial annual pension.

1852 First meeting with Otto and Mathilde Wesendonck.

Conducts four performances of *Der fliegende Holländer* in Zurich.

Poem (first version) of *Die Walküre* completed.

One month's holiday with Minna in Italy.

Poem (first version) of *Das Rheingold* completed.

He reads the four poems of *Der Ring des Nibelungen* to friends in Mariafeld, near Zurich.

1853 His intimate friend Theodor Uhlig dies in Dresden, aged 31.

Second reading of *Der Ring des Nibelungen* to friends in Zurich.

Conducts three concerts in Zurich, including sections from *Rienzi, Der fliegende Holländer, Tannhäuser* and *Lohengrin*.

Polka for Mathilde Wesendonck completed.

Piano Sonata for Mathilde Wesendonck completed.

Alpine walking tour with the poet Georg Herwegh.

At a meeting with Liszt in Paris, he sees Liszt's daughter Cosima, aged 16, for the first time.

Composition sketch of *Rheingold* begun.

1854 Begins work on composition of *Walküre*.

Minna travels to Germany to visit relations.

Rheingold completed.

Minna returns from Germany to Zurich.

Conceives plan for *Tristan und Isolde*. ('On returning from one of my walks I jotted down the contents of three acts into which I intended to concentrate the whole material': *Mein Leben*.)

1855 *Faust Overture* (second version) completed.

Travels, alone, to London (26.2).

Conducts eight concerts in London, receives public acclaim but poor press notices (March to June).

Friendly reception, during interval of seventh concert, by Queen Victoria and Prince Albert.

After returning from London, Richard and Minna take a month's holiday by Lake Lucerne.

He is plagued by facial erysipelas.

1856 *Walküre* completed.

Prose sketch for projected drama, *Die Sieger* (The Victors), with Buddhist background.

Continued health problems (erysipelas), followed by another water cure which brings some relief.

Begins work at composition of *Siegfried*.

On Liszt's 55th birthday, the first act of *Walküre* is performed privately, with Liszt at the piano and Wagner singing the parts of Siegmund and Hunding.

1857 First conception of *Parsifal*.

Move to Asyl (Sanctuary), a villa on the Wesendoncks' property near Zurich.

Work at *Siegfried* interrupted, after finishing orchestral sketch of second act, only to be continued after twelve years.

Hans von Bülow and Cosima Liszt are married (18.8). They spend three weeks of their honeymoon with the Wagners. Thus, the three most important women in Wagner's life are together: Minna, Mathilde and Cosima.

Poem (first version) of *Tristan und Isolde* completed.

Close relationship with Mathilde, based on mutual love and admiration. He gives her the first version of his poem of *Tristan und Isolde*.

Begins work on composition of *Tristan und Isolde*.

Composition of three of the *Wesendonck Lieder*, settings of poems by Mathilde.

1858 Estrangement between Minna and Mathilde. ('I had to inform Minna that because of her disobedience and her foolish behaviour towards our neighbour, Frau Wesendonck, our remaining here had become most doubtful': *Mein Leben*.)

Wagner travels to Paris and obtains the gift of an Erard grand piano from Mme Erard.

Returns to Asyl.

Two further *Wesendonck Lieder* complete the cycle.

Intolerable situation at Asyl, provoked by Minna's interception of Wagner's letter to Mathilde.

Minna leaves, to take a three months' cure for heart trouble at Brestenburg, by Lake Hallwyl.

Bülow and Cosima stay as guests at Asyl (21.7 to 16.8).

Wagner leaves Asyl (17.8) and travels to Geneva and Venice.

Minna returns to Germany (2.9).

Continued work in Venice on *Tristan und Isolde*.

1859 Travels from Venice to Milan and Lucerne, then stays for 24 hours with the Wesendoncks.

Returns to Lucerne and works on *Tristan und Isolde*.

Tristan und Isolde completed.

Four days as guest at the Wesendoncks'.

Plans for performing *Tannhäuser* in Paris.

Travels to Paris, where Minna joins him.

1860 Conducts three concerts in Paris, with music from *Der fliegende Holländer*, *Tannhäuser*, *Lohengrin* and *Tristan und Isolde*. Berlioz, Meyerbeer, Auber and Gounod attend.

Wilhelmine Schröder-Devrient dies, aged 55.

Minna takes health cure in Bad Soden (Rhineland).

Partial amnesty for Wagner: he may enter Germany with the exception of Saxony. He travels to Bad Soden, Frankfurt, Darmstadt, Heidelberg, Baden-Baden, Mannheim and Cologne, then returns with Minna to Paris.

Essay: 'Music of the Future'.

Paris Opera begins to rehearse *Tannhäuser*.

Daniela, Bülow's and Cosima's first child, is born (12.10).

Typhoid fever incapacitates Wagner for five weeks.

1861 Alterations to first act of *Tannhäuser* (extended Venus scene with Bacchanale) for Paris staging.

Tannhäuser at Paris Opera, but Wagner withdraws it after three performances. Hostile reception interrupts music, at times for over ten minutes. ('Minna had been recognised as my wife by her neighbours who proceeded to insult her; our faithful servant girl silenced one of the hooligans with a resounding *Schweinehund*': *Mein Leben*.)

Attends *Lohengrin* rehearsal and performance in Vienna and receives ovations.

Celebrates his 48th birthday with the Wesendoncks in Zurich.

Minna takes another cure at Bad Soden.

Tristan und Isolde rehearsals in Vienna.

Reads his prose sketch of *Die Meistersinger von Nürnberg* to friends at Mainz.

1862 Moves to Biebrich (Rhineland) where Minna joins him ('Ten days of hell': *Mein Leben*). Minna leaves again.

King of Saxony grants full amnesty.

Works at composition of *Meistersinger*.

First meeting with Mathilde Maier, aged 29, in music publisher Schott's house in Mainz.

Close relationship with this 'second Mathilde'.

Bülow and Cosima visit him at Biebrich.

With Bülow's help he studies the parts of Tristan and Isolde with Schnorr von Carolsfeld (tenor) and his wife Malwine (soprano).

Otto Wesendonck commissions Cäsar Willich to paint portrait of Wagner. Cosima reads to him during the sittings, and Otto presents the finished painting to Mathilde, while Wagner has a copy made for Minna.

Conducts his first *Lohengrin* at Frankfurt.

Visits Minna in Dresden, before final separation.

1863 Successful concert tour ($3\frac{1}{2}$ months) to Vienna, Prague, St Petersburg and Moscow.

Blandine, Bülow's and Cosima's second child, is born (20.3).

Moves into new home in Penzing, near Vienna, and furnishes it extravagantly.

Mathilde Maier resists his requests to move in. ('My invitation seemed to have alarmed her': *Mein Leben*.)

Further concerts in Budapest, Prague, Karlsruhe, Breslau and Vienna.

Visits the Bülows in Berlin. Richard and Cosima decide 'to belong solely to each other' (*Mein Leben*).

1864 Growing debts mislead him into issuing uncovered cheques.

Ludwig II (1845–86), aged 18, becomes King of Bavaria.

Evades creditors and debtors' prison.

First meeting between King Ludwig and Wagner. Outcome: friendship, cancellation of debts, special allowances, fixed salary and free housing.

Moves into Haus Pellet by Lake Starnberg.

Cosima visits him with both daughters and stays for two months. Bülow also arrives, one week after Cosima.

Essay: 'On State and Religion'.

Composition: *Huldigungsmarsch* (Homage March) for Ludwig's 19th birthday.

Moves to Munich.

Ludwig commissions *Der Ring des Nibelungen* for 30,000 gulden (appr. £90,000).

Bülow appointed Court Pianist, settles in Munich with family.

Wagner conducts first Munich performance of *Der fliegende Holländer* for Ludwig.

1865 Isolde, Wagner's and Cosima's first child, is born (10.4).

First performance of *Tristan und Isolde* at Munich, in presence of King Ludwig, with Schnorr von Carolsfeld and wife, conducted by Bülow. Public success but hostile press.

First meeting with Bruckner, who visits third performance of *Tristan und Isolde*.

Cosima begins Wagner's autobiography, *Mein Leben*, from his dictation.

Schnorr von Carolsfeld dies suddenly, aged 29.

Wagner begins his diary, *Das braune Buch* (The Brown Book).

Press attacks Wagner for his 'immoral' life and for draining the Bavarian exchequer; the dejected King advises Wagner to leave Munich temporarily.

Wagner departs to Switzerland.

1866 Minna dies in Dresden (25.1).

Ludwig wants to abdicate, but Wagner persuades him to persevere.

Wagner settles in Haus Tribschen by Lake Lucerne, financed by Ludwig.

Cosima moves, temporarily, into Tribschen, with Daniela, Blandine and Isolde. After a month, Bülow joins them. Three months later, all Bülows leave for Munich, but after another four weeks Cosima rejoins Wagner.

Ludwig visits Tribschen on Wagner's birthday and stays for two days.

Work continues on composition of *Meistersinger*.

1867 Ludwig engaged to cousin Sophie Charlotte.

Eva, Wagner's and Cosima's second child, is born (17.2).

Bülow appointed Court Conductor and Director of the Royal Music School (not yet established).

Cosima and children return to Bülow in Munich.

Series of articles: 'German Art and German Politics'.

Ludwig breaks his engagement to Sophie Charlotte.

Meistersinger completed. Wagner presents the score to Ludwig as Christmas gift.

1868 Essay: 'Recollections of Schnorr von Carolsfeld'.

Cosima returns to Tribschen, but leaves again after a few days.

Wagner travels to Munich to supervise *Meistersinger* rehearsals. He stays with the Bülows.

Wagner and Ludwig take a trip on Lake Lucerne in steamboat *Tristan*, to celebrate Wagner's 55th birthday.

First performance of *Meistersinger* at Munich, conducted by Bülow, with Wagner sharing the King's box.

Cosima returns to Tribschen.

With Cosima to Italy for a three weeks' stay.

Cosima joins her husband in Munich for the last time.

Sketches for projected drama, *Luthers Hochzeit* (Luther's Wedding).

Ludwig lays foundation stone to Castle Neuschwanstein.

First meeting between Wagner and Nietzsche.

Cosima and children settle in Tribschen.

Essay: 'A Remembrance of Rossini'.

Wagner presents the *Rienzi* score to Ludwig for Christmas.

1869 Cosima begins her diaries.

Composition of *Siegfried* taken up again, after twelve years.

Nietzsche's first visit to Tribschen.

Siegfried, Wagner's and Cosima's third child, is born (6.6).

First meeting with Judith Gautier (1846–1917), French novelist who is to have close relationship with Wagner between 1876 and 1878.

Ludwig orders first performance of *Rheingold* in Munich, against

Wagner's wishes, who does not want to split the *Ring*. (To the conductor: 'Hands off my score, sir, or may the devil take you!')

Work at composition of *Götterdämmerung*.

Essay: 'On Conducting'.

Composition: *Motto for the German Fire Service*.

Ludwig begins to build Castle Linderhof.

1870 Ludwig orders first performance of *Walküre* in Munich, again in spite of Wagner's protest.

Bülow and Cosima divorced (18.7).

Wagner and Cosima married (25.8).

Essay: *Beethoven*.

Play: A *Capitulation*, a somewhat cheap caricature of the French, who were losing the Franco-Prussian war.

Composition: *Siegfried Idyll*.

Performance of *Siegfried Idyll* on Tribschen staircase for Cosima's 33rd birthday (25.12).

1871 Poem: 'To the German Army before Paris'.

Siegfried completed.

Composition: *Kaisermarsch*.

Paper: 'The Destiny of Opera', read to the Royal Academy of Arts, Berlin.

Conducts Berlin concert, with German Emperor attending.

Article: 'On performing the Stage Festival *Der Ring des Nibelungen*'.

Views Bayreuth opera house, but rejects it as unsuitable for his works. Plans to build his own Festival Theatre in Bayreuth.

Bayreuth town council donates land for building.

1872 Moves from Tribschen to Bayreuth.

Foundation stone ceremony in Bayreuth, on Wagner's 59th birthday, with performance of Beethoven's Ninth Symphony, conducted by Wagner.

Essay: 'On Actors and Singers'.

Liszt visits Richard and Cosima in Bayreuth.

Extended travel with Cosima, visiting many opera houses in search of suitable artists for future Bayreuth Festival.

1873 Reads poem of *Götterdämmerung* to friends and patrons in Berlin.

Concert tour: Hamburg, Berlin and Cologne.

Essay: 'On Performing Beethoven's Ninth Symphony'.

Bruckner visits Bayreuth and dedicates his Third Symphony to Wagner.

Composition: *Kinderkatechismus* (Catechism for children), for four children's voices and piano, in praise of Cosima.

1874 Bayreuth building crisis, owing to lack of funds.

Ludwig guarantees further building operations with a generous credit.

Wagner and family move into their newly built Haus Wahnfried (*Wahn* = illusion, delusion; *Fried(e)* = peace, rest).

Preliminary *Ring* rehearsals with the first batch of singers and conductor Hans Richter.

Götterdämmerung completed, and with it the whole *Ring* cycle, 26 years after the first sketch.

1875 Extended concert tours in aid of Bayreuth building fund: Vienna, Budapest (together with Liszt), Vienna, Berlin, Vienna.

Series of rehearsals for next year's opening of the Festspielhaus, ending with banquet for 140 artists in the gardens of Haus Wahnfried.

He produces and attends performance of *Tannhäuser* in Vienna, conducted by Richter.

He produces and attends performance of *Lohengrin* in Vienna, conducted by Richter.

1876 Composition: *Grand Festival March in Celebration of the Centenary of the American Declaration of Independence*, commissioned by Philadelphia for a fee of 5,000 dollars. ('Richard is unable to visualise anything for this composition . . . except the 5,000 dollars': *Cosima's Diaries*.)

Performance of *Tristan und Isolde* in Vienna, in aid of Bayreuth fund.

Intensive Festspiele rehearsals at Bayreuth.

Nietzsche publishes *Wagner at Bayreuth*.

Ludwig attends dress rehearsals of the *Ring* in Bayreuth.

Bayreuth Festspiele open with first performance of *Ring* cycle, followed by two further cycles, all conducted by Richter. Kaiser Wilhelm I, Emperor Dom Pedro II of Brazil, the King of Württemberg, Tchaikovsky, Bruckner, Otto and Mathilde Wesendonck, Mathilde Maier and Judith Gautier are amongst the guests.

Ardent relationship with Judith Gautier. ('How I wish I could kiss you again, dear one, sweet one!': Letter to Judith.)

Wagner's and Cosima's joy over the artistic success of the Festspiele gives way to deep depression over the massive deficit (almost £800,000).

Wagner and family travel to Italy for three months.

1877 Festspiel plans for this year are dropped, owing to disastrous financial outcome.

First performance of *Der fliegende Holländer* in New York.

Continued work on *Parsifal*.

With Cosima to London, where he conducts eight concerts at the Albert Hall (7.5 to 29.5).

Queen Victoria receives Wagner at Windsor.

First plans to emigrate to the USA.

Return to Germany and reading of *Parsifal* poem to friends in Heidelberg.

In his Bayreuth speech to Festspiel supporters he envisages performing all his works, from *Holländer* to *Parsifal*, from 1880 to 1883 (he will only live to see one more Festspiel season, in 1882).

1878 Nietzsche breaks with Wagner. ('How bad the world has become. It has infected a promising person like Nietzsche with its own badness': *Cosima's Diaries*.)

King Ludwig begins to build Castle Herrenchiemsee.

Essays: 'Public and Popularity'
        'The Public in Time and Space'
        'A Retrospect of the Stage Festival of 1876'.

He conducts first and private performance of the Prelude to *Parsifal* in the salon of Haus Wahnfried.

1879 Continued work on *Parsifal*.
Essays: 'Shall We Hope?'
        'On Poetry and Composition'.

Next year's Festspiel season declared impracticable.

Liszt stays at Wahnfried for ten days.

1880 Wagner and family in Italy, from January to October: Naples, Ravello, Rome, Perugia, Siena and Venice.

Essay: 'Religion and Art'.

Ludwig puts orchestra and chorus of his court opera at Wagner's disposal for next Festspiel season.

Wagner and Cosima attend Munich performances of *Der fliegende Holländer*, *Tristan und Isolde* and *Lohengrin*.

He conducts the Prelude to *Parsifal* in Munich, with Ludwig as sole guest. This is their last meeting.

Continued work on *Parsifal*. ('*Parsifal* I want to finish, and then symphonies': *Cosima's Diaries*.)

1881 Essay: 'Know Thyself'.

Wagner and Cosima attend first Berlin performances of the *Ring*.

Essay: 'Heroism and Christianity'.

Autumn visitors at Wahnfried: Liszt and Judith Gautier.

Frequent indispositions (heart complaints) delay completion of *Parsifal*.

Extended stay in Italy, from November 1881 to April 1882, with family: Palermo, Acireale, Venice.

1882 *Parsifal* completed (13.1) in Palermo.

Renoir paints Wagner.

Return to Bayreuth (1.5).

Parsifal rehearsals in the Festspielhaus.

Wagner's last (platonic?) attachment: Carrie Pringle, English singer, flower maiden in *Parsifal* (circumstances not reliably documented).

Wagner's last Festspiel season: 16 performances of *Parsifal*, conducted by Hermann Levi and Franz Fischer, with Wagner conducting the final scene of the third act in the last performance.

A fortnight after the end of the Festspiel season, Wagner and family travel to Venice, where he is to die early next year.

Liszt stays with the Wagners for eight weeks.

Wagner conducts his Symphony in C major (after almost 50 years) for Cosima's birthday in the Teatro la Fenice.

1883 He intends to revise *Tannhäuser*.

Hermann Levi visits Venice and stays until the day before Wagner's death.

Fragment: 'The Feminine Element in Mankind'. After the words *Liebe-Tragik*, the pen drops from his hand.

Wagner dies at half past three in the afternoon (13.2).

Funeral in Bayreuth (18.2).

1884–1906 Cosima directs the Festspiele.

1886 King Ludwig drowns in Lake Starnberg.

Daniela marries Henry Thode.

Liszt dies in Bayreuth.

1894 Bülow dies in Cairo.

1900 Nietzsche dies in Weimar.

Isolde marries Franz Beidler.

1902 Mathilde Wesendonck dies in Traunblick (Austria).

1907–30 Siegfried directs the Festspiele.

1908 Eva marries Houston Stewart Chamberlain.

1910 Mathilde Maier dies in Mainz.

1914 Daniela divorces Thode.

1915 Siegfried marries Winifred Williams.

1917 Judith Gautier dies in St Enoyat.

1919 Isolde dies in Munich.

1930 Cosima dies in Bayreuth.

Siegfried dies in Bayreuth.

1940 Daniela dies in Bayreuth.

1941 Blandine dies in Berlin.

1942 Eva dies in Bayreuth.

PRINCIPAL CHARACTERS

Hans von Bülow

8.1.1830–12.2.1894

Outstanding pianist (pupil of Liszt) and conductor (pupil of Wagner). Takes up music as career against his parents' wishes. Admires both his teachers, and marries Liszt's daughter Cosima in 1857. Children: Daniela (1860–1940) and Blandine (1863–1941). Bavarian Court Kapellmeister, he is the first conductor of *Tristan und Isolde* and of *Meistersinger* at Munich. Divorced in 1870, when Cosima marries Wagner. Second marriage to actress Marie Schanzer (1857–1941) in 1882. Becomes chief conductor of Berlin Philharmonic Orchestra. Dies in Cairo.

Judith Gautier

25.8.1846–26.12.1917

Of French-Italian parentage, marries writer Catulle Mendès, whom she later divorces. Visits the Wagners at Tribschen and during the Bayreuth Festivals. Has love affair with Wagner between 1876 and 1878. Translates *Parsifal* into French, writes poetry, novels and recollections, *Wagner at Home*.

Jessie Laussot

born 1829*

Daughter of London solicitor. First husband Eugène Laussot, wine merchant. Second husband, Karl Hillebrand, historian. Falls in love with Wagner in 1850, but breaks with him, after their planned escape to Greece or Asia Minor fails.

* The date of her death is unknown.

Hermann Levi

7.11.1839–13.5.1900

Son of rabbi, studies conducting and composition. Court Kapellmeister at Karlsruhe and Munich, conducts *Parsifal* at Bayreuth from 1882 to 1894. Excellent translator of Italian opera libretti into German. Wagner's attempts to convert him to Christianity were unsuccessful.

Franz Liszt

22.10.1811–31.7.1886

Composer, conductor and leading pianist of his time. First liaison with Countess Marie d'Agoult (the novelist Daniel Stern): children Blandine, Cosima and Daniel. Second liaison with Princess Carolyne Sayn-Wittgenstein: childless. Meets Wagner in Paris in 1840, later becomes his intimate friend and supports him financially and spiritually. Dies during Bayreuth Festival 1886. Compositions include Symphonic Poems, Symphonies, Piano Concertos, Hungarian Rhapsodies and Piano Transcriptions.

Ludwig II

25.8.1845–13.6.1886

Ascends Bavarian throne in 1864, aged 18. Summons Wagner to his Munich Court, gives him substantial material help and, in 1874, saves the Bayreuth Festival with a generous credit. Builds castles Neuschwanstein, Linderhof and Herrenchiemsee. Declared insane, deposed, and drowns (suicide, murder or accident?) in Lake Starnberg.

Mathilde Maier

1833–1910

Highly intelligent lawyer's daughter in Mainz, meets Wagner at the house of Schott, the music publisher. Ardent friendship with Wagner mirrored in his letters to this second Mathilde (Frau Wesendonck was the first), but declines several invitations to keep house for Wagner. Some of her character traits can be found in young Eva in *Meistersinger*.

Giacomo Meyerbeer

5.9.1791–2.5.1864

German Jewish composer, lives in France. First meets Wagner at Boulogne in 1839. Tries to help by giving him introductions to influential persons, and by promoting *Rienzi* and *Der fliegende Holländer*. Wagner later misjudges Meyerbeer's motives and abuses him in his writings. Composer of grand operas, including *Robert le Diable, Les Huguenots, Le Prophète, L'Africaine*.

Cosima Wagner

25.12.1837–1.4.1930

Daughter of Franz Liszt and Countess Marie d'Agoult. Meets Wagner in 1853. Marries Hans von Bülow in 1857. Close attachment to Wagner begins 1862. Has two children by Bülow, Daniela and Blandine. Leaves Bülow and lives with Wagner in 1868. Has three children by Wagner, Isolde (1865–1919), Eva (1867–1942) and Siegfried (1869–1930). Divorces Bülow and marries Wagner, both in 1870. Begins her diaries in 1869 and ends them the day before Wagner's death. Takes charge of the Bayreuth Festivals from 1883. Dies aged 92, in the same year as her son Siegfried, and is buried in Wagner's grave, at the back of Haus Wahnfried, Bayreuth.

Minna Wagner

5.9.1809–25.1.1866

Popular actress, first meets Wagner in 1834. Already has illegitimate daughter, Natalie, aged 9, whom she passes off as her younger sister. Her marriage to Wagner in 1836 is childless and passes from crisis to crisis. Final separation in 1861. Natalie marries a Herr Bilz after Minna's death, but is soon widowed. Hands over, for payment, numerous documents concerning Minna and Wagner to Mrs Burrell, for biographical purposes. These form part of the Burrell Collection.*

Siegfried Wagner

6.6.1869–4.8.1930

Wagner's only son (nicknamed Fidi), trains as architect, studies music with Humperdinck. Conducts and produces at Bayreuth, later becomes sole Festival director. Marries Winifred Williams, adopted daughter of Wagner's London friend Karl Klindworth. Their children: Wieland, Friedelind, Wolfgang, Verena. Amongst his operas: *Der Bärenhäuter, Der Kobold, Schwarzschwanen-reich*. Dies in the same year as his mother Cosima.

Mathilde Wesendonck

23.12.1828–31.8.1902

Married to Otto Wesendonck, wealthy businessman. Meets Wagner in Zurich (1852) and later has close relationship with him. Wagner and his wife Minna moved into the Asyl (Sanctuary), put at their disposal by the Wesendoncks, in 1857. She inspires his *Walküre* and *Tristan und Isolde*, and writes the poems to Wagner's *Five Wesendonck Lieder*.

* Formerly in the Curtis Institute of Music, Philadelphia. Most of it purchased in 1979 by Nationalarchiv der Richard Wagner Stiftung Bayreuth.

INTRODUCTION
THE REAL
WAGNER

A provocative title. How can the author possibly know who Wagner really was? Did Wagner himself know?

In its nine chapters this book searches for the answer. This is neither a life story nor a documentary biography. Of the former we have a superabundance, and the latter is a risky undertaking. The choice of documents may well throw light upon the author, but not necessarily upon his subject. Both categories have to rely on the copious correspondence of Wagner and his contemporaries, on the evidence of people who knew him, on press reports of the time, on diary entries etc. He who writes on Wagner must decide on the use and evaluation of the documents, on what to include and what to exclude. He can, if he so wishes, regard Wagner as an eminent artist and a trivial human being, or consider him eminent both as an artist and as a man, or dismiss him as trivial in both roles. Such cases have been made out. Or he can saddle his hobby horse and reveal Wagner as a nationalist, a socialist, an enemy or a friend of the Jews, a faithful or deceitful husband, or as a forerunner of either Lenin or Hitler.

I am the most German of all Germans. (DB 86: *11.9.1865*)

A nationalist then.

Here I am, once more treading German soil, and I must confess that the event makes not the slightest impression on me. The only thing worth noting is the way people talk – ill-mannered and stupid. Believe me, we have no fatherland, and if I am a German, it is because Germany lives within me. (Wagner to Franz Liszt, BWL II 280: *13.9.1860*)

No, not a nationalist.

I am neither a republican, nor a democrat, neither a socialist nor a communist. I am an artist, and being an artist I am nothing but a revolutionary by instinct, by choice and by resolve. A destroyer of the old, a creator of the new. (First draft of *A Communication to my Friends*, published in *Zeitschrift für Musik*, No. 7, 1931)

An artistic anarchist?

Splendid horses, noble, willing and dashing, a proper coachman, skilled, upright and firm, and who sits inside the carriage and lords it over man and beast? A bloated Jewish banker! (CWT II 837: *1.12.1881*)

Plainly, an antisemite.

27

You said in your letter you would like to be able to feel kindly towards Wagner. That you can and that you shall! He is the best and noblest of men. . . . As for his campaign against 'Judaism' – so he calls it – in music and in modern literature, his motives are entirely high-minded. He is not stupidly anti-Jewish, like the landed gentry or like some protestant churls. You can tell by the way he treats me and by the way he treats Joseph Rubinstein. As for poor Tausig, he was his intimate friend whom he loved very dearly. (HL 9)

Plainly not an antisemite.

The dangers are evident, and many a biographer has, wittingly or unwittingly, made use of the masses of documents to prove his own idea of Wagner. This book wants to know who Wagner really was. What kind of man was it whom Thomas Mann described as 'that dwarfish snuff-taker from Saxony with his immense talent and his shabby character';* who could be outrageously unfaithful and ungrateful, but who received steadfast gratitude and loyalty from those around him; who radiated so much light and cast such wretched shadows?

An extensive documentary compilation might enable the reader to find the real Wagner, provided the selection process is rigorous and the evidence comprehensive and balanced so that nobody could complain – not even Wagner himself – that important documents had been withheld, or that attempts had been made to blacken or to whitewash.

This is what the author has attempted here.

All documents in this volume have been newly translated, some for the first time. Since the quoted letters, diary entries, newspaper reports etc. constitute evidence, it was necessary to strive for accuracy in translating passages which might be obscure even to a modern German reader, on account of stylistic or grammatical idiosyncrasies. In translating passages from Wagner's own librettos,† accuracy and clarity were again two of the guiding principles. The others concern Wagner's poetic language and the mode of expression of each individual character. From *Der fliegende Holländer* onwards, Wagner's opera texts are characterised by their weighty, often dignified and imposing diction. If a translation fails to convey this, it will have missed one of the chief ingredients of Wagner's texts. It is equally important to follow the author in allowing each

---

* Thomas Mann: *Wagner und unsere Zeit*, Frankfurt/M. 1963, p. 30.
† Wagner, who wrote his own opera texts, preferred the term 'poem' to the more usual 'libretto'.

character his or her personal manner of speech. Alberich must sound different from Loge, Hagen from Siegfried, Elsa from Ortrud, Beckmesser from Sachs, and not only in their choice of vocabulary but in their way of presenting it.

In its first half (Chapters 1 to 5), the book considers Wagner's early experiences and experiments, which had a formative influence on his personality, confirming, strengthening or otherwise modifying his character traits, while the second half (Chapters 6 to 9) examines the many-sided, often contradictory nature of the man, as revealed in his life and work. His singular capacity for attracting patronage, his comprehensive artistic talents, his self-assurance, his powers of persuasion, his craving for luxury, his need for indulging in the absurd, the grave substance of his works, his belief in the *artificiality* of real life and the *reality* of his art, his single-mindedness in pursuing vital as well as trivial objectives, his harsh treatment of friends and loved ones, are examined by perusing his own testimony and that of his contemporaries. The final chapter, or Envoi, assembles some forty opinions on Wagner, aired by representatives of his and of our own century. They form a mixed garland of laurel and of poisoned ivy. Having absorbed Chapters 1 to 9, the reader may enjoy savouring the one and evaluating the other.

In treating each of these topics separately, it has been necessary to abandon biographical continuity. To assist the reader therefore, a Chronology and brief biographical sketches of the Principal Characters precede this Introduction, while genealogical tables of the Wagners and the Bülows are provided for Chapters 1 and 6. Chapter 4, which deals with Wagner's financial achievements, mentions an uncomfortably wide variety of nineteenth-century currencies, such as louisdor, friedrichsdor, gulden, thaler, ducat and franc. The chapter is preceded by a table giving the approximate present-day value of these denominations. The list of Sources and Abbreviations on p. 302 provides the sources of documents, together with their abbreviations, as they appear immediately following the passages quoted. For example, CWT II 320: 23.3.1879, refers to:

Cosima Wagner: *Die Tagebücher* (The Diaries), vol. II, p. 320, dated 23 March 1879.

It is the *biographer's* business to survey the available material, and to establish, first in his own mind and then in his reader's, a picture of his subject. Not so in this case. Here, the author provides the evidence, he comments, connects, sums up, and occasionally permits himself the luxury of his own opinion, but he does not give a final verdict. This he leaves to the reader.

I

PRODIGIOUS APPRENTICE

WAGNER'S FAMILY

Mother
Johanna Rosine Pätz
1774 ~ 1848

First Marriage (2nd June 1798)

Friedrich Wagner
Police actuary
1770~1813

Children

Albert, singer/actor/producer
1799-1874

Gustav
1801~2

Rosalie, actress
1803~37

Julius, goldsmith
1804~62

Luise, actress
1805~72

Klara, singer
1807~75

Maria Theresia
1809~14

Ottilie
1811~83

Wilhelm Richard
22nd May 1813 to 13th February 1883

Second Marriage (28th August 1814)

Ludwig Heinrich Christian Geyer
Actor/writer/painter
1779~1821

Child

Cäcilie
1815~93

Sir,

Beethoven's magnificent last symphony has long been the object of my deepest study. The more I came to realise its greatness, the more it saddened me that it should remain so misunderstood, so neglected by the majority of the musical public. A suitable piano arrangement seemed to me the best way to make this masterpiece more accessible. To my great regret I have so far not found one (for the inadequacy of Czerny's arrangement for four hands is obvious). My own enthusiasm then prompted me to undertake an arrangement of this symphony *for two hands*, and so far I have managed to set the first and perhaps most difficult movement, with the greatest possible clarity and attention to detail. I therefore approach your respected publishing house now, to enquire whether you would be interested in such an arrangement (for you will appreciate that without your encouragement I should not feel inclined to persevere with this laborious task). As soon as I hear of your interest, I shall proceed and complete what I have begun without delay. I therefore ask you most respectfully for an early reply, humbly assuring you of my most earnest diligence.

I am, Sir, Your obedient servant, Richard Wagner

(WSB I 117: 6.10.1830)

So writes Wagner, aged seventeen and quite unknown, to the house of Schott, the music publishers in Mainz. He receives no answer and, when he sends them a reminder, they turn him down. Wagner is unperturbed and completes his 'laborious task'. To ensure that his efforts are not wasted, he now approaches Schott for a third time:

I am sending you herewith a piano arrangement, two hands, of Beethoven's Symphony No. 9 which you had already seen last year and returned to me on account of having a backlog of manuscripts. I now offer you my arrangement once more, asking you to use it as and when you see fit. I require no fee, but I should be much obliged to you if in return you were to make me a gift of music. . . .

1. *Missa Solemnis* (D major), full score and piano score.
2. Beethoven's Ninth Symphony, full score.
3. idem: Two Quartets, score.
4. Beethoven's Symphonies in the arrangement by Hummel.

(WSB I 129–30: 15.6.1832)

*Wagner's transcription of Beethoven's 9th Symphony:
opening of the vocal section of the last movement*

Schott can resist no longer. Even though he does not publish the manuscript, he dispatches the music. The transaction reveals the young Wagner's tenacity and self-assurance. Today it is a publisher who yields to his powers of persuasion; financiers, women, artists and a King will succumb tomorrow.

Wagner knows he will be a musician. The schoolboy hears Beethoven's Seventh Symphony in Leipzig and recalls its impact on him in his autobiography, *Mein Leben*, about forty years later:

> The effect was indescribable, especially since I had already been deeply affected by Beethoven's appearance, as seen in lithographs of the time, by the news of his deafness and of his solitary, withdrawn life. An image soon formed within me of the sublimest, unearthly originality which was in every way unique. This image merged in my mind with that of Shakespeare. I encountered both of them in ecstatic dreams; when I awoke I was bathed in tears. (ML I 37)

Then he hears the Ninth Symphony. He immediately copies the whole score, line by line, and in so doing familiarises himself with the composer's craft: the compass and characteristics of the various instruments, the principles of harmony and counterpoint, the treatment of the human voice. And above all, the exercise draws him closer to Beethoven:

> This Ninth Symphony became the mystical centre of attention for all my weird and wonderful musical thoughts and aspirations. . . . This symphony, I felt sure, must contain the secret of all secrets. (ML I 42–3)

'The secret of all secrets'. Wagner seeks it in Beethoven, as later generations have sought it in Wagner.

As a rule, Wagner reacts to a stirring experience by bestirring himself. He encounters Beethoven, he copies the score. He encounters Shakespeare, he learns English:

> My trying to learn English sprang from the desire to understand Shakespeare more thoroughly. I soon made a metric translation of Romeo's monologue. After a short time I abandoned English again, but Shakespeare remained my ideal. (GS I 5)

From now on Beethoven and Shakespeare determine the artistic development of the boy. They also haunt his subconscious world in dreams. The authoress Eliza Wille,* a friend of Mathilde Wesendonck, records:

---

* Elizabeth Wille (1809–93), a novelist of English descent, was Wagner's confidante in the affair with Mathilde.

Wagner told me that he remembered a dream of his early youth, in which he saw Shakespeare and spoke with him, as though in real life. This made an incredible impression upon him and caused him to meet the departed Beethoven, too. (EW 134)

The spirit of Shakespeare, or what the fifteen-year-old regards as such, directs his attention to dramatic art. He begins to write a tragedy in five acts, *Leubald*, and actually finishes it within the space of twelve months. He proves, to himself at least, that he is serious about writing, and acquires in the process that tireless persistence which he will call upon when erecting the gigantic structure of *Der Ring des Nibelungen*, a labour spanning a quarter of a century. The cast list of *Leubald* conveys the turbulent imagination of the schoolboy:

Leubald
Werdulst, friend of Siegmar, Leubald's deceased father
Roderich
Bärting, a robber knight
Astolf, betrothed to Adelaide
Albert
Lothar, steward at Leubald's castle and his tutor
Breischald, companion to Bärting
Wulst, servant to Leubald
A Hermit
The ghost of Leubald's father Siegmar
Flamming, a vagabond
Bäringer
Schrammenbald
Schenk, an innkeeper
Agnes, wife of Roderich
Adelaide, daughter of Roderich
Gundchen, her confidante
Siegfried and Albrecht, Roderich's sons, ten and twelve years old
A Witch
The Witch's Spirits   (OD 24)

Wagner admits in *Mein Leben* that *Hamlet*, *Macbeth* and *King Lear* had been *Leubald*'s godparents:

The plot was really based on a variation of *Hamlet*. The difference was that my hero, confronted with the ghost of a father murdered in similar circumstances and crying for vengeance, is roused to such violent action that he commits a series of murders and finally becomes insane.

(ML I 32)

Shakespeare's influence lends him wings, and versifying seems to set him no problems:

> But see, here comes young Leubald,
> With eyes of brilliant flame!
> By God, I ne'er yet saw him thus;
> The lion's glare
> It seems he borrows;
> His fiery cheeks
> Would almost singe his beard,
> And sin, it does appear,
> He crushes underfoot! (OD 25)

The tragedy ends, somewhat clumsily:

> He lived with love and hate;
> To murder was his fate;
> Till sick in mind with rue,
> Torment brought madness too. (OD 29)

Despite the awkward phraseology, one glimpses Kurwenal's lament over Tristan:

> Here lies he now,
> The fairest of men
> Who did love as no other could love.
>
> (Tristan und Isolde, Act 3, Scene 1)

Leubald was to win its author little credit. In his own words:

I neglected my school work to such an extent that I had to anticipate a discontinuation of my scholastic career. While my dear mother had no inkling of this, I awaited the catastrophe not with fear but with longing. To face the coming crisis with dignity, I finally decided to give my family a surprise and confronted them with my completed tragic drama. . . . I sent my voluminous manuscript [to my uncle], together with a detailed letter which informed him of my intentions with regard to school life, and of my unshakable decision not to allow my independent development to be inhibited by scholastic pedantry. I was

Wagner's mother painted in 1813, the year of Wagner's birth,
by her second husband, Ludwig Geyer.

certain my uncle would be overjoyed, but I was wrong. He was greatly alarmed, . . . paid a visit to my mother and my brother-in-law . . . and gave a report of the disaster that had struck the family. (ML I 31–2)

It is unlikely that Wagner's headmaster regretted the laggard's departure. The School Chronicle records his dismissal, and under *Further Data* merely reads, 'Died 13.2.83 in Venice.'

To pay his debt to Shakespeare and Beethoven, Wagner determines to continue along the chosen path: *Leubald* must be set to music. Thus had Beethoven ennobled Goethe's *Egmont*. An even greater achievement would be Wagner's music to Wagner's text. He does not even consider asking someone else to undertake the composition. The ex-schoolboy knows already what he is to formulate thirty-four years later in his *Meistersinger*, when Walther asks David to explain to him what a 'master' is. A master, David replies, is a poet who:

> *To words and to rhymes which he has found,*
> *Can masterly fashion his own new music.*
> (*Die Meistersinger von Nürnberg*, Act 1, Scene 2)

But how does one fashion one's own new music? His copying of the Ninth Symphony has taught him much, but his good sense tells him that the art of composing can only be learnt from a master of the art. Christian Gottlieb Müller, merely thirteen years older than Wagner, is a composer, conductor, violinist and organist. It is he who is to teach the fifteen-year-old boy the principles of harmony, secretly at first and free of charge, a Wagnerian achievement in itself. Soon Müller becomes his official and paid tutor, but his pupil's attempts at composition are carried out in secret. Following his own instinct, Wagner composes two Piano Sonatas and a String Quartet, while – like an obedient pupil – working through Müller's harmony exercises. He composes in advance of his knowledge and is convinced that the technique of harmony, counterpoint and instrumentation, once studied and absorbed, will confirm his experiments. Three and a half decades later, Hans Sachs is to advise the equally speculative Walther von Stolzing:

> *The rules of masters will provide you*
> *With everything you need to guide you.*
> *What youthful passion planted,*
> *In summer shall be granted.*
> *Sweet springtime's ringing*
> *Shall teach you singing.*

So lock them safely in your heart,
That they may nevermore depart.
(*Die Meistersinger von Nürnberg*, Act 3, Scene 2)

Rules of masters and youthful passion – the former are taught by Herr Müller, but the pupil follows the latter and celebrates his seventeenth year by composing a Trio for Female Voices, a Soprano Aria, a Tenor Aria, and his first orchestral work, the Overture in B flat major. He shows this to the conductor Heinrich Dorn, but conceals it from his teacher. On Christmas Eve 1830, Dorn gives its first performance in the Leipzig theatre, against the wishes of the orchestra, who think the composer a madman. Wagner describes the world première:

> The concert began with a piece which the programme called, provocatively, 'New Overture', no more. I had attended the rehearsal with fear in my heart, but had been greatly impressed by Dorn's composure, which he maintained in the face of the ominous unrest among the players who had to come to terms with this enigmatic composition. The principal theme of the Allegro was in four bars. At the end of each four-bar sequence, however, I had inserted a fifth bar which was quite unrelated to the melodic theme, but stood out by a peculiar whack on the kettle drum, on the second beat of that bar. . . . On the evening, this ever recurring effect aroused first the attention, then the amusement of the audience. I heard my neighbours count the bars and predict each repeated drum beat. I was only too well aware of the correctness of their calculations, and my torment was indescribable, causing me to lose all consciousness. I regained my senses when the Overture, which I had disdained to furnish with a conventional ending, came to a sudden standstill. . . . I could hear no sounds of displeasure, no hissing, no criticism, not even laughter as such, but only utter consternation at this unusual event which appeared to all, and to me, like an astonishing dream. (ML I 60–1)

'Unusual event', 'astonishing dream' – one will come across those words many times, in descriptions of performances of Wagner's later works.

The Christmas concert is over, and it is high time to come clean with Herr Müller and, if at all possible, obtain his forgiveness. This recently discovered letter from pupil to teacher reveals the fledgling diplomat.

> I expect you are displeased and angry with me and, truly, I cannot blame you. You will reproach me for having acted behind your back and for

having hurt and offended you, only to boost my vanity. Rest assured that many details are different from what you may suspect. So please listen to my explanation. About nine months ago I made the acquaintance of Herr Dorn, the director of music, and I can only say that he proved a kindly friend. He asked me, among other things, whether I felt inclined to hear one of my compositions performed. He suggested I should try my hand at a piece for orchestra, and it was that proposition which tempted me, in my youthful passion, to hatch this Overture. I did not dare show it to you because I thought you, as my teacher, would laugh at me. . . . I duly forgot all about the Overture and my other orchestral scribbles, and since last summer I have had no further contact with Herr Dorn, until he recently sent word through my sister, to ask whether I would like to hear my Overture at Christmas. This caused me such a surprise that, unfortunately, I overlooked consulting you, and took my Overture straightway to Herr Dorn. It was really only yesterday that I realised how wrongly I had acted towards you, and how foolishly towards myself. There was not enough time, however, to correct my error. Therefore, all I can do now is to beg you most sincerely to forgive me and not to blame my intention but my negligence which, I do hope, does not merit too harsh a sentence. . . . I assure you of my affectionate obedience for the future. Please forget my negligence and, as a welcome Christmas gift, present me with your profound forgiveness.*

Müller forgives and Wagner remains his pupil until the following autumn.

The art of diplomacy, practised here by the seventeen-year-old, is to become an increasingly important skill with the passing years, when Wagner will have to impress sponsors, temporise with creditors, make small operatic parts palatable to great singers, persuade opera directors to let him have their best singers and players for a whole season, and charm offended prima donnas into unpacking their already packed luggage.

The July uprising of 1830 in Paris, however, offers little scope for diplomacy. Social justice and civil liberty are the slogans which enflame the young Wagner:

> I naturally became a firm supporter of the revolution which I saw as a courageous and triumphant struggle of the people, unstained by the terrible excesses of the French Revolution. (ML I 47)

---

* J. Deathridge: *Wagner und sein erster Lehrmeister* (Programme booklet: *Die Meistersinger* 1979, Bavarian State Opera). Letter dated probably 25.12.1830.

There is no more composing to be done, at least not for the time being:

At once I became a revolutionary and I was convinced that no reasonably alert person could help occupying himself exclusively with politics. (GS I 7)

Wagner at 22: the first known likeness

Here one encounters a recurring pattern in Wagner's life. He is busy composing, when an event in the political, social, cultural or military sphere overwhelms him to such an extent that he has to put his work aside. The particular set of problems created by the event has to be solved before he can get back to work, and preferably solved by Richard Wagner himself. He does so either by thinking aloud in the presence of his family and friends, or in writing, and if the latter process requires his full attention for days, weeks or months, so be it. From that compulsion spring numerous pamphlets and essays, among them:

'The Artist and the Public'	1841
'Account of the Return of Weber's Remains from London to Dresden'	1844
'What is the Relation between Republican Ambitions and the Monarchy?'	1848
'The Revolution'	1849
'A Project for the Organisation of a German National Theatre for the Kingdom of Saxony'	1849
'Man and Existing Society'	1849
'Art and Revolution'	1849
'The Art-Work of the Future'	1849
'Judaism in Music'	1850
'The Vienna Court Opera Theatre'	1863
'State and Religion'	1864
'Report to His Majesty King Ludwig II of Bavaria upon a German Music School to Be Founded in Munich'	1865
'German Art and German Politics'	1867–8
'To the German Army before Paris' (Poem)	1871
'What is German?'	1865/1878
'The Public in Time and Space'	1878
'Public and Popularity'	1878
'Religion and Art'	1880

'Heroism and Christianity'   1881
'The Feminine Element in Mankind' (Fragment)   1883

In 1830, however, Wagner's enthusiasm for the revolution takes a sensible course for a future artist, it sublimates itself into creative effort. In that and in the next year he composes:

Overture to *The Bride of Messina*
Piano Sonata for four hands in B flat major
Overture in C major
Overture in E flat major

Christian Theodor Weinlig (1780–1842), who succeeds Müller as Wagner's teacher in autumn 1831, is a late successor to Johann Sebastian Bach, as Cantor at Leipzig's Thomas-Schule. He not only encourages his new pupil's compositions – after half a year's strict training – but sees to it that one of them is published by Breitkopf & Härtel:

SONATA
FOR PIANOFORTE
composed and
respectfully dedicated to
HERR THEODOR WEINLIG
by
RICHARD WAGNER

The grateful student works his way through Weinlig's textbook, *Theoretical and Practical Guide to Fugue*, and without this intensive study, the fugue illustrating the nocturnal brawl at the end of the second act of *Meistersinger* (*Prügelfuge*) would be hardly conceivable. Wagner, though, had not found it easy to persuade Weinlig to teach him.

> He long resisted all urgent pleas, but in the end he seemed to take pity on me, in a positive, kindly way, on account of the sad state of my musical training. This he ascertained from a fugue I had shown him, and he agreed to teach me, stipulating that I must not compose another note for the next six months, but patiently follow his instruction. (ML I 63)

Soon Weinlig recognises that this is no ordinary pupil:

Weinlig summoned me one morning at seven o'clock to work out, under his supervision, the framework of a fugue by midday. He actually devoted the whole morning to me, scrutinising each single bar as I wrote it, advising and instructing me all the time. At twelve o'clock he sent me away with the assignment to finish the framework at home, by filling in the other parts. When I brought him the completed fugue, he gave me in return his own version of a fugue on the same theme, for comparison. This joint fugal work resulted in a most fruitful and affectionate relationship between myself and my kindly teacher. (ML I 63)

Such a 'fruitful and affectionate relationship' between teacher and pupil recurs in the third act of *Meistersinger*, when Hans Sachs instructs Walther how to

Theodor Weinlig

create the master-song which will win him Eva's hand. The cobbler poet's teaching is unselfish, because it loses him his beloved Eva; so is Weinlig's, for, fully conscious of what he is doing, he teaches his pupil to overtake him:

Within two months I had worked out a number of most complicated fugues and all manner of extremely difficult contrapuntal exercises. I

then handed my teacher a particularly elaborate double fugue and was quite taken aback when he told me I could have it framed, and there was nothing more he could teach me. . . . Weinlig himself did not seem to attach much importance to what he had taught me. He said, 'You will probably never again write fugues or canons, but what you have acquired is *independence*. You are now able to stand on your own two feet . . .' From that time on he gave me a free hand. My first reward was his permission to compose my Fantasia for Piano in F sharp minor, exactly as I liked. I allowed myself complete structural freedom, melody interchanging with recitative, and altogether pleasing myself immensely with this work, especially since it gained Weinlig's approval.
(ML I 63–4)

This Fantasia is of special interest, for it looks back to Beethoven and forward to *Tannhäuser*, *Tristan und Isolde* and *Der Ring des Nibelungen*. Beethoven haunts the recitatives, several chord sequences, the adagio section and the allegro agitato. But as early as bar 4 one finds:

Twenty-three years later this figure returns, note for note, in the same key, as the motif of 'Wotan's Dejection' in the second act of *Die Walküre*:

The Ring motif is anticipated in bar 12, while the lengthy 60th bar – almost a recitative by itself – offers:

which will later be transformed into the Love motif in *Tristan und Isolde*:

In the recitative section of the Fantasia one encounters:

Twenty-seven years later Tristan will ask, 'How could I safely guide this vessel to King Marke's country?':

Bar 213 of the Fantasia:

will be reborn as 'Brünnhilde's Plea' in the last act of *Die Walküre*:

The adagio theme of the Fantasia (bar 220) foreshadows *Rienzi* in melody, key and ornament:

FANTASIA

RIENZI (Overture)

The Fantasia ends:

This phrase will be heard again in the Rome Narration of the third act of *Tannhäuser*:

Like Hans Sachs, Weinlig evidently knew how to mix instruction and inspiration. When Walther wants to know how to begin his song 'by the rules', Sachs replies, 'Make your own rules and follow them.' This will be Wagner's motto for the future, greatly encouraged by his teacher's wise words:

The composer's individuality will always insist on freedom as his birthright. This entitles him to find his own way, provided he does so in the spirit of the recognised basic principles.

So Weinlig pronounces in his *Theoretical and Practical Guide to Fugue, written and fully illustrated with musical examples by Christian Theodor Weinlig, formerly Cantor and Director of Music at the Thomas-Schule in Leipzig, and Master of the Academia dei Filarmoniei of Bologna* (Dresden 1845, para. 191).

Weinlig's words are music to Wagner's ears, and he writes to his sister Ottilie:

O, how it hurts me to have to tell you that for a while I really let myself go and allowed some student friends to distract me from my studies, causing our dear mother a great deal of trouble and grief. I finally pulled myself together . . . and became a pupil of Cantor Weinlig who can justly be regarded as the *greatest living contrapuntist,* and who is also such a wonderful person that I love him as a father. He has instructed me with such loving care that, according to his own words, I may regard my apprenticeship as already over, and he now simply acts as my mentor and friend. You may measure the extent of his love for me by the answer he gave to mother, when she asked him after the first six months to name his fee; he said it would be unreasonable to accept payment for the pleasure he took in teaching me, and that my industry and his hopes for my future rewarded him amply. (WSB I 126: 3.3.1832)

Weinlig does not live to rejoice in his pupil's success with *Rienzi* – he dies in March 1842, missing the first performance by seven months. But one year later Wagner dedicates his choral work, *Das Liebesmahl der Apostel* (The Love Feast of the Apostles), to 'Frau Charlotte Emilie Weinlig, widow of my unforgettable teacher'. Gratitude is not one of Wagner's outstanding virtues. When he does show it, it is to be savoured.

In his letter to Ottilie, Wagner also tells her proudly about the first performance of his Overture in D minor, in the hallowed Leipzig Gewandhaus, in February 1832:

I was so scared and apprehensive that I nearly died (if only you had been with me!). So just picture my delight and astonishment, when at the end of the Overture everybody began to applaud, just as though they had heard the greatest masterpiece. I can assure you I hardly knew what was happening to me! Luise [their sister, who lived in Copenhagen] was moved to tears. How I wished you could have been there; it would have pleased you, I think. (WSB I 127: 3.3.1832)

This is a busy time for Wagner. His compositions are being heard. In the same letter he informs Ottilie:

> This week one of my Piano Sonatas which I dedicated to Weinlig has been published. They gave me 20 thalers' worth of music for it. I would gladly send you a copy, only the postage would cost more than the music, so go to a music shop in Copenhagen and ask for *Sonata for Pianoforte, Richard Wagner's first composition, published by Breitkopf & Härtel, Leipzig.*

There is more to come:

> Recently I composed an Overture *King Enzio*, a new tragedy by Raupach, which is given at every performance of the play in the theatre. Everybody likes it. (WSB 1 128: 3.3.1832)

Raupach? Little known today, he was the celebrated author of 117 dramas in the first half of the nineteenth century. In *King Enzio*, the captured king languishes in a dungeon, together with his beloved Lucia, who had succeeded in entering the prison in disguise. This reminded Wagner so much of similar circumstances in Beethoven's *Fidelio* that it induced him to write his Overture in the same key as Beethoven's, E major. Since his sister Rosalie played the part of Lucia, he also provided the music for the end of the fifth act.

It is not, however, Beethoven alone who inspires the young composer. Wilhelmine Schröder-Devrient, whom he had seen as Fidelio three years ago, is to be his first Adriano (*Rienzi*), his first Senta (*Der fliegende Holländer*) and his first Venus (*Tannhäuser*). *Mein Leben* describes their first encounter, when he was sixteen:

> She appeared in *Fidelio*. Looking back, I can hardly find any event in my entire life which has produced a greater impression on me. Anyone who can recall this wonderful woman at that period in her life is bound to bear witness, in one way or another, to the almost demonic fire kindled in him by the utterly convincing, warm-hearted, ecstatic performance of this unique artist. At the end I rushed to the house of one of my friends, to compose a short letter in which I declared to the great artist that henceforth my life will be given relevance, and if in the future she should hear people praise my name, she should remember that it was she who on this evening had made of me what I herewith vowed to

49

become. This letter I took to her hotel and then I ran out into the night like a wild thing. Later, when I came to Dresden in 1842, for the first performance of my *Rienzi*, and was frequently able to visit the house of this artist who had taken a liking to me, she surprised me one day by reciting that letter word for word.* (ML I 44)

Such is the magic which, over a century later, affected audiences when a Maria Callas, an Anja Silja were on stage. Wagner himself is to experience it once more, with Ludwig Schnorr von Carolsfeld, his first Tristan. They are 'singing actors', the type he always prefers to mere singers who might never fully understand their parts. Even shortly before his death the thought bothers him that his Bayreuth singers, and the public with them, might not grasp the meaning of *Parsifal*. Cosima notes in her diary:

> The great scene between Kundry and Parsifal will probably never be done as he visualised it. R. is disappointed with his performers who are insensitive to all that is in that scene. He thinks of Schröder-Devrient, how she would have uttered the words, 'So war es mein Kuss, der hellsichtig dich machte' ['Was it my kiss then, that made you understand the world and yourself?'] (CWT II 977: 9.7.1882)

Wagner does not acknowledge many preceptors, but Shakespeare, Beethoven and Schröder-Devrient he will never deny. When the great singer proclaims, as Leonore in *Fidelio*, 'Ja, es *gibt* eine Vorsehung!' ('There *is* a divine providence!'), Wagner echoes this in his *Lohengrin*, where Elsa affirms, 'Es *gibt* ein Glück' ('Happiness *is* alive'). And just as Leonore rushes forward, 'shielding Florestan with her body', and cries, 'Away!' so, in *Tannhäuser*, Elisabeth rushes forward, 'shielding Tannhäuser with her body', and cries, 'Away!'

Strangely enough, in 1849 Wagner and Schröder-Devrient share the same fate. Both, independently of one another, take an active part in the Dresden uprising, and both have to flee the country – Wagner to Switzerland and towards the *Ring*, *Tristan*, *Meistersinger* and *Parsifal*, the singer downhill, into marriage disasters and other catastrophic liaisons and her death in 1860. Wagner is to dedicate his essay, 'On Actors and Singers', to her memory, and the figure of Tragedy on the façade of his Haus Wahnfried† in Bayreuth bears her features.

---

* Recent research suggests that Wagner is unlikely to have seen *Fidelio* in 1829, but confused this with a performance by Schröder-Devrient five years later, in Bellini's *I Capuleti e i Montecchi*.

† The name of his later Bayreuth residence (*Wahn* = illusion, delusion; *Fried(e)* = peace, rest).

*From left to right: Schröder-Devrient as Tragedy. Ludwig Schnorr
von Carolsfeld as Wotan, personifying Ancient Myth.
Cosima Wagner, with little Siegfried by her side, as Music.*

While Schröder-Devrient, Shakespeare and Beethoven intoxicate the artist in
Wagner, the young man has also begun to experience the enchantments of
Woman. From these emotions spring his early stage works. *Die Hochzeit* (The
Wedding) is his first opera project. The nineteen-year-old writes his own text in
Pravonin, near Prague, where he spends time with Jenny and Auguste, the
illegitimate daughters of Count Pachta. He writes to his friend Theodor Apel:

> Picture Jenny as an immaculate beauty, and you know everything. My
> passion elevated her prettiness into a manifestation of excellence. My
> idealising eyes saw in her all they wanted to see, and that was
> unfortunate! I thought I saw my feelings returned and that it only
> needed a bold advance to ensure her response. But what a response! . . .
> Alas, Theodor, imagine all those things that can wound a burning
> passion; but that which can kill it is too dreadful for words. Listen then
> and lend me your sympathy – she was not worthy of my love! A deadly
> chill gripped my spirit. If only I could instantly have renounced all fair
> hopes, my feelings numb with icy cold, I should have counted myself
> happy! But to witness the gradual dying away of every single spark of
> what had once been a bright flame, that brings tears to the eyes. . . .
> Enough, enough, more than enough! In spite of the infinite emptiness
> in my heart, I do long for love, and what really annoys me is that I still
> manage to look so healthy! Such are the conditions under which I wrote

51

the poem of my opera, *Die Hochzeit*, which I took back with me to Leipzig, about a fortnight ago. (WSB I 133–4: 16.12.1832)

Art, as so often with Wagner, flourishes in adversity. But shortly afterwards he tells Apel:

I have discarded my opera text and have torn it up.
(WSB I 134: 3.1.1833)

What had happened? *Mein Leben* tells us:

[At Pravonin] the old gentleman and his beautiful daughters received me very graciously, and I enjoyed their most stimulating hospitality till late autumn. As a youth of nineteen, already with a healthy growth of beard, which had been advertised to the young ladies in my sister's letter of introduction, the constant, close association with such pretty and well bred young ladies could hardly leave my imagination unaffected. . . . Their relations with me were uninhibited, sisterly and good-natured, but it was clear to me that I was expected to fall in love with one or the other. (ML I 71–2)

He flirts with both, but the dark-eyed Jenny (as we already know) is his favourite. The young man now commits a grave error, or rather he exhibits a failing which will be a source of annoyance to others throughout his life – he tries to impose his ideas on them:

I held forth against the deplorable lending library novels which were their sole reading matter, against the Italian operatic arias which Auguste was in the habit of singing, and against the empty-headed horse-loving cavaliers who called from time to time and paid court to both Jenny and Auguste in an indelicate manner which offended me. My anger at this last point soon gave rise to considerable unpleasantness. I became severe and offensive, lost myself in sermonising on the spirit of the French Revolution, and even gave them advice – which to their ears was 'fatherly' – to the effect that they should, in heaven's name, make friends with well educated commoners rather than with such haughty, coarse suitors whose company could only harm their reputations. . . . So, one cold November day I took my leave of those lovely girls, undecided whether I was in love or indignant, though we parted on good terms. (ML I 72)

Uninvited attempts at educating others and frequent tantrums constitute part of Wagner's psychological make-up; in a temper tantrum he can tear up the libretto of *Die Hochzeit*, in his evangelical mood he will attempt to baptise Jews or try to persuade perfectly healthy people to undergo a rigorous water cure that has taken his fancy. Even Cosima will not always be able to divert his tantrums. Here she describes an instance from late in their marriage. By this time the Wagner family travels in style. For their Italian sojourn he has booked a private railway coach:

> He goes to the railway station . . . to book the special coach. . . . R. is very upset and works himself into a rage, after having been out in the miserable weather to inspect the special coach which he dislikes very much. . . . We leave at six in the evening. The special coach is far more comfortable than was thought at first. (CWT II 615–16: 29/30.10.1880)

When the rage subsides, one plays cards:

> I am convinced that when he makes a scene and flares up, or when he seeks to hurt people, it is his malaise which takes possession of him to such an extent that my words, however conciliatory, only pour more oil on the flames. When I leave the room for a while, he follows me, soon calms down and explains the reasons for his bitterness which are all too convincing, and we play whist. (CWT II 858: 28.12.1881)

But, back to Pravonin. As it turns out, his heart is not broken. 'She was not worthy of my love': thus, characteristically, he renounces his first love, though the excitement of the senses will not soon be forgotten. By such abdications will he master similar situations in both his life and his works. Thus will he renounce a Jessie Laussot, a Mathilde Wesendonck, a Mathilde Maier, a Judith Gautier. Thus the Dutchman renounces his Senta, Lohengrin his Elsa, Wolfram his love for Elisabeth, Sachs his Eva, and Wotan the world.

It is only to be expected that certain experiences of his youth will determine the growth or curtailment of certain character traits. While still in Pravonin, for instance, he is persuaded to join a hunting party. What follows affects him so deeply that he still remembers it after forty-one years. He and Cosima have roast hare for lunch, and before going to bed that night she writes in her diary:

> R. says that when he was young he once went hunting in Bohemia, on Count Pachta's estate. He had fired at random, without taking aim, and was told that he had hit the rear leg of a running hare. At the end of the hunt, a hound had discovered the poor animal and had dragged it along. Its cries of terror had pierced him to the core. People told him, 'That is

your hare', and he vowed to himself never again to take part in such an entertainment. (CWT I 762: 13.12.1873)

Although it did not stop him dining on roast hare, his compassion for animals persisted, and may go some way to compensating for his lack of sympathy with many of his fellow men.

Soon he is to write his new opera, *Die Feen* (The Fairies), in which we come across this passage:

You, huntsman, be on your way!
Hoho, blast loudly your horn!
O see, how tired is the beast!
Set to! The arrow, it flies!
See how it flies! My aim was good!
Haha! It pierced his heart!
But see, the beast can weep!

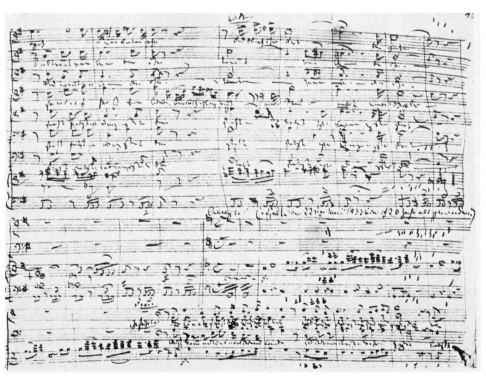

Composition sketch for Die Feen *with these words (centre right):*
Today, 22 May 1833, I have become 20 years old

A tear is glistening in its eye!
With broken glance it looks at me!
(*Die Feen*, Act 3)

This was written at the age of nineteen. Fifty years later Gurnemanz remonstrates with the young Parsifal who has just shot a flying swan:

So you could murder in this sacred forest,
Where gentle peace enfolded you?
The woodland beasts came close and trusted you,
Greeting you, friendly and tame.
From their branches, what warbled the birds to you?
What harm did the faithful swan?
. . .

Here, see here! You pierced him here.
The wound is all blood, his wings are all lifeless,
His snowy plumage crimson defaced.
Quite broken his glance – look at his eyes!
Now does your evil action haunt you?

(*Parsifal*, Act 1)

Both these passages may well owe their existence to these lines from Shakespeare's *As You Like It*:

Today my lord of Amiens and myself
Did steal behind him as he lay along
Under an oak, whose antique root peeps out
Upon the brook that brawls along this wood;
To the which place a poor sequestered stag,
That from the hunter's aim had ta'en a hurt,
Did come to languish; and indeed, my lord,
The wretched animal heaved forth such groans
That their discharge did stretch his leathern coat
Almost to bursting, and the big round tears
Coursed one another down his innocent nose
In piteous chase; and thus the hairy fool,
Much marked of the melancholy Jaques,
Stood on the extremest verge of the swift brook,
Augmenting it with tears.

(Act 2, Scene 1)

Cosima's diaries bear frequent witness to the whole family's involvement with the animal world:

> The children thought they had found two dead birds in the morning, but we soon saw that the little things were still alive and had probably been thrown out of their nest by some other bird. Now they are embedded in cotton wool and we feed them. God knows whether we can help them to survive. They are robins. (CWT I 100–1: 30.5.1869)

> The gnats and flies, growing rigid as they die, arouse R.'s pity. He cannot recall any poet having written about this; they usually only deal with the fading of flowers. (CWT I 449: 15.10.1871)

Although, as we know, Wagner lost interest in his projected opera, *Die Hochzeit,* his account of the plot is worth reading:

> Two great families had long lived in a state of feud, but had at last found their way to swearing an oath of peace. The ancient father of one of the families now invited the son of his erstwhile enemy to the wedding of his daughter to one of his faithful followers. The wedding feast is to celebrate their reconciliation. While the guests are still suspicious and afraid of some treachery, their leader feels a dark passion for the bride of his new confederate. His sombre glance pierces her heart too, and when the festive procession has conducted her to the bridal chamber, there to await the arrival of her beloved, she suddenly beholds this same glance at the window of her chamber high in the tower, scorching her with fearful passion. She realises immediately that this is a matter of life or death. The intruder embraces her with insane ardour, but she pushes him back to the balcony and hurls him to the ground, where his companions find his crushed body. . . . The bride begins to show signs of incipient madness. She flees from her bridegroom, refuses their union and locks herself up in her chamber in the tower, allowing nobody to approach her. Only when the rites of death are celebrated with great splendour at night, does the bride make her appearance, pale and silent at the head of her maidens, to attend the ritual, when its solemnity is shattered by news first of the approach of hostile forces, and then by an armed attack of the murdered youth's kinsmen. When the avengers of the apparent treachery at last rush into the chapel and call for their friend's murderer, the petrified burgrave points to his dead daughter who, turning away from her bridegroom, has sunk lifeless upon the coffin of the man she had murdered. (ML I 75–6)

'Festive procession to the bridal chamber' – thirteen years later such a festive procession is to conduct Elsa and Lohengrin to their bridal chamber. The 'armed attack of the murdered youth's kinsmen' foreshadows a similar incident in the first act of *Die Walküre*. The interrupted ceremonies recur in *Der fliegende Holländer*, Act 3; in *Lohengrin*, Act 2; in *Götterdämmerung*, Act 2. The end of *Die Hochzeit*, with the daughter sinking lifeless upon the dead body, anticipates Isolde's death by love in *Tristan und Isolde*, and Brünnhilde's death by fire at the end of *Götterdämmerung*. In *Die Hochzeit* the bridal chorus sings:

> *See, o see where they approach,*
> *In flush of youth, in boldest grace;*
> *Newly wed, the noble pair*
> *In love and lasting faith are joined.*

In *Lohengrin*, the bridal chorus sings:

> *Follow our steps, fortunate pair,*
> *Enter in peace under love's guiding spell.*
> *Courage so bold, loving so fair*
> *Leads you where faith everlasting shall dwell.*

In *Die Hochzeit* we find:

> *My husband, speak, who is that stranger?*

Words and metre are lodged in Wagner's mind. Nine years later, Senta asks in *Der fliegende Holländer*:

> *My father, speak, who is that stranger?*

Of the music to *Die Hochzeit* three numbers survive, a maestoso Introduction, a Chorus in seven parts and a Septet. His treatment of the choral parts is still quite conventional.

But a short theme, occurring several times in the orchestra, foreshadows a number of *Ring* motifs:

(A) is to make a reappearance as 'Brünnhilde's Appeal', in *Die Walküre*:

It will also constitute the second half of the Siegfried motif which pervades the *Ring*:

The falling minor second (B) can be met again, also in the *Ring*, as the Woe motif, one of the most frequent ones in the whole tetralogy.

The orchestra which Wagner had in mind for *Die Hochzeit* demands four French horns and three trombones, an unusually large number for opera orchestras of the time, but his standard requirement for *Rienzi, Der fliegende Holländer, Tannhäuser* and *Lohengrin*.

In January 1833 Wagner is appointed chorus master at Würzburg, a position conducive to securing performances of his own music, and now he is quite determined to launch out on a career as a composer of operas. In the next two years he is to write *Die Feen* and *Das Liebesverbot*. His Würzburg contract of employment requires the signatures of three older members of his family, since he is still under age:

> Frau Johanna Geyer; Rosalia Wagner, actress, of Pichhof, Leipzig; and Herr Albert Wagner, singer, actor and producer*, resident in Würzburg, undertake to act as guarantors for the punctuality and obedience of the minor Richard Wagner, hitherto student of music in Leipzig, son of Johanna Geyer, an actor's widow, the said Richard Wagner's appointment to run until the Sunday before Palm Sunday 1834. Richard Wagner's chief duties will be as chorus master, but if need be he will also be expected to make himself useful as actor in spoken and silent parts, in plays, tragedies and ballets, and for this both he and the guarantors of his diligence have given their permission and consent. In case of disobedience or insubordination the management reserves the right to penalise Herr Richard Wagner in accordance with the theatre regulations. If, in such an event, Richard Wagner's income does not cover the imposed fines, the above-mentioned guarantors undertake to pay them to the theatre management on his behalf. (*Allgemeine Musik-Zeitung*, Berlin 14.10.1910)

By the look of it, the new chorus master's duties are going to keep him more than fully occupied, but in fact he finds sufficient leisure to work at his first opera, and after only twelve months, on 6 January 1834, he can write 'Finis. Laudetur Deus' underneath the final chord of *Die Feen*. In his *Communication to my Friends* (1851) he describes the plot:

> A Fairy renounces immortality for the sake of a human lover, but she can attain mortality only through the fulfilment of certain severe conditions. If her mortal lover were unable to comply with those conditions, she herself would be threatened with the direst consequences. Her lover fails the test which required him to cling faithfully to his beloved, however evil and cruel she might be compelled to appear to him. . . . The Fairy, now changed into a stone, is released from her spell by her lover's wistful song, while he – instead of being allowed to leave his own country together with the bride he has won – is invited by the King of the Fairies to enjoy the everlasting delights of Fairyland, together with his Fairy wife. (GS IV 252–3)

The story contains signposts pointing in the direction of *Der fliegende Holländer*,

---

* Wagner's oldest brother.

Siegfried and *Tannhäuser*, for 'renouncing immortality' will be Brünnhilde's own choice, while the love union in another world is the destiny of Senta and the Dutchman, Brünnhilde and Siegfried, and Isolde and Tristan. The first act anticipates the forbidden question in *Lohengrin*:

Die Feen	Lohengrin
Above all else,	*Vow not to ask me ever,*
for eight long years	*seek for an answer never*
you must not ask me	*from whence to you I came,*
who I am!	*nor what my birth and name!*

In both operas that fatal question is asked.

Hamlet and Wagner's own *Leubald* have inspired the statement in the first act of *Die Feen*:

> *Your father am I nevermore,*
> *I only am your father's ghost.*

The unknown father will play an important part in several later works. Siegmund, Sieglinde, Tristan, Parsifal – they all are fatherless. Wagner himself, incidentally, was never quite certain which father's son he was, police official Carl Friedrich Wilhelm Wagner's, or Ludwig Heinrich Christian Geyer's, the actor and poet whom his mother married after her husband's death.

Further echoes and premonitions are discernible in *Die Feen*. Thus, the duet between Gernot and Drolla in the second act is unthinkable without the Pagageno–Papagena duet in *Zauberflöte*, while Ada's great aria is a descendant of Leonore's in the first act of *Fidelio*. Ada's Narration finds its later counterpart in Lohengrin's Narration, and the shrieking horns in Arindal's hunt solo ('Halloo! Untether all your hounds!') recur in Sieglinde's vision of the pack of hounds in *Die Walküre*. It is in this the first of his operas that one finds the prototype of his later leitmotifs. During the Song of the Witch in the first act ('I tell you of an evil witch, Dame Dilnovaz her name'), the orchestra sounds a two-bar motif:

This appears first when the suspicion is aired that the Fairy Ada might be a witch, and flits thereafter in various keys through the whole scene. The orchestra sounds this motif several more times later on, when it will speak directly to the audience, without explanatory words, as will be Wagner's practice in the *Ring*

Ludwig Geyer: self-portrait by Wagner's stepfather

and his later works. A remarkable little tune is played by the violins in bars 441 to 444 of the Overture to *Die Feen*:

In the second act the flute plays it, to console Ada's grief:

And now this fairy tune is lodged in Wagner's brain, so much so that it will ghost its way into three subsequent operas. It can be heard in the second act of *Rienzi*:

It appears at the conclusion of the second act of *Der fliegende Holländer*:

It enters again, only slightly modified, at the end of the first act of *Tannhäuser*:

Shortly before completing the *Feen* score, Wagner tells his sister Rosalie about the rehearsal of a Würzburg concert which is to feature several extracts from their chorus master's first opera. He makes a point of mentioning that their brother Albert had to stop singing, because he was so moved. The writer himself is too moved, too engrossed still in the frenzied aftermath of creation, to write coherently:

> But why am I telling you all this? Because I simply long to share everything with you. God, dear God, it will not be long now, I shall soon be with you. . . . I am always in such a state of excitement these days, – again I could not sleep last night, – but what am I saying, – I have long given up my peace at night, – I am always thinking of you all – and – in my presumptuous way, of my opera! (WSB I 139: 11.12.1833)

He will soon learn to see nothing wrong in thinking of his works 'in a presumptuous way'. The jungle in which composers try to persuade directors and singers to perform their works unfortunately demands from its inhabitants the thick hide of an elephant, the cunning of a fox and the ruthlessness of a Bengal tiger. For the present he is still the caring brother, the loving son. His letter to Rosalie continues:

> How is mother, how are you all? – Ah, I shall soon see you all again! – I really am a spoilt child, because I fret every moment that I am away from you! – I hope, my Rosalie, that we two shall yet spend *much time* together in this world! – Would you like that? – . . . Heavens! I am really only twenty! – Give them all my love, but above all much, much love to my dear mother, and do tell everybody about their Richard who gives them so much concern. But you – you will always be my angel, my one and only Rosalie!

One would like to see the later Wagner, occasionally at least, as he appears in this letter – friendly and modest. But, who knows, his works might then have turned out the same – friendly and modest.

It is easier to compose *Die Feen* than to have it performed. Wagner tries Leipzig, where all manuscripts by aspiring composers of opera are examined by Franz Hauser, singer and producer, who reads and rejects *Die Feen*. Harmony, instrumentation and treatment of vocal lines, he says, are not solid enough. What is Wagner to do next? How does a young, little-known composer persuade a widely respected expert to change his mind? He turns diplomatist, as he did at fifteen, when begging Herr Müller's forgiveness for concealing his Overture from him. He now writes to Hauser:

> With this letter I follow your recent advice to set down in writing any observations, rejoinders and conclusions regarding your remarks of three days ago, which were penetrating and sincere, knowing that in so doing I should gain the necessary detachment for a lucid reply. But I cannot proceed without first conveying to you my warmest and most heartfelt gratitude for your excellent criticism and for the attestation of your generous friendship which makes me forever beholden to you.
>
> (WSB I 149: *March 1834*)

He assures Hauser that Herr Weinlig, his former teacher, had given him thorough instruction in harmony and counterpoint and continues:

> He dismissed me with these words, 'I herewith discharge you from your course of instruction, as a master releases his apprentice who has learnt all that his master could teach him.' . . . During and after my period of study, several of my Overtures and, more recently, a Symphony of mine were performed at our subscription concerts, and I am pleased to be able to say that no harm ever came from this. . . . I now entertain the same intentions and hopes for my opera. You, my esteemed friend, now apparently wish to follow your deepest conviction and dissuade me from cherishing such hopes. You dislike my opera and, what is more, you dislike the direction in which I am going, since it is not your artistic direction. . . . You ask me why I do not orchestrate like Haydn. . . . You reproach me with total ignorance of compositional technique and of the practice of harmony, and with my lack of thorough training. You have found nothing in my music that comes straight from the heart, nothing that could have sprung from real enthusiasm. . . . Any attempt

to refute such censure or even to offer explanations, does not become the person so criticised, nor is it really possible! I shall be silent, because any contention would seem to me presumptuous. . . . Now that the life or death of my opera depends on my response to you, you will not take it amiss if, like a shipwrecked person, I cling to the smallest plank that could sustain my life and my hopes. . . . Do not place, I beg you, any obstacles in the way of the present negotiations, and allow me to observe the normal formalities and have the score collected, so that I can place it officially in the conductor's hands. Let me tempt providence, just this once. At the same time, it would grieve me immensely if you thought that I might carelessly disregard the advice you so warmly and persuasively gave me. It all resides deeply within me, and I hope that a fresh, securely founded and purer artistic endeavour on my part will spring from your words. . . . I regard these lines as a basis for a mutual relationship in which advice is freely given and eagerly accepted. (WSB I 149–55)

The young man's compositions may be immature, but his letter shows a knowledge of human nature and cunning in equal measure. That it fails to move its recipient is not Wagner's fault but Hauser's, and in fact the composer will not live to see the first triumphant performance of *Die Feen* which takes place in Munich, five years after his death, in 1888 (the conductor, incidentally, being not Hermann Levi as is commonly supposed, but Franz Fischer). Between 1888 and 1899 Munich stages seventy performances. Prague, Cologne, Zürich, Stuttgart and Leipzig follow, and Bayreuth sees the opera as late as 1967 as part of the International Youth Festival, though not in the Festspielhaus; the BBC broadcasts it in 1976, and in the centenary year of Wagner's death, 1983, Munich gives the opera in concert performance. The manuscript, though, remains untraced. Its last owner was Adolf Hitler.

Wagner's position in Würzburg lasts one year. In July 1834 he becomes director of music in the much smaller town of Lauchstädt, exchanging the status of a small fish in a big pond for its opposite. In the summer of that year, he begins writing the poem for his next opera, *Das Liebesverbot* (The Ban on Love), after Shakespeare's *Measure for Measure*. He will never again make such a vast artistic leap as that from *Die Feen* to *Das Liebesverbot*. The first inhabits an insubstantial fairy land, while the second turns its back on the supernatural, and extols the sensual pleasures of this world and rebellion against the established order. Wagner relates in his *Communication to My Friends*:

I felt enthusiastic about the novice Isabella who leaves her convent, to plead with the hard-hearted governor for her brother's pardon who, in pursuance of a draconian law, has been sentenced to death, for the crime of indulging in a love bond with a maiden which, though forbidden, had been blest by nature. . . . Shakespeare settles the resulting conflicts through the public return of the Duke who had hitherto been a hidden observer. His judgement is severe, based on the judge's precept, 'measure for measure'. I, however, untied the knot without the Duke's aid, by means of a revolt. I transferred the action to the capital of Sicily, to enable me to make use of the hot-blooded southern temperament. I also made the governor, a puritanical German, ban the proposed carnival celebrations. An intrepid young man, in love with Isabella, incites the people to put on their masks and to keep their weapons at hand:

> Who will not share what we love best,
> Shall have the steel thrust in his breast.

Isabella persuades the governor to come, masked, to their rendezvous where he is discovered, unmasked and ridiculed. The brother is freed by force, just in time before his imminent execution, while Isabella renounces her noviciate and gives her hand to her young carnival companion. A procession, fully masked, goes to meet the returning Duke who is confidently expected to be less mad than his governor.

(GS IV 254–5)

Die Feen and *Das Liebesverbot* live in irreconcilably different worlds which Wagner finds it imperative to inhabit simultaneously. He comments:

It is plain to see that there was a possibility of my developing in one of two very different directions: the profound seriousness of my earlier inclinations, or the disrespectful fancy for unbridled sensuality. . . . Anyone comparing this composition [*Das Liebesverbot*] with *Die Feen* would find it difficult to understand how in so short a time such a conspicuous change of direction could have taken place. My further artistic development was to create a balance of both tendencies.

(GS IV 255–6)

Numerous echoes from the past and pointers to the future can be detected in the poem of *Das Liebesverbot*. Particularly noticeable is its relationship with Mozart's *Marriage of Figaro*. In both operas, the *jus primae noctis* plays an

Franz Stassen's cover design for libretto of Das Liebesverbot

important part. In *Figaro*, Count Almaviva intends to deflower Susanna before handing her over to her bridegroom. In *Das Liebesverbot*, Friedrich intends to deflower Isabella before returning her to the convent. In both operas the men are outwitted and cheated of their nocturnal sport. In both operas secret messages are handed to the governor and to the Count, and both flirt with their masked wives, in place of their supposed paramours. In both operas, exposure results in public disgrace. Both operas, incidentally, require three principal female parts, all soprano.

As in *Die Feen*, Beethoven's *Fidelio* too has left its imprint on *Das Liebesverbot*:

Fidelio	Liebesverbot
LEONORE (rushes forward): . . . *First kill his wife!*	ISABELLA (rushes forward): *First kill me!* *I am his sister!*
PIZARRO: *Lock up the prisoners once again.*	ISABELLA: *Lock up the prisoner once again.*
PIZARRO: *Triumph! Triumph! The victory is mine!*	ISABELLA: *Triumph! Triumph! The plan is now complete.*
JACQUINO: *My hair now stands on end.*	BRIGHELLA: *With fear my hair now stands on end.*

Both operas conclude with the King's representative appearing as *deus ex machina*.

Certain phrases in the text of *Das Liebesverbot* also recur in his more mature works:

Liebesverbot	Tannhäuser
FRIEDRICH: *and life to you is naught but lust and pleasure.*	TANNHÄUSER: *and love to me is naught but pleasure.*
Liebesverbot	Siegfried
FRIEDRICH: *But you who lit a thousand fires within me, how will you now put out those flames?*	SIEGFRIED: *The blaze that burned round Brünnhilde's rock, will fiercely burn in my breast. O maid, now put out those flames!*
Liebesverbot	Meistersinger
BRIGHELLA: *A painful task, I must confess.*	BECKMESSER: *A painful task, and more so now.*

It seems that a verbal phrase and its rhythm, once formed, wants to reassert itself, after several years or even decades. Review and preview in the text, echoes and augury in the music. With *Das Liebesverbot* Wagner rids himself of the operatic conventions current at that time among the lesser Italian and French composers. With his next opera, *Rienzi*, he echoes Meyerbeer's heroic pathos, and in *Der fliegende Holländer* he finds himself, the real Wagner.

In the volatile Overture to *Das Liebesverbot* – what a brilliant concert piece, if only orchestras would play it today – Wagner employs tambourine, triangle and castanets, the same percussion blend which can be heard in the Bacchanale of *Tannhäuser* (Paris version). In the Nuns' Chorus of *Das Liebesverbot*, a 'Salve regina coeli' makes its appearance:

This is a clear forerunner of the theme of forgiveness in the third act of *Tannhäuser*:

On the whole, the *Liebesverbot* music is pleasant enough and should have found a grateful public in the 1830s and 1840s, but Wagner encounters, for the first time, the public censor who objects to the 'immoral' title. The resourceful composer renames the opera, giving it the highly respectable name, *The Novice of Palermo*, which is sufficiently acceptable to censor and operatic management for it to appear for the first time on the Magdeburg stage, in March 1836, under Wagner's baton. Of the two scheduled performances, only the first takes place. The composer describes the second:

> I cannot tell whether a few people may have turned up in the theatre by the beginning of the Overture, but about fifteen minutes before the intended commencement I could only see Frau Gottschalk with her husband and, most conspicuously, a Polish Jew in full regalia in the front stalls. Undismayed, I was still hoping for further customers, when suddenly the most extraordinary scenes began to take place behind the

curtain. Herr Pollert, the husband of my leading lady (Isabella), had come upon my second tenor (Claudio), a very young, handsome singer against whom the resentful husband had long harboured secret feelings of jealousy. Apparently the leading lady's husband who had peeped through the curtain with me to ascertain the attendance, felt that the long awaited hour had struck in which he could, without damage to our operatic enterprise, wreak vengeance on his wife's lover. *Claudio* was badly pummelled and so severely used that the poor fellow had to retreat into the dressing room, with blood all over his face. When *Isabella* was informed of this, she made a desperate dash towards her husband, only to be so soundly spanked by him that she went into a fit. The confusion among the cast soon knew no bounds. . . . The producer was sent before the curtain to inform the curiously assorted small gathering that 'owing to unforeseen circumstances' the performance of the opera could not take place. And so my career as conductor and opera composer at Magdeburg, begun with so much promise for the future and with quite a few sacrifices, came to an end. (ML I 128–9)

The surreal events of that night find their way into *Die Meistersinger*, where Hans Sachs shakes his head over the unrestrained behaviour of the normally well-behaved citizens of his peaceful Nürnberg. He calls the frenzy which overtakes them '*Wahn*' or 'delusion':

> *How soon from lane and byway*
> *Delusion takes to the highway.*
> *Man, prentice, wife and child*
> *Charge and launch out, all blind and wild.*
> *Encouraged by delusion,*
> *The town is in confusion,*
> *And scuffling, spanking, smiting*
> *Must quench their thirst for fighting.*
> *God knows how that befell.*
>
> (Act 3, Scene 1)

It is the same *Wahn* which is to plague ill-fated Nürnberg once again, in the twentieth century, when it becomes the playground for Nazi thugs. Wagner himself is not free from *Wahn*, as Cosima who shares his last fifteen years with him will learn.

The composer's immediate concern is to rescue his *Liebesverbot* from oblivion. He writes to Robert Schumann, then editor of the influential *Neue Zeitschrift für Musik*:

I herewith send you a report, or rather a certain kind of report on Magdeburg. . . . If you do not like it, change it as you see fit. With the best will in the world I could not avoid saying a few things about myself. . . . I mention my own opera, because nobody else does, and I would dearly love to have it discussed. It is a shame that one has to resort to self-help! However, I do not feel I have written too much about myself. Nevertheless, I think you will agree that the article must be anonymous and that my name must not be divulged to anyone, else heaven help me! I shall probably soon see you again in Leipzig. I am really looking forward to that. Here in Magdeburg there are far too many Shits [*Scheisskerle*]. (WSB I 260–1: 19.4.1836)

Schumann publishes the article, in which Wagner uses his journalistic flair for beating mightily on his anonymous drum:

Magdeburg – . . . I can assure you that their concerts occasionally feature worth-while music. A well-manned orchestra which, when it is in the mood, can play superbly; a notable singer, Frau Pollert, . . . a conductor full of fire and passion, heightened by his recent engagement [to his future wife Minna], and what more do you want? . . . A talented young artist, the music director Richard Wagner, has built up a strong ensemble, with skill and imagination, and consequently we were offered some genuine artistic delights. . . . The season ended with a new opera by R. Wagner, *Das Liebesverbot* or *The Novice of Palermo*. Disaster, however, had already struck before the performance; the ensemble had practically broken up, and the composer was only just able to rush his opera on to the stage, but in great haste and under adverse circumstances. . . . This much is clear, the opera will succeed, provided the composer manages to have it performed by first-rate theatres. It has much to offer, and what I particularly like about it is its sheer musicality and tunefulness, which is more than can be said about today's German operas. (*Neue Zeitschrift für Musik*, Leipzig. 3.5.1836)

The expected response fails to materialise. German opera houses reject *Das Liebesverbot*, while Leipzig takes umbrage at its 'indecency'. Wagner travels to Berlin, where the opera management procrastinates for six weeks, alternately raising and dashing his hopes, sending him from one official to another before finally rejecting it. He is to remember for ever these mortifying weeks.

*   *   *

Thirty years later, Wagner is to present the score of *Das Liebesverbot* to King Ludwig II of Bavaria. He writes on the title page:

> *In boyish ignorance I strayed a little.*
> *What penance for my juvenile caprice?*
> *Permit this work to sue for its acquittal.*
> *May Your good grace secure it lasting peace.*
>   (KL II 119: Christmas 1866)

Much later still, in 1879, he discusses the opera with Cosima, who notes in her diary:

> He says he was quite astonished at the poverty of that music. 'We go through strange phases! One might hardly believe that one is the same person.' (CWT II 301: 1.2.1879)

Only in 1923 will *Das Liebesverbot* be performed in Munich. Encouraged by its success, it is taken up by Hamburg, Stuttgart, Berlin, Leipzig, Magdeburg (!), Bremen, the BBC, and Bayreuth (International Youth Festival), with a fair number of performances in 1983, the centenary year of Wagner's death.

Wagner has now learnt, for a second time, that the difficulties attending the composition of an opera are not to be compared with those of launching it upon the public. Since he knows his goal, he also knows what is to be done. If his operas are to be more important, their subject matter must be weightier. *Rienzi, Der fliegende Holländer, Tannhäuser, Lohengrin, Der Ring des Nibelungen, Tristan und Isolde, Die Meistersinger, Parsifal* – they do not exist yet but he is already determined that they will be performed – must find their stages; if not in Germany, then in France; and if not in France, then he will build his own opera house, and the world shall make a pilgrimage to that place, wherever it will be. He will give the pilgrims what Church, State and Art have denied them. In his works he will speak to them about life and death, about the beginning of the world and its possible ending, about love's bliss and its despair. He will set out not to entertain them, but to stir their innermost being with unheard of music and with dramatic symbols which will speak to them as immediately, as starkly and as reassuringly as Moses was spoken to by the voice from the burning bush. This he must achieve, and to achieve it any means will be fair. If in the process his own image becomes tarnished in the eyes of the world, so be it.

He is still alive – no, he is at the height of his powers. . . . We are awaiting the new works which his genius will yet bring to light! (wsb i 65–6)

Wagner writes this of Giacomo Meyerbeer, in an unpublished article which he had prepared for a French journal in 1839. Two years earlier he had tried to make contact with the influential composer, by first approaching Eugène

Giacomo Meyerbeer

Scribe, Meyerbeer's librettist. He sends his *Das Liebesverbot* and asks him to show it to the composer. Scribe does not reply. Wagner now writes to Meyerbeer himself:

I trust it will not cause you too much displeasure to be importuned by a letter from so far away and from a person as unknown to you as I am. . . . I am not yet 24 years old, born in Leipzig, and when I attended the university there I decided to pursue a career in music. My passionate admiration for Beethoven impelled me to take that step, which also explains why my first works were extremely one-sided. Since then, and since I have gained experience of life and of the musical profession, my views about the present state of music, particularly of dramatic music, have changed considerably. Need I deny that it was your works, more than anything else, that showed me a quite new direction? (WSB I 323: 4.2.1837)

He then mentions Scribe and the unacknowledged *Das Liebesverbot*:

> I have sent him my grand comic opera, *Das Liebesverbot*, with the request to pass it on to you for your perusal. . . . You will readily understand the decisive influence of your judgement on my future career and on my whole life, provided you would take the trouble and pronounce your opinion on my modest work. My most ardent desire, to which all my efforts are directed, is to be able to go to Paris, for I feel that within me which should come to fruition there. . . . You yourself can hardly rise to greater artistic fame, for you have already reached the most dazzling heights. Where people sing, your melodies are heard; you are almost a god on earth. How wonderful it must be for one who has attained such a position, to look down and hold out his hand to those whom he has left so far behind, and allow them to come at least a little closer to him. (WSB I 324–6: 4.2.1837)

Meyerbeer does not reply, and it is two and a half years before they are to meet. When they do, the composer of *Robert le Diable* and *Les Huguenots* receives the newly arrived Wagner in Boulogne, gives him letters of introduction to take to Paris, and later negotiates the acceptance of *Das Liebesverbot* by the Théâtre de Renaissance. The theatre, unfortunately, goes bankrupt. Wagner is now in Paris, with Minna, and together with other equally penniless artists he tries to make a living. Once again he turns to Meyerbeer:

> My sincerely esteemed Lord and Master,
> When you left Paris you gave your protégé permission to keep you informed of his progress there. And you, my dear Master, who are goodness and benevolence itself, will be less angry with me than anyone else would be, if cries for help – alarming as they might be – disturb your peaceful retreat. . . . I implore you to create an avenue for me, through your recommendations and support, to the Paris public. . . . With all my sins and weaknesses, worries and misery weighing me down, I

respectfully take my leave, praying for deliverance from all evil through God and yourself. If I remain in your favour, God will also be with me, so remember me occasionally, who am

In glowing admiration Your devoted servant

Richard Wagner.

(WSB I 378–9: 18.1.1840)

Meyerbeer obliges. He pulls a few strings and achieves a rehearsal at least of Wagner's *Columbus* Overture by the Paris Conservatoire Orchestra. Its composer thanks him:

Wagner at the time of the Meyerbeer episode

My sincerely esteemed Lord and Protector,

My need for help cries to heaven! So let me at once sound my strings and sing the ancient, all too familiar original melody, 'Please help me!', in the Wagnerian mode of course, lyrical, tender and melancholy. . . . It gives me great pleasure to report that, thanks to your recommendation, I succeeded in persuading Habeneck to rehearse my Overture. The entire orchestra showed by their repeated and lengthy applause that they were not dissatisfied. . . . The gratitude I carry in my heart for you, my noble Protector, knows no bounds. I foresee that I shall be pursuing you, muttering my thanks, in this world and the next. I assure you that even in hell I shall still be muttering it.

> Your subject, forever bound to you, body and soul,
> Richard Wagner.
> (WSB I 380: 15.2.1840)

But, just as doors seem to be opening to Wagner, so they are shut in his face, and he and Minna stay poor. In May 1840 he writes a further letter to Meyerbeer which is to prey on his mind for years to come and which throws light on Wagner's later attitude towards Meyerbeer and the Jews. It is an extraordinary outburst:

> The time has come for me to sell myself to someone, in order to exist in the most basic sense of the word. But my head and my heart are no longer my own – they are already your property, my Master; all I have left are my hands. Would you like to make use of them? I realise that I shall have to be your slave in mind and body, if I am to gather food and strength for the work which shall one day express my gratitude to you. I shall be a faithful and honest slave. I feel immensely happy when I can give myself unconditionally, recklessly, and in blind faith. . . . Therefore buy me, good sir, your purchase should be worth your while! Unpurchased, I should perish, and my wife with me. Would that not be a pity? (WSB I 388: 3.5.1840)

'My head and my heart are no longer my own' – this phrase is to be so firmly lodged in his memory that he reproduces it twelve years later in *Das Rheingold*, when Alberich cries from the depth of his utter despair, 'Hand and head, eyes and ears are no longer my own.' Wagner, too, must have been in utter despair when he found it necessary to abase himself so profoundly. Where most people would hate themselves for having written in that vein, Wagner chooses to hate the recipient, and his whole race to boot. But for the present it is imperative for him – and his future works! – to remain on good terms with the protector who has responded favourably to his cry for help and instructed his secretary to look after the needy composer:

> This young man interests me. He is talented and ambitious, but fortune does not smile on him. He has written me a long and very moving letter

which is the reason for my request: please let him have the means of assistance enclosed in this letter. (WSB I 397: 15.7.1840)

Meyerbeer does more. The following year, in a letter dated 18 March 1841, he recommends Wagner to Baron von Lüttichau, director of the Dresden opera:

Herr Richard Wagner from Leipzig is a young composer who not only had a sound musical training, but is also very inventive and possesses a wide knowledge of literature. His present position deserves altogether a great deal of sympathy from his native country. He has written the text and composed the music of his opera, *Rienzi*, and it is his greatest wish to have it performed by Dresden's new Royal Opera. He has played me several numbers which I found full of inspiration and dramatically most effective. I hope the young artist may enjoy Your Excellency's protection and find an opportunity for his great talent to be more generally recognised. (J. Kapp: *Giacomo Meyerbeer*, Berlin 1932: 98)

Dresden is to perform *Rienzi* a year and a half later. Meyerbeer again intercedes for Wagner over his next opera, *Der fliegende Holländer*. On 9 December 1841 he writes to the director of the Berlin Royal Opera House:

I herewith take the liberty of sending you the score and text of the opera, *Der fliegende Holländer*, by Richard Wagner. I already had the honour, the day before yesterday, to converse with Your Excellency about this interesting composer who deserves, both on account of his talent and of his extremely difficult circumstances, that the great court stages, as protectors of German art, should not close their doors on him. (*Die Musik*, Berlin 1903, vol. 11: 331)

Berlin takes no notice, but Dresden does. In 1842 Wagner and Minna leave Paris and return to Germany. In October, *Rienzi* has its first performance, with Schröder-Devrient, and only eleven weeks later Dresden gives *Der fliegende Holländer* for the first time, again with his admired soprano. Wagner's star has risen, and in February 1843 he is appointed Royal Saxon Court Conductor. In a letter to Franz Liszt, written eight years later, he looks back at that period in his life:

I do not hate Meyerbeer, he only fills me with immense loathing. This man, forever charming and obliging, reminds me of the most awkward, not to say immoral time of my life, when he still pretended to be my protector. That was the period of pulling strings and of back stairs, when we are hoodwinked by our patrons whom in our hearts we resent. This is a totally dishonest relationship; neither is sincere with the other; each simulates feelings of affection, and both make use of each other as long as it is to their advantage. (WSB III 545: 18.4.1851)

For a very long time to come – Meyerbeer died in 1864 – the former protector, the 'Lord and Master', is to disturb the dream world of the 'faithful and honest slave', the 'subject forever bound to you, body and soul'. Cosima notes in her diary:

He told me several times of his 'idle dreams' during the night. In one we were out driving with the King of Bavaria who had been very ostentatious in bestowing favours on us; in another he had been walking arm in arm with Meyerbeer in Paris, and M. was smoothing the paths to fame for him. (CWT I 576–7: 26.9.1872)

On another occasion:

R. had a good night, though he dreamt of Meyerbeer, whom he had met again in the theatre and who said, 'Ah yes, I know, my long nose!', as though R. had made fun of his nose, whereupon R. more or less apologised, while the audience applauded their reconciliation. (CWT II 515: 3.4.1880)

'More or less apologised' – 'applauded their reconciliation'. Wagner asleep redeems Wagner awake.

There will be no more Meyerbeers in Wagner's life, and no more bending of knees. His apprenticeship is over.

II

WEDDED WIFE
AND
MAGIC MUSE

older than he is. He does not mind. Her intellectual capacity does not measure up to his. He does not mind that either. She has a daughter, Natalie, by a former lover, a Captain Ernst Rudolf von Einsiedel. Wagner accepts this too, for he is deeply in love. Since Minna was only sixteen when her child was born, Natalie

Minna Planer in 1835 painted by her then suitor Alexander von Otterstedt.
By the following year she was married to Wagner

is passed off as her much younger sister, not only to all the world, but to the child herself; the situation appeals to Wagner's dramatic instinct and he finds it easy to forgive. He woos her passionately for two years:

Berlin, 21.5.1836

My poor, poor Minna! If you could only know what prompts these words! My eyes are flooded with tears, my strength is broken by sadness!

You are so far, so very, very far away, amongst strangers, amongst unfeeling people. . . . I keep on weeping and am truly not ashamed of my tears; . . . Oh, how glad I should be, if *I* could, for once, contribute something to our happiness, so that *you* may at last have something to thank *me* for, because so far I have to thank *you* for *everything*, for *everything*. My *poor, poor* girl, – I have already given you so much trouble, so much worry . . . and do you love me still? do you still love me? Well then, nothing, nothing in the whole world will make me part from you. By the eternal God, nothing, nothing will tear you, my Minna, from your Richard. I must close, I can say no more, but you know me, you know me as I am! (WSB I 263–6)

Would this tender-heartedness be preserved for the years of marriage? In *Meistersinger*, Hans Sachs sings:

> *But when you're wed, you soon will see,*
> *One sings a different melody.*
>
> (Act 3, Scene 2)

Both Minna and Richard soon learn the 'different melody'.

The wedding ceremony takes place in Königsberg, on 24 November 1836. Wagner records:

The preacher proclaimed there were hard times ahead for us, and he recommended to us a friend, whom neither of us knew. I looked at the priest with interest, eager to learn more about this unknown, influential patron whose existence was intimated to me in this strange way. However, the preacher announced in a particularly strict tone of voice that our unknown friend was – Jesus. I did not take umbrage at this, as was surmised in the town. I was merely disappointed, whilst I assumed that admonitions of this kind were usual in nuptial addresses. (ML I 142)

Minna's marriage brings her, on the whole, more sorrow than joy. There is not enough household money. There is not enough consideration on his part, and not enough sympathetic understanding on hers. Their best times together are the years before Wagner's exile. She writes to him from Dresden to Zurich, in August 1849:

You will remember that I hardly ever missed a performance which you conducted. I saw only you and I was happy! I believed that everything I heard came from you alone. Don Giovanni was your *last* opera here; it will be a sad memory for me for a long time to come. But the Ninth

Symphony will *remain forever in my memory*, because of you. You seemed to me like a god, ruling the mighty elements and bewitching his audience. (SB 349)

Having played a leading part in the 1849 Dresden uprising, Wagner has to run for his life, a warrant for his arrest pursuing him into Switzerland. Now Minna is expected to share his exile. But she is uncertain. What can he offer her?

Dresden, 11.8.1849

Really, you must not think badly of me, but I am worried. How are we going to manage? I just cannot face again what I have been through with you before. When I remember those stupid anxieties about our food, when sometimes I did not know what to put into the boiling water, because there was nothing to put in, I have to shudder when I think of my future, when similar things are likely to await me. I will not hide it from you – I have lost my courage. (SB 348–9)

Wagner is to hear this anxious tone again and again. No wonder he will get tired of it. And yet she has reason to worry.

One year later Minna joins him in Switzerland, only to face fresh vicissitudes. Wagner has discovered Jessie Laussot, aged twenty-two, the wife of a Bordeaux wine merchant. He intends to elope with her to Greece or even further east. The sensible merchant's counter-measures prevail, but Minna suffers, as always. She writes to him in May 1850:

All my labour of love in our home was meant to please you, was done for your sake. Right from the beginning I did *everything* for *love* of you. My *independence* which I treasured so much, I gave up gladly, so that I really *could be yours alone*. As for your intellectual development, I am happy in the knowledge that *all* the beauty you created had come to life in the *home I had made*. I understood, I appreciated you completely. You know how happy you used to make me when you sang and played nearly each new scene to me. But then, two years ago, you wanted to read me that essay in which you *offended whole generations of people* who had really shown you nothing but kindness,* and ever since that day you have been angry with me, and have punished me so very severely that you never again read or played any of your works to me.

(SB 391)

* R. Wagner: 'Das Judenthum in der Musik' (Judaism in Music).

Jessie Laussot stays with her husband, but Minna informs Wagner:

> May 1850
>
> . . . I should forever blame myself, if I were to hinder you in your decision and insisted on being reunited with you. . . . But I cannot decide how long I shall be able to stay here, nor *where* I shall go to live out my sad life. If I go to Germany I shall have no reason to keep our separation a secret. I have committed no crime, so the world cannot find me guilty. (SB 392)

The world, and Dresden in particular, will soon know the secret. Wagner's Bordeaux escapade is all over the town, and Minna is looked upon as practically divorced and once more free to marry. One Herr E. – we do not know his identity – proposes to her by letter, probably in June 1850:

> My dear, highly esteemed lady,
> Although I only had the pleasure on two occasions of meeting you in company, and talking with you, and although I may not even be so fortunate as to be still remembered, I nevertheless make so bold as to approach you today in a matter on which will depend my whole life's happiness. I am not unaware of the fact that your husband has left you, and it is not for me to consider which party will eventually be the more deserving of sympathy. Please let me assure you that your husband is severely criticised here, as everyone appreciates the excellence of your character – which is so rarely to be found amongst women. I do realise that you will find it hard to make a decision to enter into the bonds of marriage for a second time, when you have had such bitter experiences, yet I feel that, as an honest and upright man, I may venture to offer you my heart and my hand. Although I am not a man of great wealth, I feel confident that my savings and my thriving shop will suffice to provide you with many of life's pleasures, which might recompense you for past privations. (SB 399)

There is no record of Minna's reply, if indeed she gave one, but she must have been impressed with the contrast between the unfaithful genius and the suitor with his thriving shop. In July Minna and Richard re-establish their household in Zurich.

Wagner works on *Der Ring des Nibelungen*. He writes his essay, *Oper und Drama*. He completes *Rheingold*. He completes *Die Walküre*. He lays aside his work on *Siegfried* and begins *Tristan und Isolde*. He conducts in Zurich and in London. But, two years after the Jessie Laussot débâcle, he falls in love with Mathilde Wesendonck. In April 1857 he and Minna move into the small house which adjoins the Wesendonck residence and which the generous Otto puts at their disposal. Mathilde enchants and inspires her *master*, and under his spell she becomes his muse, with Minna as a gloomy spectator.

Does Wagner think his wife duller or blinder than she is? Or – and this would be a pity – is she no longer worth his consideration? In April 1858, Minna takes a health cure at Brestenberg by Lake Hallwyl. He entreats her:

Zurich, 23.4.1858

Poor dear Minna,
Once more I call to you and repeat it a thousand times, be *patient*, and above all, *trust me*! If you only knew how much your distrust torments me, you would surely regret it. Recently, when you assured me that you really did love me, I implored you to prove this, by refraining from mixing with [the Wesendoncks] and by not flouting your status, at least until the end of your convalescence. *I for my part* promised to do everything in my power to reassure you. But the tempter has seized hold of you for a second time, and this time you have openly shattered our love and our faith. But I forgive you, first of all on account of the deplorable state of your health, which is responsible for your clouded brain, and what is more, I forgive you for all time to come. (RWM I 265)

Four days later he goes berserk:

Zurich, Tuesday, 27.4.1858

This, dear Minna, is the date on which I have decided not to let myself be committed to a hydropathic establishment, but to a lunatic asylum, for that seems to be the only place I am fit for. Everything I say or write, even if it is with the best intentions, causes nothing but unhappiness and misunderstanding. If I do not mention certain things, you become suspicious and imagine I am acting behind your back. If I write seriously and frankly and, as I believed – ass that I am – to allay your fears, I am told that I am thinking up nasty tricks, in order to cause your immediate demise. At the same time you tell me to be a *man*! Quite so, I do not want to be just *any* man, I want to be *yours*. Just tell me always and exactly how I am to speak, to think and to look upon the world. I will always obey you and neither speak, think nor see anything you do not approve. Does this satisfy you? Advise me too, what and how I am to compose, write and conduct. I will follow you in everything, so that you can no longer harbour the slightest doubts about me. . . . Heaven knows whether this will cheer you up, as I intended, or whether I seem to you hypocritical and malicious again. . . . My God, what am I to do to win your approval? (RWM I 266–7)

The couple are falling apart. Not surprisingly, Minna saw in Mathilde the sole reason for their impending separation, although they had long gone their different ways, physically and mentally, and the separation would surely have come to pass even without Mathilde.

Minna writes a sombre letter to Frau Schiffner, her Dresden friend:

> 2.8.1858
>
> It is no small matter when one is faced with a separation, after nearly 22 years of marriage. I, for one, shall not get over it easily. Let me assure you that this is not my own choice. Where my understanding of men is concerned, I am just as enlightened as other women, and I have understood and not wanted to notice a good many things. After all, I have carried on like that for six whole years, with my eyes shut. . . . R. has two hearts. He is ensnared by the other woman, and clings to me out of habit, that is all! I have therefore decided, since this person will not tolerate my staying with my husband and since he is weak enough to give in to her, to stay alternately with the Tichatscheks in Dresden, and then in Berlin, perhaps also in Weimar, until either Richard or God will call me. . . . What weak creatures we are, and how we torment each other.
>
> (FH 257–8)

Later that month, on 19 August, Minna advertises in the *Zürich Tagblatt*:

> *For sale*, on account of removal:
> One large elegant mirror in beautiful gold frame, the glass being 4ft 8ins
>   high and 2ft 7ins wide.
> One new walnut card table with carved pedestal.
> One large round ditto.
> One ditto extending dining table for 14 people, 12 ditto chairs.
> Walnut bedsteads, feather mattresses, silk covered sofas, armchairs,
>   carpets etc.
> One lock-up wine cabinet, easily holding 300 bottles.
> Apply to Frau Wagner on the Gabler, in Enge, next to Herr
> Wesendonck's house. (FZ II 144)

Two days earlier, on 17 August, Wagner has left his Asyl,* alone. The magic muse has done her duty: *Die Walküre* is completed, and the score bears the letters 'g.s.M.', 'gesegnet sei Mathilde' (blessings on Mathilde), and *Tristan und Isolde* is begun.

It was as far back as 1853 that he had first met Cosima, Liszt's daughter. Later, in August 1857, she and her husband, Hans von Bülow, spent part of their honeymoon – symbolically? – with Wagner in Zurich. Now, in Minna's autumn of adversity, young Cosima von Bülow sends her a discarded garment. Mischief or pure kindliness? The reader must decide:

> As for my old dress, I am very grateful to you, dearest madam, for having put it to such good use. I did not think it would serve for anything better than wiping the stairs, and so I feel very proud that it will still function as a dress. (SB 690)

Wagner travels to Italy, Minna returns to Germany. *Tristan und Isolde* is completed. In November 1859 the couple attempt once more to live together. They share the distressing experience of the Paris *Tannhäuser* fiasco in March 1861, when his work is hissed off the stage, but in the summer they separate again. He begs her to submit to the inevitable. She tries, but in February 1862 she pays him a hopeful visit on the Rhine. She should have resisted the impulse, for the reunion is a harrowing experience for both of them. She writes to her daughter Natalie:

> 6.3.1862
>
> Richard wrote me an emotional letter saying that he was definitely going to stay in Biebrich, a ghastly place, so that he could compose his new opera undisturbed. However, he had no one who would make his life a little easier and look after his comfort. He had to borrow some sticks of furniture as bare essentials, and he really sounded rather gloomy. So I made a quick decision and went to him. . . . Richard was hugely delighted when I arrived, he nearly pulled my head off for joy and was really very sweet. But next morning at breakfast he received a letter from that Wesendonck woman, and everything was changed, though I had not uttered a *single* word. He raged and roared without reason, that it was no concern of mine, that he could correspond with whomever he

* *Asyl* = sanctuary, Wagner's name for his temporary refuge on the Wesendoncks' property.

pleased, etc. The following day we went with the Schott family from Mainz to Darmstadt, where *Rienzi* was performed with Niemann, and we did not return to B. until the day after. As before, we were just having our breakfast, when another bulky letter arrived from that Wesendonck hussy. Again I did not say a single word. But Richard once more began

Minna and her dog Peps in 1853, the year Wagner first met Cosima

to shout himself into a mad fury. . . . I said that he could insult me as much as he liked, and that I would not answer back, and so he really went on raving for three quarters of an hour, until I finally said to him that apparently he did not know of the rights of a woman and wife, which admittedly I had never referred to before, partly out of consideration for him and partly because I am too modest for such proclamations, and that for the sake of God and for the sake of his marital obligations towards me, I could not allow this correspondence, as it was so obviously having a bad influence on him. I said all this

calmly, although I was really thunderstruck. Next day . . . an official
called to inform me that a box was waiting to be collected which had
arrived by post a few days before. Meaning well, because I know that R.
does not like to bother with such things, and assuming that it contained
music, I had the little case opened, in order to pass it through the
customs, and – what do you know – it was again from that bitch: an
embroidered cushion, tea, Eau de Câlange [Minna's spelling], and
boxed violets. Of course this provoked another outburst, but I do not
like to repeat what I had to hear, in spite of the fact that I entreated him,
for heaven's sake not to put me to shame in front of other people.

(SB 539–40)

How jealous Minna must have been to risk provoking Wagner's rage by
opening the box, and how the poor woman must have got on his nerves to make
him lose all self-control. So Minna leaves for Dresden, but nothing goes right.
Even Natalie, still believing herself to be Minna's younger sister, is dogged by
bad luck. She cannot find a husband. Minna counsels her:

Dresden, 6.3.1862

If your suitor has not declared himself by the autumn, he never will.
Then you can come to me and we shall manage somehow. You attach
too much importance to a few kind words . . . such things mean
nothing and should never be taken seriously. They are only idle chatter,
hiding the real purpose which is to find out how much money one has.
In any case, you really are a little too old for him, and it is no great good
fortune to get a husband with a salary of 320 thaler. You still do not
know how to economise. On the other hand, if you love him, you would
learn that too. Only try not to be affected, my dear Natalie, do not pull
such ugly faces, or you may not even get this poor fellow. (SB 705)

The poor fellow takes to his heels, and Natalie continues to pull ugly faces.
  In June 1862 Wagner appeals to their mutual friend and family doctor, Anton
Pusinelli, to discover what Minna would think of a divorce. She is appalled:

Chemnitz, 16.6.1862

I received your letter. . . . My heart pounded like a galloping horse, and
it took me a long time to calm myself. I do hope you will excuse me from
coming to Dresden. A week ago I thought I might be able to travel, but I
am still not strong enough to undertake this short journey, and least of
all to take part in discussions regarding Richard and his intentions
towards me. . . . I have begged Richard repeatedly, not only now, but

years ago, that he should do what he likes, correspond with whom he likes, but also that he should respect me as a person, and not insult me. I do not ask for more, and I cannot ask for less. . . . My replies to Richard's possible demands are as follows: if he wants a divorce, my answer is No. He will have to be patient until God parts us. A separation? He already has that, as I have been pushed around on my own for many years. He can come to Dresden whenever he wishes, he will always find his home here. I have already proved that I am able to suffer his outbursts in silence. I therefore favour the arrangement that he should come to me in Dresden from time to time, and that he can do so whenever he wishes. I beg of you, dear friend, . . . to inform him of my opinion and to advise him to treat the old companion of his life with the forbearance which I trust to be my due. Farewell, I send a thousand kind regards to you and your dear family, especially to your wife.
In gratitude
    Your friend M. Wagner.
    Please excuse my writing. I am trembling . . .   (FH 313–15)

If Minna objects to a divorce, so Wagner argues, let her at least agree to a silent truce and terminate their correspondence. He explains why in this letter to Natalie, with its disingenuous ending:

Penzing, 20.6.1863
Believe me, dear Natalie, my heart has been bleeding for many a year; for I see quite clearly that I can no longer live with Minna. . . . Of course, I do not hate her. I want to be decent to her, but the differences between us are too great, and the split, caused by bitter experience, so wide that no attempt at deceiving ourselves about its true nature would succeed. So I must ask myself to what purpose I should keep the poor woman in a state of uncertainty which is hurtful to her and to me? Even our letters can never be quite without a sting. There will always be misunderstandings which in their turn demand explanations, and all this causes ever greater distress. I have, therefore, come to the conclusion that it would be better to stop writing. In saying this, believe me, I have to do battle with myself, and my heart suffers more from this seeming show of hardness than any of you can possibly imagine. It is better if I keep my softer feelings to myself. Were I to show them to Minna, it would only bring about more confusion. . . . She is the unquestioned owner of all the possessions at present in her keep; it is for her to dispose of them as she pleases . . . I shall never dream of asking

her for a divorce. I shall remain single, and no one is to take her place.

(SB 546–8)

Minna has to endure this existence for another two and a half years. Yet, in February 1864, Wagner writes her this note:

Penzing, 15.2.1864

Life is such a serious matter and so terribly difficult. Who can tell with certainty what to do for the best? Poor Minna! Fate has tied you to one of the strangest of men. Every day I realise anew how little I am understood, how much I stand alone and forsaken. No wonder that your suffering is so great. (SB 552)

In his works, Wagner shows an understanding of the most complex traits of his characters and their predicaments. In his private life, he has rarely succeeded better than with this letter. He blames neither Minna nor himself, but rather life itself.

Perhaps it did Minna's bruised heart good, when others confessed to her their own distressing experiences with Wagner. Cäcilie, his half-sister, neglected by him for years, grumbles to Minna:

22.10.1864

Many thanks for your news about Richard. I am glad he is not ill, but much of what you wrote about his life and his activities did not exactly please me. When you say, for instance, that the Bülow clan is in fact also moving to Munich, I feel absolutely with you that his star will soon wane again, as those people will surely contribute to the immoral side of his character. . . . Moreover, he will grow in arrogance through these Bülows, who do everything to support him in it. Bülow himself is after all a shameless scoundrel – I have always hated his guts. . . . But tell me, dear Minna, do you not write to R. any more? . . . Alas, his heart seems to be dead. How sad, for he once had such a good, gentle heart.

(SB 679–80)

Cäcilie is right. He did once have a good, gentle heart. But she is also wrong. His heart is not dead. Its passionate beats will yet give life to *Meistersinger*, *Siegfried*, *Götterdämmerung* and *Parsifal*.

Even a fortnight before her death, Minna has to suffer from press rumours which suggest that Wagner had failed to support her. The harassed woman issues a disclaimer :

The True Facts
A misleading article in the *Münchner Weltbote* makes me issue the following correct statement of facts:
I have always received financial support from my husband, Richard Wagner, during his absence, which has provided me with a decent, comfortable standard of living.

Frau Minna Wagner née Planer
Dresden, 9.1.1866   (SB 565)

A few days later she is dead. Wagner is in Marseilles and either cannot or will not attend the funeral. In her will she states:

As I leave neither descendants nor other persons qualified to inherit, and as – especially in view of the absolute renunciation of all claims on my estate by my husband, the composer Richard Wagner – I am entirely free to dispose of the same, I herewith name my dear sister, Natalie Planer, as sole heiress to my whole estate, including all effects, whatever they be.

Dresden, 11.5.1865   (SB 720)

So the sister-daughter deception continues posthumously.

After her death, Minna meets the same fate as some other women once close to Wagner's heart – in Cosima's diaries she is disparaged:

15.8.1870

In the evening our conversation turns to Minna, R.'s first wife. Some of Fräulein Meysenbug's observations had given me an insight into a veritable abyss of vulgarity. (CWT I 271)

1.10.1870

Yesterday he read to me from his biography, and I had to shudder at his wife's shameless behaviour towards him. (CWT I 293)

29.7.1878

R. proceeds to other memories, sad ones; how 'bad' Minna had been, when she made use of their meeting in Dresden, only to go to the law courts with him, to file proceedings against the Einsiedels and procure alimony for Natalie. This lack of sensitivity shocks R. even now, whereas at the time, and after she had betrayed him, his good nature made him ignore it. (CWT II 148–9)

Minna had seen in the Wagner of the *Rienzi* period a popular, well-salaried conductor and composer but his development took a course mysterious and troublesome to her. Life had marked Wagner for artistic flights which Minna was unable to share.

The eagle does not care to be reminded that he was once too feeble to soar.

MAGIC MUSE

Natalie does not care for Minna's rival, Mathilde Wesendonck, and she finds some choice terms to describe her in letters which she sends to Mrs Burrell, Wagner's biographer. 'That disreputable creature', 'that slippery cold snake', 'that irresponsible, flirtatious, heartless beast'. The Wesendonck house she calls 'the magic palace of the she-devil superior' (SB 424, 23, 23, 653). Mrs Burrell corresponds with both ladies, in order to obtain material for her book, and Natalie naturally takes her mother's part – she still believes herself to be the younger sister of the now deceased Minna* – and protests in her letter to Mrs Burrell, nine years after Wagner's death:

> 24.11.1892
> Yes, dear esteemed lady, this notable devilish sprite, pious as a lamb, this precious little Mathilde, has told you nothing about all those infernal injuries which were cleverly and deliberately inflicted upon Minna. She has kept quiet, so as not to sink in your estimation and lose her crown of perfection. (SB 24)

Just how devilish was Mathilde? At the age of nineteen she marries Otto Wesendonck, a successful merchant. Wagner meets the couple in Zurich, in 1852. Five years later, they invite him and Minna to live in the house on the green hill, on their property. Wagner is forty-four, Mathilde is twenty-nine. In January 1857 she sends Minna her letter of welcome:

---

* Neither Minna nor Richard ever disclosed the truth to Natalie, who inherited Minna's family papers and was left to draw her own conclusions as to the real nature of the relationship.

Paris, 11.1.1857

Oh may this little house be a real shelter of peace and friendship, a sacred abode, in a world full of envy, hatred and ill will, a safe refuge from all the troubles and tribulations of life. I wish I could give the house my blessing, that only beauty, goodness and love should dwell in it, so that the serenity and the peace of its inhabitants should never be disturbed! . . . I myself can hardly wait for the day when I shall take you

Otto Wesendonck

there, and in my mind I have already arranged the rooms. . . . I wish you farewell for today! I am very much looking forward to seeing you again soon, to convince myself, with my own eyes, that possession of the little house will make you happy. Wagner will have to think of a suitable name for it. He has already conceived so many beautiful utterances that he will not fail to find a fitting one. Let us celebrate the christening together. Adieu, I send a thousand kind regards to you and to Wagner, with the assurance of my warmest friendship.

Yours Mathilde Wesendonck   (SB 484–5)

The Asyl does not last long, barely sixteen months, but it proves a particularly fruitful period in Wagner's creative life. He continues and then abandons his *Siegfried* and he begins *Tristan und Isolde*. He composes five songs to Mathilde's words, 'Der Engel' (The Angel), 'Träume' (Dreams), 'Schmerzen' (Grief), 'Sausendes, brausendes Rad der Zeit' (Restless, thundering Wheel of Time), and 'Im Treibhaus' (The Hothouse). In April 1858, Wagner sends a messenger

The Asyl

with a letter to Mathilde, which the hapless Minna intercepts. She gives it the same cavalier treatment which she accorded the little box in Biebrich – she opens it, and peace and creativity are shattered:

7.4.1858 [Minna's pencilled date]
The day before yesterday an angel came to me at noon, blessed and comforted me. That made me feel so wonderful and serene that I greatly longed for the company of friends in the evening, as I wanted to share

my happiness with them. I knew I was in the mood to be really pleasant and convivial. Then I heard that they had not dared to deliver my letter to you personally, because De Sanctis was with you. . . . Now in the morning I have come to my senses again and am able to pray to my angel

*Unfinished sketch by Kietz of Mathilde Wesendonck
and her son, Guido*

with heartfelt emotion, and this prayer is love! Love! Profound joy in this love, the source of my salvation. . . . When I look into your eyes, there is nothing more to say; then everything I could utter becomes meaningless! Look, everything is then so clear to me, and I feel so sure of myself when this wonderful, sacred gaze rests upon me and envelops me quite! It is there that the distinction between the object and the subject ceases. There all is one and all at one, profound, infinite harmony! Oh, there is peace, and in that peace perfect realisation of life! A fool is he who would gain his world and his peace from elsewhere! Blind is he who, gazing into your eyes, did not find his soul in them! Only from within, from our innermost self, only from the very depth does salvation spring! Now I find that I can only speak and explain myself to you when I cannot see you, or – when I am not allowed to see you. Think well of me, and forgive my childish behaviour yesterday – you were quite right to call it that! Today the weather seems mild. I shall walk in your garden. Perhaps I may find you undisturbed for a little while! Receive my soul with this morning greeting! (SB 490–3)

Intended for one pair of eyes, the letter now finds three, for Minna acquaints both Wesendoncks with its contents. Then she pens her own, undated, farewell letter to Mathilde:

Esteemed Madam,

With a bleeding heart I must tell you before I leave, that you have succeeded in alienating my husband's affections, after nearly 22 years of married life. May this noble deed contribute to your comfort and joy. I am sorry that I feel compelled, after your most spiteful remarks about me, to put before you an exact copy of that fateful letter which my husband took upon himself to address to you, and which prompted me to see you, in order to discuss the matter *as between friends*. Perhaps you should ask yourself what you would have done in my place. Feeling convinced that you did not misunderstand my good and generous intentions when I saw you last, I had, however, to discover all too soon that, unfortunately, you had betrayed my confidence and had made common gossip of it. You repeatedly incited my husband against me and even made unjust and indiscreet accusations about me to your good husband. When I returned after an absence of three months, my husband told me that I should approach you personally. I yielded after some unpleasant scenes and wanted to spread the mantle of oblivion over the incident, just to quell some horrible gossip and, quite honestly, merely to preserve our Asyl. But it was all in vain. I was in any case too late, for you did not wish it, and you were right, it is the only thing I can thank you for. Now Wagner will start working again, from which he had for so long – and to my great pain – been so shamefully prevented. Having only discovered this recently, in addition to everything else, this is the only wish of an unhappy woman.

M. Wagner   (SB 496–7)

Minna's frenzied mind clearly vexes her style, which was erratic even at the best of times. Also, she seems to be alluding to a possible projected understanding between the two women the nature of which may have been too delicate to be spelt out in writing.

Wagner leaves his sanctuary and travels to Venice, without Minna. There he completes the second act of *Tristan und Isolde*. To begin that miraculous score, Mathilde and the peace of the Asyl were needed. Now its own momentum will enable the composer to manage without magic muse and private paradise. What matters is the mood of the moment, and Wagner is adept in conjuring it up, usually by creating barriers between the world outside and his imagination. Costly tapestries, splendid curtains, subdued light, perfumes, silk undergarments – midwives all to the act of creation. As for Mathilde, her image in his mind suffices. He who wants to compose the second act of *Tristan*, with its fathomless nocturnal love music, must be possessed by the double ecstasy of music and love. Did Mathilde beget the ecstasy, or the ecstasy Mathilde? The first act was written in a state of intoxication which Wagner now salvages and carries with him to Italy. He continues writing to his distant beloved. But what letters are these? They form part of the diary which he keeps in Venice and Lucerne. Between August 1858 and April 1859 he writes thirty-three diary letters to Mathilde. Thus he keeps alive both the image of his muse and the ecstasy which had called their love into being.

Diary entry, four days after the Asyl catastrophe:

21.8.1858

That last night in the Asyl I went to bed after eleven. I was to leave the following morning at five. Before I closed my eyes, I clearly saw pictures pass through my mind of how I had always evoked sleep in this position, imagining that I should die one day in such a place. Thus would I lie, and you would come to me for the last time, you would hold my head in your embrace, for all to see, and with a last kiss you would receive my soul. (RWW 33)

Tristan und Isolde

Mild und leise	*Tranquil, tender,*
wie er lächelt,	*Gently smiling,*
wie das Auge	*Sweet the gaze*
hold er öffnet –	*And sweet the vision –*

MS of first page of Tristan und Isolde

seht ihr's, Freunde?	*Have you eyes*
Säht ihr's nicht?	*Or are you blind?*
Immer lichter	*Ever fairer*
wie er leuchtet,	*See his lustre,*
Stern-umstrahlet	*Soaring skywards,*
hoch sich hebt?	*Star-enwrapt.*
. . .	. . .
In dem wogenden Schwall,	*In the eddying tide,*
in dem tönenden Schall,	*In its sonorous pride,*
in des Welt-Atems	*In the vaporous*
wehendem All –,	*Void to abide –,*
ertrinken,	*Abiding,*
versinken –,	*Subsiding –,*
unbewusst –,	*Life shall cease –,*
höchste Lust!	*Timeless peace!*

(Act 3, Scene 3)

Diary entry, 3.9.1858:

To live with your image is to live for my art. It becomes me, as an artist, to gladden your life. That is in tune with my nature, my fate, my will – my love. Thus I am yours; thus should you also find renewal through me! *Tristan* will be completed here, in spite of the world's hostility. And with *Tristan* I can and I shall return, to see you again, to comfort you, to bring you joy. I see this clearly before me, and this is my ardent and sacred desire. Well then! My hero Tristan, my heroine Isolde! help me! help me! help my angel! Here you shall bleed to death, and here the wounds shall be healed. From here the world shall receive the message of the exalted, noble anguish of the most sublime love, the tears of grief and joy. (RWW 38)

Diary entry, 1.1.1859:

Ah, I still breathe it, the magic scent of those flowers which you culled from their resting place at your bosom. Here are no seeds of life; this is the scent of the miraculous flowers of heavenly death, of life eternal. Thus they once adorned the dead body of the hero, before the flames reduced it to divine ashes; the loving woman would throw herself into this grave of fire and fragrant odours, to unite her ashes with those of her beloved. Now they are one! One element! Not two living beings: one divine primeval substance, living in eternity! (RWW 84)

Tristan und Isolde

So stürben wir,	*I die for you*
um ungetrennt,	*And you for me,*
ewig einig,	*Deathless to*
ohne End',	*Infinity,*
ohn Erwachen,	*Without waking,*
ohn Erbangen,	*Without sighing,*
namenlos	*Wondrously*
in Lieb' umfangen,	*In love undying,*
ganz uns selbst gegeben,	*One on one depending,*
der Liebe nur zu leben!	*Our love shall be unending!*

(Act 2, Scene 2)

Mathilde was his magic muse, and *Tristan* owes much to the mood which her presence created in Wagner. He encapsulates his debt in the sketch to the first act which she had received from him on the last day of 1857:

Marble bust of Mathilde by Keiser

Hochbeglückt,	*Blissful pair,*
schmerzentrückt,	*Freed from care,*
frei und rein	*Pure, sublime,*
ewig Dein –	*Ever thine –*
was sie sich klagten	*Their sighing,*
und versagten,	*Their denying,*
Tristan und Isolde,	*Tristan and Isold,*
in keuscher Töne Golde,	*In notes of chastest gold,*
ihr Weinen und ihr Küssen	*Their kisses and their tears,*
leg' ich zu Deinen Füssen,	*Are for Mathilde's ears,*
dass sie den Engel loben,	*Placed at the angel's door,*
der mich so hoch erhoben!	*Who gave me wings to soar!*
R. W.	R. W.
	(RWW 23)

For the third act of *Tristan* Wagner discovers a most unlikely stimulant – rusks. Not the ordinary kind of rusk, but rusk – Zwieback – sent by Mathilde.

9.5.1859

Child! Child! The rusks have done it. They helped me with a jolt over a bad patch, in which I had been stuck for eight days without making any progress. . . . When the Zwieback arrived, I realised straight away what I had been missing: my rusks here were nowhere near sweet enough, and of course they could produce no proper inspiration; but with those sweet, familiar rusks, dunked in milk, I was at once back on the right track. And so I put the sketches on one side and continued with the composition of the story of the healer in her distant land. Now I am perfectly happy: the transition is successful beyond words, with a most wonderful concord between two themes. All this is due to the Zwieback, I assure you! Zwieback! Zwieback! the only medicine for fretful composers – but they must be the right sort! Now I have a good supply of them. When you notice that I am running out, do please send a new consignment. I know they are my vital medicine! . . . Dear Lord! Zwieback! (RWW 133–5)

His enthusiastic response produces changes in Mathilde's shopping list. She sends more Zwieback than he can consume, dunked or otherwise, and the fate of the sorcerer's apprentice begins to frighten him. He ponders:

21.6.1859

Many beautiful boxes of Zwieback arrived yesterday. They have produced an avalanche in my larder. What is going to happen to all the boxes? We shall have to think of something. (RWW 152)

But Mathilde is more than a provider. She still receives the confessions of his heart. The letter he sends her from Lucerne is a revealing document, a Credo:

24.8.1859

But child, what makes you see or wish to see a 'Wise Man' in me? Surely you know that I am the maddest person imaginable? . . . But I do possess a sense of humour which again helps me over abysses that the wisest man does not even see. For I am a poet, and – what is worse – a musician. Now think of my music, whose most subtle and mysterious fluids seep into the finest pores of sensibility and penetrate to the very marrow of life, there to annihilate anything that smacks of common sense or complacent daily routine, and only leaves that strangely sublime sigh that is uttered in the knowledge of our helplessness. How can *I* be a wise man, I who am myself only when in a state of raving frenzy?

But I want to tell you this. Princes and their people came from all parts of the world to the temple at Delphi, to gain information about themselves. The priests were the wise ones who imparted this information; but they themselves had first ro receive it from the priestess Pythia, as she, seated on the tripod of inspiration, passed through the wildest convulsions of ecstasy. Thus she pronounced the utterances of the gods with awestruck moans, which the wise priests had merely to translate into a language understood by the world. I believe that he who has once sat on the tripod, can never be a priest again, for he has been too close to the god. (RWW 170)

Thus he, the ecstatic artist, is seated on his tripod. Thus he translates the utterances of the gods into musical and dramatic language. Like Prometheus, he tethers his own heart to human souls who, for a while, may share his ecstasy. When he lets them go – for ecstasy is a private experience and tolerates no lasting ties – they fall like Lucifer.

For some time now he has dispensed with the familiar *Du* in his letters to Mathilde. Soon he finds it possible to tease, perhaps even to hurt her:

Paris, 12.2.1861

You asked me about the ladies among my friends? I have made new acquaintances, but no new friends. Madame Ollivier is very talented and also shows a dazzling personality, and is rather more good-natured than her sister. . . . There is amongst others an elderly democratic spinster, Fräulein von Meysenbug, who is exceedingly unappealing. . . . In the so-called higher world, a lady whom I knew slightly from earlier days, has drawn more of my attention than she had done before; this is the Countess Kalergis. . . . I have already commented on the Princess Metternich. She certainly is a strange creature. They tell me that she dances most charmingly and that she has an unusual singing voice. Recently she asked me if I had written any Fugues? She said she liked playing Fugues! I just looked at her. . . . Frau von Pourtalès, the Prussian ambassador's wife, seems to have a fund of wisdom and a cultivated taste. I discovered quite a bonny creature in the wife of the Saxon ambassador, Frau von Seebach. She is quite frumpish and coarse looking. I was surprised by a certain gentle flame glimmering under the lava. She did not understand how anybody could fail to see the immense passion in my works, and thought it risky to take her young daughter to *Tannhäuser* . . . (*Die Musik*, Berlin, September 1931: 882–3)

Mathilde cannot have failed to notice the lukewarm tone of his next letter, also from Paris. He tells her about his *Meistersinger*, in the resigned manner of his cobbler poet:

[Paris, end of December 1861]

Life and all its fuss and bother means nothing to me any longer. Where? In what way? I do not care at all. I want to work, nothing else! . . . That painful, final step is a thing of the past now – Venice, the return journey and the following three weeks – terrible! – all this is now behind me. Courage! One must and will manage somehow! I shall often send you samples of my work. You will open your eyes at my *Meistersinger*! Hold on to your heart when you meet Hans Sachs, or you will fall in love with him! . . . Oh, one must have been in paradise to know what lives in such a work! Of my life you will always hear just the essentials, the outer facts. Within me – I assure you! – nothing at all takes place any more; nothing but artistic creation. So you will lose nothing, but receive the only thing of value, my works. But we also want to see each other from time to time. Am I right? And then without ulterior motive, and so free as air! Well, this is a strange letter! You have no idea what a relief it is for me to know that you know, that I know what you have known for some time! (RWW 293–4)

He is ready for fresh encounters. Indeed, there is a new Mathilde. Fräulein Mathilde Maier of Mainz, somewhat hard of hearing, is young and attractive. She feels at ease in the company of the almost fifty-year-old Wagner, but she declines – and later probably regrets having declined – a more intimate relationship. There also is Friederike Meyer, the worldly-wise actress, and Cosima is beginning to move from the periphery of Wagner's life towards the centre of his heart. Yet, for some time the first Mathilde continues to seem irreplaceable. In 1858 he had left her.·Five years later, she sends him a poem for his fiftieth birthday:

> *A grave I have provided,*
> *And therein would I hide*
> *My hopes and my desires,*
> *My love and all its fires,*
> *And all my grief and pride.*
> *And when I had duly bestowed them,*
> *I lay down by their side.*
>
> (RWW 351)

Has Mathilde's sad poem moved him? He confesses to his older, platonic friend and confidante, Frau Eliza Wille, what he feels, or at any rate what he feels at the time of writing:

> Penzing, 5.6.1863
> I cannot write to her how I feel in my heart, without betraying her husband whom I hold in warm esteem and respect. What can one do? Nor is it possible to keep this secret entirely to myself; at least *one* person must know how I feel. So I shall tell you – she is and remains my first and only love! I feel that with ever greater certainty. It was the fulfilment of my life; those demure, beautiful, uneasy years which I spent, ever more enchanted, in her proximity and in her affection, those years were the sweet joy of my life. . . . Alas, my dearest! One only loves once, whatever else life may offer us by way of intoxication and delight. Yes, it is only now that I know for certain – I shall never stop loving her, and her alone. (RWW 309–11)

So much for his words. But he knows that it is wise to refrain from attempts at resurrecting departed love, and that it is important to live without illusions. Indeed, he will name his last home *Wahnfried* ('Free from delusion'), and it will

Wagner in 1871

be Cosima who helps him to cope with his past. Just as her diaries record disparaging memories of Minna, so too they contain unsavoury passages about Mathilde, his 'first and only love', 'the fulfilment of his life':

> 22.8.1870
> I write to Frau Wesendonck and ask R. whether he agrees with the letter; he thinks it is too much, he had cast a poetic veil over this relationship, to cover up its trivial nature. But even the poetry has now faded, and he does not like to be reminded of it . . . (CWT I 275)

> 8.2.1871
> Frau Wesendonck sends me a copy of her *Frederick the Great*. R. is not at all in favour of women making themselves conspicuous by publishing, and sees signs of bad taste in this. (CWT I 353)

9.2.1871

I thank Frau W. for having sent me her book; I avoid praising the book itself, but write seriously and warmly about its subject. I read the letter to R., but he reproves me severely and says, 'What words are left to us for original thoughts if we use them for absurdities?' When I answer that I find it impossible not to take people seriously who had been kind to him, and towards whom he had felt sympathy, he answers, 'If you write like this out of consideration for me, I feel positively degraded. Let there be no sentimental misunderstanding – I have returned the lady's letters and had mine burnt, as I do not want anything to remain that could lead to the assumption that this was a serious relationship.' (CWT I 353)

Mathilde's fate is shared by many who had once been close to him. It is not a case of Wagner dismissing remembrances of former friendships from his heart, but of his surrendering his heart – his whole heart – to his works and finding little to spare for friendship and kind thoughts. He confesses to Cosima:

20.9.1879

I know I was irresistible. I drove people mad, and then I ran away from them. (CWT II 412)

Thirteen years after Wagner's death, Cosima records what she had told her daughter Eva, concerning her father's relationship with Mathilde:

The publication of the Five Poems [*Wesendonck Lieder*] was unavoidable, and your father told me, in the friendliest manner, that Mathilde Wesendonck had obviously enjoyed their joint public acclaim. Later he wrote to me, with bitterness, 'She put on the market what ought to have been most sacred to her, so that these songs are worth nothing to me. I now assign them to singers who are past their prime.'
(CWZ 406)

Almost simultaneously, in February 1896, the *Allgemeine Musikzeitung* publishes reminiscences by Mathilde. She says:

Richard Wagner loved his Asyl, as he called his new home in the Enge near Zurich. He left it, sad(ly) and dejected, and of his own volition! Why? It is an idle question! *Tristan und Isolde* was created at that time. The rest is silence and humble reverence! (RWW x)

III

EROS

*Women are life's music.**

🌿 THERESE 🌿

Wagner is not yet twenty when he becomes chorus master at the theatre in Würzburg. It is a mixed chorus, and while he pays professional attention to both the male and female sections, it is the sopranos and altos who attract his personal interest:

> It was a gravedigger's daughter, Therese Ringelmann, whose pretty soprano voice led me to believe that I should train her to become a primadonna. I told her about my plan, whereupon she appeared at the chorus rehearsals particularly neatly dressed, and she made sure that the string of white pearls which adorned her hair should pleasantly stimulate my imagination. During the summer vacation I remained in town and gave Therese regular singing lessons according to a method which has remained a mystery to me to this day. I also visited her a number of times in her home, always in the presence of her mother and sister, although I never saw the gruesome father. We also met in the public gardens, but my rather ungallant sense of modesty kept me from divulging this love affair to my friends. This may have been due to her family's lowly status, or to Therese's somewhat alarming educational deficiencies, or possibly to my own doubts as to the candour of my affections; I do not really know. But then I was pressed to declare myself, while at the same time I was beginning to feel jealously suspicious of Therese, and that was the end of our affair. (ML I 84)

🌿 FRIEDERIKE 🌿

Exit gravedigger's soprano daughter with pearls in her hair, enter hot-blooded Italian chorus member:

> A more serious love affair developed with Friederike Galvani, a mechanic's daughter of unmistakable Italian stock. Very musical and gifted with an attractive, easily trained voice . . . very petite and with big

* UFH 19, letter to Uhlig, 27.12.1849

dark eyes, she had already captured the heart of a fine musician, the excellent first oboist of our orchestra. . . . As the autumn of this Würzburg year approached, several friends – amongst them our oboist and his bride – invited me to a country wedding a few hours away from Würzburg. The peasants were having the time of their lives. There was drinking and dancing, while I tried, unsuccessfully, to recapture my former skill on the violin, but I could not manage even the second fiddle to the satisfaction of my fellow musicians. My success with the compliant Friederike, however, was all the greater. We danced several times madly right through the crowds of peasants, until the heated atmosphere created an excuse for everybody – and that included us two – to abandon all restraint. We hugged and kissed each other quite spontaneously, while her official lover was providing the dance music. He took due note of the uninhibited tenderness with which Friederike was favouring me, and he accepted his position, sadly but with good grace. This gave me, for the first time in my life, a flattering feeling of self-assurance. (ML I 84–5)

It must be doubted whether that was really the first time he had felt that 'flattering feeling'. It was more probably his from birth. The oboist's reaction, however, certainly does set a precedent for later events both in Wagner's life and in his works. Sadly but with good grace will Wotan hand Freia to the giants, will King Marke give up Isolde, Sachs his Eva, Bülow his Cosima, and Otto Wesendonck – temporarily – his wife Mathilde.

The dizzying number of moves that Wagner made after leaving his Magdeburg post show him, like the Flying Dutchman, restlessly seeking an anchorage:

Lauchstädt (July 1834) – Rudolstadt (August 1834) – Magdeburg (October 1834) – Berlin (May 1836) – Königsberg (July 1836) – Riga (July 1837) – London (August 1839) – Paris (September 1839) – Dresden (April 1842) – Weimar (May 1849) – Zurich (May 1849) – Paris (February 1850) – Bordeaux (March 1850) –

Stop! The last is noteworthy.

❀ JESSIE ❀

In March 1850 the Laussot family invite Wagner to stay with them. *Mein Leben* records:

The handsome young husband spent most of the day looking after his business, and while Jessie's mother was usually excluded from our conversations on account of her poor hearing, Jessie and I had copious animated talks concerning various important topics, and we found that our relationship was marked by mutual confidentiality. Jessie, then about twenty-two, showed hardly any resemblance to her mother at all, but seemed to take entirely after her father, about whom I heard much that was likeable. (ML I 450)

'While Jessie's mother was usually excluded' – the *while* is significant. The opportunist in Wagner knows how to turn situations to his advantage. Does this *while* not recall his adventure with Friederike Galvani, whom he hugged and kissed, 'while her official lover was providing the music'?

At the age of sixteen, Jessie Laussot had attended the first performance of *Tannhäuser* at Dresden. That was her initiation and it was probably not unlike that of the fifteen-year-old Ludwig, future King of Bavaria, who was so overwhelmed by his first experience of Wagner's music (a performance of *Lohengrin*) that he too felt irresistibly drawn to the composer. For the present, Jessie becomes to Wagner what Mathilde Wesendonck is to become later – devoted acolyte and divine enchantress. Fate has chained both Wagner and Jessie to the wrong spouses, and both now see an opportunity which may never recur for ridding themselves of their fetters. They decide to escape together.

It is to *Mein Leben* that we must turn for an account of this incident, bearing in mind that the occasional harshness with which he tempers his praise of Jessie is perhaps in deference to Cosima, to whom the autobiography was dictated. Originally designed as an 'official' account for the eyes only of King Ludwig and the next Wagner generation, today's readers play a curious multi-dimensional game as they turn its pages. How far did Wagner 'adapt the truth' to his audience? How were King Ludwig and the Wagner children supposed to react? And how did he see each event after so considerable a lapse of time (the dictation of *Mein Leben* begins on 17 July 1865)? He describes Jessie thus:

Her instant receptivity was astonishing; she would immediately and, as it seemed, correctly understand things which I barely hinted at. That was also her way with music; she could read at sight with the greatest of ease and she was a remarkable pianist. When she was in Dresden she had learned that I was still looking for a pianist who could play Beethoven's great B flat major sonata for me, and now she really surprised me with an exquisite rendering of that extremely difficult music. My admiration, aroused by the discovery of such an outstanding, natural talent, turned of a sudden to embarrassment when I heard her sing. Her harsh, shrill falsetto voice was fierce and gave no evidence of genuine feeling. I was so taken aback that I could not help begging her to refrain from singing in the future. (ML I 450–1)

Wagner and Jessie are in love, and now Minna must be gently prepared for what is to come. He writes to her from Paris in March 1850:

It is inconceivable that anyone could be more kind-hearted, noble-minded and sensitive than our friend Jessie Laussot. I think you would be truly surprised, my dear wife, if you could witness the deep impact which your husband's works are making on healthy, unspoilt, generous minds. (WSB III 244: 2.3.1850)

Eleven days later:

Will you be angry with me if I tell you that I have decided, all at once, to accept the most urgent and cordial invitation coming from my friends at Bordeaux? They have even sent the travelling expenses, and I shall therefore leave for Bordeaux tomorrow morning. (WSB III 252: 13.3.1850)

His next letter on the subject comes from Bordeaux:

Here I am now in Bordeaux and am longing for a letter from you which should tell me, I very much hope, that you are not cross about my trip. . . . I arrived last Saturday in Bordeaux which, compared with Paris, is heaven indeed! You have no idea of this family's kindness and their devotion to me! . . . I am thoroughly happy here, but in spite of it all I am longing with my whole heart for you and our home! Believe me, I know of no greater bliss than to be able to live in peace and quiet, together with you, in our cosy nest. . . . I cannot describe the divine kindness and love of these people here! Perhaps they, or at least the wife, will visit us some time in Switzerland, to see for herself that we are happy and want for nothing. (WSB III 255–9: 17.3.1850)

Minna knows her husband too well not to suspect some ill wind blowing from the South of France, and she weighs his protestations of love against the proposed visit of the female representative of those 'divine' hosts.

Wagner remains in Bordeaux for another eighteen days, then he leaves in order to gather the wherewithal and the necessary courage for his flight with Jessie who, for her part, also addresses a letter to Minna:

Herr Wagner has made us extremely happy with his visit. I believe that his stay here has not been disadvantageous to him either. The weather has always been at its best, and I do hope he will retain happy memories of his visit. (SB 377: 7.4.1850)

Minna's reaction to this is unequivocal. 'O false, treacherous creature' are the words that she scribbles at the foot of the page.

Wagner takes stock of the situation in Montmorency, outside Paris. Minna has reacted coldly to his glowing news from Bordeaux, and he now composes a much more drastic farewell letter to her. Printed in full it would require approximately thirteen pages:

Dear Minna,
Yes, this is what I call you, in spite of the ending of your letter in which you requested that I should address you by 'Sie' in future.* . . . Your letter has now destroyed everything, and you stand before me with all your vindictiveness. . . . You remain true to yourself. Every word in your letter clearly proclaims that you do not love me, for you disdain everything that is dear to me, even my use of the 'Du' which I love to reserve – following my own inclination – for the person who ought not to be a stranger to me. . . . I have broken with everything old and I fight it with all my strength. You cling to some*body*, I to some*thing*; you to individual people, I to mankind. Thus there is a world of difference between us, and we can only irritate one another, without hope for mutual happiness. Perhaps it is you who are the more unhappy, for I understand you well enough, but you do not understand me! . . . Let us go our separate ways, forget me as I am *now* and be happy without me! For *with* me there can no longer be any happiness for you! . . . I do not know where I shall be going! Do not search for me! But I shall always do my utmost to find out whether you are well. . . . For the last fortnight I have wept a thousand bitter tears over this wretched parting! But it must be! (WSB III 275–88: 16.4.1850)

Minna now alerts two of his Zurich friends, Wilhelm Baumgartner and Jakob Sulzer, who in their turn petition Wagner:

Dear Friend,
You can easily imagine how deeply your last communication has

* *Sie* = the formal 'you', in contrast to *Du* = the personal 'you'.

saddened your wife and us. . . . For your sake and in the interest of your own future we beseech you: examine yourself once more without prejudice and examine the reasons which led to your recent decision, before taking any irrevocable steps. A third party, though motivated by the warmest sympathy, could only create further upset by meddling in such circumstances. We shall therefore not attempt to influence your ultimate decision by arguing the case, much as we should like to do so, but we trust that you will consider the request of your loyal friends to make the manly resolution not to oppose your wife's reasoning by an unalterable decision, but lend her a willing ear. . . . Whatever you decide, always remember that you will never find more faithful friends than us in Zurich. (SB 384: 21.4.1850)

The two persuade Minna to travel to Paris and hand their letter to Wagner in person. When he hears that she is on her way, he immediately takes himself off to Geneva and from there he sends her a second letter of farewell:

I must write to you once more before going far away from you. . . . I am about to set out for Marseilles, where I shall straightway board an English ship for Malta, and then on to Greece and Asia Minor. . . . For the present the world of today no longer exists for me, for I detest it and want no more to do with it, nor with what people nowadays call 'art'. . . . During the recent critical weeks, therefore, I conceived the plan of a journey to Greece and the East, and now I am fortunate enough to have the necessary means placed at my disposal by a new benefactor in London. He is one of the most eminent English lawyers, who knows my works and who is going to support me on certain terms, namely my assigning to him the original manuscripts of anything I may write in the future. . . . So let us stay apart! If we thrive, if times and circumstances change, we may well cherish the hope of seeing each other again. But for the present, separation will be good for both of us.
(WSB III 295–7: 4.5.1850)

Although he does not mention Jessie by name, he must know that Minna will be able to read between the lines. As for the mysterious London protector, this is Jessie's father, but Wagner omits to mention that he is dead. Since Jessie will, in fact, be drawing on her inheritance to finance their escape, Wagner is not actually lying, although one may wonder how he intends to dispatch manuscripts to the next world. And then: 'If times and circumstances change'. Does he foresee such a possibility? Could Jessie fail to live up to her 'divine' promise? Is the skilled diplomat unwilling to burn the boat which might carry him back to his 'cosy nest'?

Another point should be considered here. Could there be another reason, apart from Jessie, for his planned escape to the East? 1850 is a watershed in Wagner's life. The world knows him as the composer of *Rienzi*, of *Der fliegende Holländer*, of *Tannhäuser*. It is soon to know him as the composer of *Lohengrin*. His audiences enjoy the melodiousness of his music, his skilful orchestration, the elaborate scenery and the intensity of the drama, but Wagner himself is no longer very interested in his earlier works. Only twelve months have elapsed since he escaped from the Dresden police to Switzerland. In his luggage was the original poem of *Siegfrieds Tod* (later renamed *Götterdämmerung*), and even before he begins working at the composition of *Der Ring des Nibelungen*, he knows that the *Ring* will be a considerable advance on *Lohengrin*. His first prose work written in exile bears the significant title, 'Art and Revolution'.

With his *Nibelungen* tetralogy Wagner will leave operatic convention far behind. He is going to discuss, on his stage, the whence and whither of life, no less; a daring leap from the known to the unknown. Such an undertaking requires a dependable springboard which Wagner lacks. As an exile without means he is perpetually searching for a secure financial base for existence. He is well aware of the forces within him which will beget his future works, but he knows that they are, as yet, invisible to the outside world. The world and, above all, his own wife expect further popular operas from him, but he has 'broken with everything old' . . . 'the world of today no longer exists for me'. In this context one might see young Jessie not as a runaway from Bordeaux but as Wagner's travelling companion, ministering to his mental and physical needs, on a journey which amounts to a search for his own self. He must leave the old world and its old songs. His hoped-for Dresden revolution had been a failure. He is now ready to create his own artistic revolution. An end to romantic opera. Arise, the myth of gods and men.

On the same day on which he sends his second farewell to Minna, Wagner also addresses friend Baumgartner:

> In our modern Europe, under prevailing conditions, there is no chance for any congenial, satisfying existence. Be content with my temporary disappearance, let me replenish my physical and moral resources, in order to resurface when the time is ripe. As things are now – I could not have gone on without all of you seeing me rot away. (WSB III 298–9: 4.5.1850)

The autobiography describes his separation from Minna in choice phrases:

> I finally brought myself to reply to my wife's urgent last letter, and I explained to her in a lengthy, friendly but frank communication the details of our whole past life together, and that I had formed the unalterable resolution to discharge her from any concrete participation in my future, since I considered myself totally incapable of planning it so as to merit her approbation. (ML I 452)

He also records the ensuing events at Bordeaux:

> Mme Laussot sent me an extremely agitated communication, informing me that she had been unable to conceal her intentions from her mother, who promptly assumed that these were not her daughter's but my own intentions. The result was that the news was passed to M. Laussot, who swore to track me down and put a bullet through my head. Taking stock of the situation, I immediately resolved to travel to Bordeaux, to settle this matter with my opponent once and for all. Instantly I sat down and wrote a detailed letter to M. Eugène, with the intention of putting the matter in the right light. I did not shrink, however, from expressing my astonishment that a man could bring himself to hold on to a wife who no longer wanted to live with him. I finished my letter by advising him that I would be arriving in Bordeaux at the same time as this letter, and that I would promptly let him know in which hotel he could find me. Furthermore, I requested that his wife should be kept strictly in ignorance of my movements, to enable him to act entirely of his own accord. . . . At the same time I addressed a few lines to Mme Laussot in which I advised her to remain calm and collected. . . . I booked in at the 'Quatre soeurs' and at once sent a note to M. Laussot informing him that I would be staying in, awaiting his call. This note I dispatched at nine in the morning, but I waited vainly for any results, until late in the afternoon I received a summons to present myself immediately at the police station. When I arrived there I was asked whether my passport was in order. I admitted that I had placed myself in an awkward position on account of an urgent family affair. Thereupon it was disclosed to me that it was precisely because of that family affair which had brought me here, that I was refused permission to remain in Bordeaux. In answer to my queries, they did not deny that this action against me had been instigated by the family in question. This strange revelation immediately restored my equanimity. I asked

the police officer to allow me a two-day extension, so that I could rest after my tiring journey. This he granted quite affably, since he was able to inform me that in any case I would not succeed in making contact with that family, as they had all left Bordeaux at noon. So I made use of my two days to recuperate, but also to compose a lengthy letter to Jessie, in which I told her exactly what had happened. I did not conceal from her that her husband's behaviour was contemptible, for he had cheapened his wife's honour by his denunciation of me to the police, and that I could on no account continue my relationship with her, until she had freed herself from her wretched bond. I now had to see this letter safely delivered. The police officer's information was too vague for me to learn whether the Laussots had left home just for the day or for a longer period. I therefore decided to go to the house myself. I rang the bell, the door sprang open, and not finding anyone inside I made my way to the first floor, stepped from room to room until I reached Jessie's lounge. There I found her work-basket and placed my letter inside, whereupon I calmly retraced my steps without meeting a soul. When my period of grace had expired, I left Bordeaux the same way I had come, having received no sign of life whatever. (ML I 455–7)

The Jessie episode ends in creative grief. He celebrates his thirty-seventh birthday (22 May) with Frau Julie Ritter* and her son Karl, at Villeneuve. Some five weeks later, towards the end of June, Wagner is in the Swiss Alps with Karl, taking long mountain walks. The little town of Thun is their base. From there, Wagner writes one of his outsize letters to Frau Ritter, playing over the unhappy episode and its humiliating aftermath, until his letter becomes his own medicine:

Five days ago Karl had a letter from Bordeaux in which Jessie told him in a very few words that – I quote – 'I am breaking with the immediate past and shall consign letters in his handwriting to the fire, unread.' She asks Karl to burn her letter immediately and acquaint me with just the main point. . . . This tells me that I had been unable to inspire Jessie with *my kind of love*. It grieves me to find that I could not win from this woman the slightest show of esteem. But into your hands I herewith place the testament of a love of which I shall never feel ashamed and which, though physically dead, will perhaps continue to evoke joyous reminiscences until my life's end. . . . He who rebels for the sake of

* Wealthy widow of a Russian merchant, Wagner's benefactress and confidante.

love, even if such rebellion were to end his life, he is my kind of person.

(WSB III 315–22: 26/27.6.1850)

A fruitful experience. He is soon to create the very person who 'rebels for the sake of love', Brünnhilde. She disobeys her father Wotan's loveless command and undertakes, on her own, for the sake of love, Siegmund's protection.

We return to the letter to Frau Ritter:

> The woman who wanted to bring me salvation has proved herself a child! Forgive me, but I can only find her pitiable! . . . She was all love and we had consecrated our lives to the god of love . . . and all of a sudden she saw the happiness of love in the light of conventional respectability. . . . The depth of her fall breaks my heart! Mother! dear, faithful woman, if only you could have seen the jubilation of love that emanated from every nerve of this richly blessed woman, as she not so much confessed as let me experience, through her own person, the instinctive, clear and naked revelation of her love, that she was mine! . . . Her kisses were the richest delight of my life! No honours, no splendour, no glory can ever match that delight! Farewell, my beautiful, blessed Jessie! You have been dearer to me than anything in the world, and I shall never forget you.

This last farewell to Jessie enables Wagner to revoke his very last farewell to his wife. The journey to Greece and Asia Minor is no longer imperative. The encounter with love has served to cure him of his world-weariness. The next thing to do is to inform Minna of the changed circumstances:

> As a sixteen-year-old girl she [Jessie] had been married to a very handsome young man with whom she had fallen in love, but it became clear to her, even before the wedding, that they, as she expressed herself, did not have three thoughts in common. . . . Long before we met, Jessie had taken a keen interest in me as an artist, and when she heard of my financial troubles, she regarded it as her mission to give me substantial aid. . . . Indeed, when I arrived at Bordeaux, her husband and her mother were uncommonly civil, as I told you at the time. The poor young woman who until then had been entirely alone, apart from her family, and without any companions in Bordeaux, that odious hagglers' den, now began to hope for a happier life. She urged her family to leave this wretched Bordeaux and, since they were not dependent on their business, to join with the Ritters and the Wagners and buy a place somewhere in Switzerland. . . . Then she suddenly wrote to me that

she was determined to leave her family and place herself under my protection. Her words were so full of glowing, desperate passion that I was quite alarmed and deeply moved. I replied with a deadly serious letter, describing my own situation in discouraging terms and putting before her the tremendously daring and fatal aspects of her decision. I urged her seriously to consider whether she was really resolved to perish in cold blood, for that was what she would have to face . . . (WSB III 337–42: *undated, probably early July 1850*)

In this compelling fiction, was Wagner perhaps drawing on one of his earlier creations? Here is the Dutchman's warning to Senta:

> *Hear tiding of the fate from which I shield you now!*
> *I am condemned to terrors without ending:*
> *A tenfold death would be a welcome boon!*
> *None but a woman can undo ill fortune,*
> *A faithful woman, true to me till death.*
> *You pledged eternal faith to me, but not*
> *Before Almighty God: this saves your life!*
> *For, hapless woman, know the fate of those*
> *Who break their faith in spite of solemn pledges:*
> *Eternal hellfire is their doom!*
> *Numberless victims paid that fearful price*
> *To me! But I shall spare your tender life.*
> *Salvation, you have fled for evermore.*
>   (Der fliegende Holländer, Act 3)

Wagner continues his letter to Minna:

I was so dreadfully perturbed and thoroughly shaken that my only thought was to go very far away, come what may. I decided to go to Greece forthwith and therefore wrote to Bordeaux, asking for the means to do this, but left everything else uncertain, even practically unspoken, all calculated to discourage her. . . . I felt the urgent need to write to you, but what I was unable to write was the truth, since everything here was uncertain; it would have been insanely cruel to disclose to you what had been going on, as I myself had not the slightest notion of the outcome of it all. All I knew was that I wanted to go away into the wide world. But I wished to give you at least some comfort, however small! My intention was to treat you as a humane physician would. . . . I was convinced that the news of my going to Greece would give you at least some peace of mind, since it made you realise that I was not just leaving *you* but rather, as it were, the whole world. Forgive me, if I assumed wrongly! My intention was good. . . . Truly, my heart was troubled, and the worst of it was that I was forced to lie. . . . If you do not believe me utterly and completely, as I should be believed, you will only make yourself very unhappy. I shall not impose any conditions for my return to you, since I am aware of your state of health; so I have decided to return *unconditionally*.

Let the reader decide whether this is a case of Wagner juggling with the truth, or whether he had a genuine change of heart. Or did Jessie's 'betrayal' so ruffle him that he needed to return to his cosy nest to lick his wounds? Or is it a mixture of all three which drives him to strive for a reconciliation regardless of such niceties as loyalty, dignity and truth?

Wagner now wishes his friends to be informed of his resurgence. His letter to Liszt is still tinged with the sadness of the recent past:

My proposed journey to Greece has come to nothing. There were too many obstacles and I could not overcome them all. If I could have had my way, I should have preferred to leave this world altogether.

(WSB III 344: 2.7.1850)

He achieves a more positive tone in his communication to Ernst Benedikt Kietz, an old comrade of the hungry Paris days:*

My wife's love for me is stronger and more explicit than her misconstruction of my intentions. Therefore, not a separation but a renewal and continuation of our life together is needed, if the dissension which has arisen between us is to be ended. I now consider, together with Minna, that the events of the past will have a beneficial effect, since they have shown us what we are and what we can be to each other.

(WSB III 349: 7.7.1850)

To Frau Julie Ritter:

She now comprehends the strength of her love which in those catastrophic, decisive days has vanquished all doubt and error. Thus she appears to me as an entirely new wife, different from the former one.

(WSB III 351–2: 10.7.1850)

* Ernst Benedikt Kietz (1816–92), a painter and draughtsman, lived in Paris from 1838 to 1870. He was the brother of the sculptor Gustav Adolph Kietz.

To Theodor Uhlig, his Dresden violinist friend:*

> I have got a new wife. . . . My friends have proved themselves indeed. I have aged considerably and I know that the second half of my life has now begun and that all idle expectations are behind me. (WSB III 360–1: 27.7.1850)

And how does Minna react to her husband's 'unconditional' return? She scribbles her comments at the bottom of his last letter to her:

> This letter is full of untrue assertions and offensive observations, but our reunion is due to my love, which is far too deep not to make me forget and forgive what has happened. (SB 412)

After her husband's death Jessie marries the historian Karl Hillebrand. She maintains her silence towards Wagner for nineteen years, then she writes to him. The letter is lost, but Cosima notes in her diary:

> Richard very unwell, which makes me sad; on top of that a silly letter from Mme Laussot, who wishes to explain to him what had happened twenty years ago! That irritates him, since it is so utterly pointless.
>
> (CWT I 47: 31.1.1869)

🌸 MATHILDE II 🌸

Wagner has returned to Minna in Zurich. Since he is wanted by the police in Germany, he is unable to attend the first performance of *Lohengrin*, in August 1850, under Franz Liszt in Weimar. In the next nine years he produces, among other works, 'Opera and Drama', his important theoretical essay; the poem of *Der junge Siegfried* (later part three of the *Nibelungen* cycle, renamed *Siegfried*); his autobiographical document, *A Communication To My Friends*; the poems of *Die Walküre*, *Das Rheingold*, *Siegfrieds Tod* (later part four of the cycle, renamed *Götterdämmerung*); the full score of *Das Rheingold*; the full score of *Die Walküre*; the full score of act one and the orchestral sketch of act two of *Siegfried*, and the *Wesendonck Lieder*. The near-breakdown of his relations with the Wesendoncks turns him into a voyager once again. He leaves the Asyl in August 1858, and during the next four years he criss-crosses Europe:

---

* Theodor Uhlig (1822–53), violinist and composer, became an intimate friend of Wagner, and they carried on a copious correspondence. He died young, of tuberculosis.

123

Venice – Milan – Lucerne – Zurich – Lucerne – Zurich – Paris –
Brussels – Antwerp – Paris – Bad Soden – Frankfurt – Darmstadt –
Baden-Baden – Paris – Karlsruhe – Paris – Vienna – Paris – Zurich –
Karlsruhe – Paris – Bad Soden – Weimar – Nürnberg – Bad Reichenhall
– Vienna – Venice – Vienna – Mainz – Paris – Mainz – Biebrich –
Karlsruhe – Biebrich.

Meanwhile he finishes *Tristan und Isolde* and he begins *Die Meistersinger von Nürnberg*. His forty-ninth birthday he celebrates in Biebrich on the Rhine (22.5.1862). He still writes to Mathilde Wesendonck, but his heart is ready to admit a fresh inhabitant, a female companion-muse to share the joys and agonies that attend the creation of his *Meistersinger*. Among his birthday guests is a second Mathilde, Mathilde Maier. This blue-eyed, flaxen-haired Mathilde from Mainz is twenty-nine. Four days after his birthday he writes to her:

> Dear Mathilde,
> That is what I *call* you. What you *are* to me, you must choose for yourself . . . (MM 8: 26.5.1862)

Or, as Wotan says to Brünnhilde, his favourite child:

> *What you are now,*
> *You must choose for yourself.*
> (*Die Walküre*, Act 3, Scene 2)

Mathilde replies:

> My dear, highly respected sir,
> That is what you are to me, and that is what I call you. I would have asked you over for a chat instead of writing to you, but mother's coffee circle meets tomorrow, Thursday, and I venture to think their company might vex you. . . . Looking back, would you agree that your great kindness towards me also included something like fatherly tenderness? Something a little patronising which might easily have hurt my pride, if seeing you in a happier frame of mind had not made me happy too. For you must know that when we first met, I carried away with me an indelible impression of the mark of profound suffering in your features. How gladly I would have gathered up all the joys in the world to help obliterate its traces, at least for a few moments. (MM 271–2: *undated, probably June 1862*)

It could be Senta speaking:

He stands before me,
His face engraved with suffering.
His profound grief speaks to my heart.
(Der fliegende Holländer, Act 2)

But the *Holländer* is far from Wagner's mind. He is working at the Prelude to the first act of *Meistersinger*. It would certainly lend wings to his labour if a tender-hearted Eva were at hand to cheer him with her chatter. In Hans Sachs style he now calls her 'lieb Kind' (dear child). He even writes her a Hans Sachs letter, for the cobbler poet could have explained their mutual love to his Eva in similar terms:

Mathilde Maier

Fear nothing, my child! Everything that can make a person dear to me is within you, and it is the whole being I love, your lovable, stalwart and yet pliable nature! You are so many-sided and always so secure and true, that I could not wish to take any part of you, to call it delightedly my own. Thus all of you is mine, although I may never possess you; but you are my last source of sublime purification! If you are that to me and if I may find fulfilment through you, then you too will not feel wholly unblest for having encountered me on your journey through life!

(MM 15: 20.6.1862)

He can also grumble like Sachs. Wishing to be close to Mathilde, he asks her to find him a pleasant residence in her vicinity. He is in Vienna, attending the rehearsals of *Tristan and Isolde*, but Mathilde reports that she has not yet found anything suitable for him. He lets fly:

O for heaven's sake! You people know how to make life difficult! Nobody does anything, they all mooch and dally. My goodness! You know full well that I shall have to leave the Rhine if you cannot find me a cosy nest! I suppose I shall have to search for one myself, from here, from Vienna, where I am up to my neck in *Tristan* trouble! Fine sweethearts I have, God knows. . . . Adieu, wicked child! No comforting, friendly words at all for you today. One does not ask much from you women, but in the end all you do is cause us grief and pain.

(MM 57–8: 25.1.1863)

He is not so much venting his anger as showing Mathilde that he loves her enough to be amiably rough with her, when he thinks the occasion calls for it. A certain amount of frustration, too, shows between the lines. His feelings are possibly those of Hans Sachs, who has made a pair of particularly pretty shoes for his Eva to wear at her wedding – not to him but to Walther:

> *To mend people's shoes is love's labour lost!*
> *If I were not a poet too,*
> *I would not mend another shoe.*
> *. . .*
>
> *A cobbler's words are wisely spoken,*
> *He puts to rights what others have broken.*
> *But pity the cobbler poet's plight;*
> *They give him no peace, not by day, not by night.*
> *The widowed cobbler's fate is dim,*
> *For all the girls chase after him.*

The prettiest damsels who want to wed,
Invite him into their marriage bed.
He knows their ways, he knows them not –
To them it matters not a jot.
Once caught, they throw him into the ditch,
The idle oaf who stinks of pitch.

(*Meistersinger*, Act 3, Scene 4)

Wagner's love for the second Mathilde is less overwhelming than his love for the first, and he remains more in touch with reality. He writes to her from Vienna:

> I could bring myself to surrender to my inclination, bear the cost and the consequences and come to you, if above all I did not need – peace! O child, I am fifty years old. At that time of life, love longs for peace after the storm, like my Flying Dutchman. But you are something quite special, and I cling to the hope to obtain that peace, together with you, in one way or another. (MM 94: 11.5.1863)

This Mathilde receives the secrets of his heart, frequently in a brief written observation where he formulates his thoughts with precision, disdains further elaboration and takes it for granted that she will understand:

> Pity us [artists] – we are the raw material of the world spirit. (MM 93: 11.5.1863)

So, at times at least, he regards himself as the instrument, not the player. When he contemplates the fundamentals of existence, the great egotist can be humble. On another occasion he speaks to Mathilde about the creative artist's lonely burden, explaining his need for home comforts:

> Next time I shall tell you about my apartment and the way I am having it furnished. God, let it be charming and spruce, for – heavens above! – that plaything, a cosy home, must compensate me for very, very much else! (MM 96: 18.5.1863)

A week later he laments:

> On the whole I am not on very good terms with men. They are not worth all that much nowadays. So few, so very few of them concern themselves with the serious aspects of life! I feel infinitely lonely among men. As for women, they always cause worries, but pleasant worries! You cause me none, but I am worried about you! You dear, precious

creature! If only I could have you with me! Yes, O yes! (MM 100: 25.5.1863)

Mathilde must have read an adverse newspaper report on something Wagner had written. He comforts her:

> Strange that you can be so angry with the critics! It does not concern me at all whether anybody reads my things or not. This is so totally unimportant to me that I am quite alarmed when I hear of people who take such matters seriously. It is amusing that they [the critics] should read my things and imagine I had written them for their approval. My good child! You too must not read anything they scribble, neither for nor against, for even the 'for' is usually stupid. What sane person writes for the newspapers? (MM 104: 5.6.1863)

The topic of possessions comes up again when he confesses to Mathilde that he has pawned a ring given to him by the Crown Prince of Russia:

> Once I am in a position to contemplate redeeming a certain flat diamond ring, all will be well. But whether I shall then still be writing such eccentric stuff as my present scores, poems and prefaces, that is another question! It is more likely that my works would then resemble my cotton dressing gowns and my savings of 300 thaler. O my child!
> (MM 107–8: 16.6.1863)

Confessions and reflections of a more serious kind abound in his letters to Mathilde:

> Look after your little dog. These animals were given to us purposely by a benevolent power, so that they should comfort us over our fellow men.
> (MM 119: 5.8.1863)

A year later:

> That I am a mystery to you, my treasure, does not surprise me. I am the greatest mystery to myself! (MM 187: 7.11.1864)

His special kind of love for the second Mathilde permits him to confide in her with great candour. She may well have felt that it was the untheatrical, the real Wagner who says this to her:

> Take courage, do not complain! No right-minded person should ever fret over health and contentment. We are all ghosts. Who lives? Who is dead? I do not know. I have already died repeatedly. (MM 224: 30.11.1865)

Several times he begs Mathilde to come and keep house for him, but by leaving it open whether he is serious or not, he always gives her sufficient latitude for a virtuous No. He accosts her from Vienna:

I am putting a question to you which for the moment is a purely theoretical one. Consider it as a moral problem, no more! When I ask myself really seriously how I am to manage my life, I can see only one hope of salvation. What I lack is a home, not some*where* but some*body*. I shall be fifty next May. Marriage is out of the question, as long as my wife is alive. If I were to divorce her at this late hour and in the present condition of her health, – heart disease in its advanced state – when the slightest shock might kill her, I might well be dealing her a fatal blow. She would, however, put up with anything as long as she keeps her legal status. Can you see that this situation, this state of affairs is hastening my end? I need a woman who will brave everything and everybody, and who will decide to be what a woman could, nay, must be to me in these wretched circumstances, if I am to survive. . . . I want a loving woman by my side, even if she is also a child. (MM 49–51: 4.1.1863)

Or, as Hans Sachs says:

> *I'd marry a child,*
> *I'd wed a wife –*
> *It would be an amusing life.*
>   (*Meistersinger*, Act 2, Scene 4)

The letter to Mathilde continues:

So I think it should not be impossible to find the one who loves me enough for that. Very well, but how would I take care of her? This is the answer I have found. . . . I rent a decent living room and bedroom in the town centre and furnish it modestly. Here I am 'at home', and people will find me there in the afternoon during certain reception hours. . . . But, tell me, where do I work? Where am I really at home? Here is the answer. In a pleasant country district, outside the town, there is a comfortable apartment inhabited by – no, not myself but by a dear child (or wife), call it what you will. My Biebrich furniture will be there, also the Erard grand piano, all looked after by this faithful soul. It is there that I shall wake up and greet the morning. The child comes to my bed, brings me my breakfast, and then I begin working, when nobody must disturb me, except the friend who may enquire how I am getting on. Later she prepares a good, simple midday meal, and then it will be time for me to go to town, receive people, pay calls and, if all goes well, return in good time to spend my evenings where I belong. In a big town this kind of arrangement is perfectly feasible, that goes without saying. But, who is She, the one who lives out there? R.W.'s last refuge, his angel, his wife – should the unhappy woman whom the rash youth had married die before him. You see, such are the speculations of a comfortless man, as the old year turns into the new. God knows what you may think of them. Anyway, I should not conceal from you what my mind is brooding. How will you take it? Ah well, perhaps it is really nothing but a theoretical problem I am putting to you. At any rate, it is interesting enough to merit consideration. What do you think, little friend?

Mathilde declines amicably, guarding her soul and her reputation. Wagner is not too disconsolate, for Cosima Bülow is moving ever closer to his heart. Eleven months after posing the 'theoretical problem' to Mathilde, he comes to quite a concrete understanding with Cosima which he describes in *Mein Leben*:

> As Bülow had to get ready for his concert, I went for another drive with Cosima, in a fine carriage along the promenade. This time we fell silent and there was none of the former banter. We gazed mutely into each other's eyes. . . . Crying and sobbing we vowed to belong to none but one another. (ML II 745–6)

Wagner gives the date of that memorable day, 28 November 1863.

His correspondence with Mathilde, however, continues. In one of his next letters he hints at some impending change in his situation. Let clever Mathilde decipher the code:

> My dear, good child,
> I find it somewhat difficult to write to you about myself just now. On the one hand, it is certain that a radical transformation of my circumstances will have to take place and that it will have to be a permanent one, but on the other I cannot foretell with any accuracy *how* it will all work out. . . . I therefore write to ask you to be a little patient with me for now. The matter in hand is uncomplicated, but its outcome is still uncertain. I shall have to establish a new mode of life, and it is possible that it will affect you to a considerable extent. (MM 139–40: 23.1.1864)

While Cosima is tied to Bülow, the 'outcome is still uncertain' indeed, but

Wagner finds it hard to forgo female companionship and solace, especially since his material circumstances are about to change radically, thanks to King Ludwig's rescue action in May 1864. Wagner is to reside in a house at Lake Starnberg, rented for him by the King, in a style quite different from the previously envisaged 'living room and bedroom' in some town centre. He now writes from Haus Pellet to Mathilde:

> Will you come and run my house for me? . . . No King, no Emperor can offer me anything, if my house is not run properly. There can be no peace for me until some female creature comes and looks after my affairs! . . . For now, the Bülows will be lodging with me for a few months. I have arranged everything so that they will be comfortable in my large house; that will help me for some time. . . . And how are things with you? Must I still fear to play havoc with your heart by asking you to come to me? Has nothing changed? . . . I live here, as in Munich, on two floors, I below and you, if you came, above. O my God! Always those wretched petty bourgeois considerations, and yet so much love! . . . I beg you, come in September, look at the house, help me, make your own conditions, have it all your own way, only come to me! (MM 162–3: 22.6.1864)

To reinforce his *cri de coeur*, he also accosts Mathilde's mother:

> You know what your daughter Mathilde means to me. She understands my requirements, such as they are and only can be at my age! If age does not sufficiently separate us, for Mathilde to fill the place of a daughter, there are other plausible degrees of relationship which would allow her to live near me in all respectability. I have several nieces of her age who would gladly come to me without anybody raising objections to their living under my roof. . . . Would you have enough confidence in me to face the world courageously and entrust your Mathilde to me? . . . Do you require my assurance that I would properly and honourably take care of her and protect her most emphatically and energetically from all smear and suspicion? Or should one envisage the possibility – I cherish no frivolous hopes, God forbid! – of my wife's death? In that case I would request your daughter's hand. . . . I can only offer you one excuse for my somewhat unusual request, and that excuse is as extraordinary as everything in my whole life. It is extraordinary that I won a King for a most lovable, dearest of sons; and so I wish, chastely but profoundly, for a dear woman by my side. (MM 165–7: 25.6.1864)

It is just as well that Wagner does not send this letter directly to Frau Maier, but asks Mathilde to pass it on, a request which she wisely ignores. Not that he is lonely at the time of writing, for the Bülows were coming to stay with him, but he must have been terrified of the desolation which would follow their departure, to hatch such a desperately convoluted scheme.

Four days later Cosima arrives at his house, preceding her husband by a week, and in the next month Isolde, her first child by Wagner, will be conceived. On the day of Cosima's appearance in Haus Pellet he writes to Mathilde:

> O my dear child,
> On no account do I want that! I will gladly bear anything in the world rather than fresh emotional storms and renewed conflicts which I now see would ensue, were you to give my letter to your good mother. . . . In any case, I must fear for the worst in every respect, since after reading my letter you could imagine that it would 'shatter' your mother, in spite of its sensible tone! . . . I now beg you with all my heart not to give your mother that letter and to keep its contents from her! It seems I have been too hasty again. It was your last letter which had encouraged me to believe that the appropriate moment had come for taking the decisive step of approaching your mother. I was mistaken. A change in our mutual relationship is now out of the question. . . . Do not fear any aberration on my part. Friends are coming to visit me presently. . . . Adieu, look after yourself and love me in spite of everything! My heart is true! (MM 168–9: 29.6.1864)

Wagner the double-dealer? Is he trying to make certain of either the one, Cosima, or the other, Mathilde? Or are we witnessing something quite different here? He creates predicaments and anguish for his protagonists, Wotan, Siegmund, Tristan, Isolde, King Marke, Amfortas – their own nature gives rise to their despair. Has the anguish of his creatures now overcome their creator, blurring his power of discernment between the real world and the one he has created? Between morality and self-preservation?

On 10 April 1865 Isolde is born. Barely nine months earlier he had informed Mathilde:

> Your coming to me *now* would have the completely opposite effect to the one I previously desired; it would be a source of torment beyond description for my heart, and that would now be unbearable. . . . Send me welcome news and love me always. (MM 171–2: 19.7.1864)

*　　　*　　　*

Concerning oneself with Wagner entails trying to square the circle. This applies to us today as it did to his contemporaries. A Jessie Laussot, a Mathilde Wesendonck, a Mathilde Maier, a Cosima is always needed to bring peace to his heart. But the feverish blood, too, must be appeased. Before we leave Mathilde, let us go back a couple of years to the time when Wagner is still living in Penzing, near Vienna, and is looking for a housekeeper/companion. He reports to Mathilde:

> A young, modest, poor girl has been recommended to me. She is supposed to be quiet, neat and not entirely uneducated. . . . I shall take her in and try her out; perhaps she will be able to fill my needs.
> (MM 106–7: 16.6.1863)

Eight days later:

> You remember the girl I told you about last time? Well, I did not hire her after all. As I grow older, I also grow more and more nervous about getting involved in any kind of relationship, no matter how incongruous. (MM 108–9: 24.6.1863)

A fortnight later:

> I shall take the girl after all. She comes with very strong recommendations, being described as gentle, modest and undemanding. She is to make tea for me, keep my clothes in order and look nice and amicable.
> (MM 112: 8.7.1863)

Twelve days later:

> I have had nothing but trouble with the girl whom I decided to take in at last. On the evening of her first day with me I asked myself how to get the poor thing out of the house again, without hurting her feelings too much. . . . My God, no, such arrangements do not really work. . . . I have got to know her older sister. . . . I might give her a try. She seems better educated, and I should be able to introduce her in all respectability to guests at an evening, let her make my tea, etcetera.
> (MM 115–16: 20.7.1863)

A fortnight later:

> The older sister has moved in yesterday and turns out to be a pleasant, clever and warm creature. She keeps me company at breakfast and in the evening, and pleases me not so much by talking but by being there. We shall see! (MM 119: 5.8.1863)

He returns from a concert tour and notifies his 'clever and warm creature', in a letter dated 6.12.1863:

Dear Mariechen,
Next Wednesday I shall be at home again, arriving at Vienna North Station at eight o'clock. Franz is to collect me with the carriage and attend to the luggage. Now, my sweetheart, make sure the house is in good order, for I am longing to relax in comfort. Everything must be neat and tidy and well heated. Most important, see to my study, make it comfortable, open the doors so that it gets nice and warm, and spray it with perfume. Buy the best you can get and make it smell beautifully. God, how I long to relax with you at long last. (The pink panties are ready, I hope??) (*Wiener Allgemeine Zeitung*, 9.10.1881)

As Alberich exclaims, in *Das Rheingold*:

> *Your arms enfold me,*
> *Snaky and slim.*
> *O let me fondle*
> *Your neck, let me nudge it.*
> *My clamorous blood*
> *Bids me cling to your billowing bosom.*
> (Scene 1)

It is worth noting that Wagner asks his Mariechen to be ready for him (pink panties and all), on 6 December, which is a week *after* he and Cosima have 'vowed to belong to none but one another'. Of course, this is not a matter of fidelity or infidelity, but of needs which are normally disavowed but which Wagner blithely acknowledges. Mathilde, as always, understands. When the time comes to send her a letter of farewell, he finds it impossible to use the word itself. He skirts it gently:

Even you, my dear, can only be that to me which you would and could be. This entailed definite restrictions, but much was left, as our letters so happily testify. I discard or revoke nothing; in fact, I welcome the serenity which our relationship has bequeathed to us. Our correspondence shows what we were to each other. No misfortune or happy event could ever come my way without my giving you a true account of it. When anything of real importance occurred, I invited you to share it with me. . . . The beautiful Rhine will never, never leave my memory. That summer makes up for many years in my life. It shall return, believe me! I shall return some time. Maybe you will have my company one day – but when, only God knows! . . . Keep your affection for me; it gave me so many dear hours for my best memories. Your heart lives in me; its beats are gentle, peaceful and pure, and they will only cease with my own. (MM 214–15: 12.7.1865)

Gentle, peaceful and pure. She might well have lost those attributes, had she followed his call and lived with him. He lost her as a potential Mariechen, but she remains the understanding, the wise one; gentle, peaceful and pure.

JUDITH

In August 1876 Wagner opens his Bayreuth Festspielhaus with the first performance of *Der Ring des Nibelungen*. Amongst the visitors is Judith Gautier, the thirty-year-old French novelist. She had already made friends with Cosima and Richard when she had visited them in Tribschen seven years earlier. Now she has left her husband, the writer Catulle Mendès, and she contributes her enthusiastic understanding of Wagner's music and her physical charms to the already turbulent life of the festival director. Wagner himself has become the owner of the magnificent Haus Wahnfried, the respected paterfamilias who is taken care of in all things by Cosima. But the intoxication of the senses which he has always craved must come from without. A few days after the final performance of *Die Götterdämmerung* he sends Judith a note:

> Must it be the last time that I embraced you this morning? No, I shall see you again. I want to, because I love you. Adieu. Think kindly of me!
>
> (JG 140: 4.9.1876)

On the same day Cosima sighs in her diary:

> The days after the final cycle were dreadful. (CWT I 1001: 4.9.1876)

Was it just the climate which she found so depressing?

Jessie Laussot had come to Wagner through *Tannhäuser*, King Ludwig through *Lohengrin* and Judith Gautier through *Der fliegende Holländer*. She relates an episode from her early days:

> By chance I came across the score of *Der fliegende Holländer*. . . . In spite of the innumerable mistakes in my piano playing, the greatness of the drama and the music suddenly revealed itself to me. I was unable to

leave the piano and I behaved quite disgracefully: I refused to allow anyone in the house to take that music away from me. That day Richard Wagner had found a new follower. (JG 24–5)

The first Bayreuth Festspiel is over. Judith has departed with the other visitors, and now Wagner arranges a clandestine correspondence with her:

By the way, you can write to me directly; I have taken care of everything. Herr Schnappauf* will be our intermediary. I would love to have just a line from you, especially since you are always before my eyes, here to my right on the sofa (my God, those eyes!), while I was writing souvenir notes for my poor lady singers. O how incredible it all is: you are the cornucopia, the overfulfilment of my life which has been so peaceful and protected since Cosima came to me. You are my largesse, my intoxicating superfluity! (Neatly put, don't you think?) But what does it matter – you understand me. Adieu, Judith! (JG 142: *early September 1876*)

So Schnappauf is to take care of their letters, so that Cosima may continue to keep his life 'peaceful and protected'. Not altogether illogical, considering the capricious nature of Wagner's needs. If the former letter owes its style to Goethe, the next one could have been penned by Schiller – both favourite authors of Wagner's:

Your embraces live in my soul as the most enthralling ecstasy, the sublimest pride of my existence. They are the last gift of the gods.

(JG 145: ?1877)

Judith remains devoted to Wagner, but she has also found a new companion who shares her life, the young composer Benedictus. Perhaps it is for his sake that she declines Wagner's invitation to accompany him on his London concert tour in May 1877. Or does she stay away because Cosima is coming too? Or is last year's festival summer with Wagner too dear to her heart to risk harming its memory? He complains to her:

How bad you were not to accept my invitation to London! And why? Alright, I know why! It really is too bad! Now – when – how? Let it be! Love me and let us not wait for the protestant Kingdom of Heaven; it is bound to be terribly tedious! Love, love, love me evermore! (JG 147–8: *1.10.1877*)

* Wagner's barber and factotum.

Soon the festive mood of Wagner and of Judith lapses into something more workaday. He asks her to go shopping for him:

For my sofa I would like a wonderful, utterly unbelievable cover which I shall name *Judith*. Listen! Try to find that silken material, I think it is called 'Lampas' or suchlike. Yellow satin, as pale as possible, sprinkled with plaited rosebuds. . . . If yellow is unavailable, then a very light

Judith Gautier

blue. White is a possibility too, and probably easier to come by. I need six metres! All for those good mornings with *Parsifal*. (JG 148–9: *undated, October/November 1877*)

He tells her about his work in hand:

You will soon see it [*Parsifal*] and it will please you. But if not? Will you still love me in spite of your dislike? I do hope so. And I shall kiss you, no

matter whether you like my music or not! O, I possess something called
'Judith'. Adieu! Adieu! (JG 158–9: 27.11.1877)

His shopping lists are getting longer:

> O my dearest Judith,
> Let us no longer torment ourselves over this wretched affair. I shall do
> without the pink satin! As for the perfumes, I leave them entirely to your
> own good taste and practical judgement. Anything you procure will be
> welcome, even the cold creams! But I could do with a rather stronger
> aroma, for my nostrils are a little insensitive. (JG 159: 30.11.1877)

Parsifal is progressing well. Although, supposedly, there is strictly No
Admittance to his study while he is working, in fact he always welcomes
stimulation, whether in the shape of favourite dogs, beloved humans, or cold
creams with rose aroma. Judith may visit him, even in the company of
Benedictus, whom he proposes to call his 'cousin':

> Be lavish with the bath essences, including the ambra varieties. My bath
> tub is underneath the study, and I like it when the odours rise up. But
> you must not think badly of me! I am old enough to take an interest
> again in puerilities. I have three years of *Parsifal* before me, and nothing
> must divert me from the sweet peace of monastic creativity. Do come!
> Come, and if you like bring my cousin along too. . . . O you dear soul!
> Deeply beloved soul! All is tragic, all that is *real* is tragic! But you will
> always love me, and I could never do otherwise, even if I wanted to. A
> thousand kisses. (JG 171–2: *December 1877*)

Judith stays away. Once more he sends her a somewhat melancholic love call. It
was to be the last:

> O you warm, sweet soul! What inspiration would I find in your arms!
> Must I forget it all? No! But everything is tragic, everything ends, at
> best – in elegy! I am yours, yours. You beautiful abundance of my life.
> (JG 189: 22.1.1878)

Having provided inspiration and injected new life into him, Judith, his
superfluity, becomes superfluous. She now receives Wagner's letter of farewell:

> I have asked Cosima to discuss with you those Paris purchases. . . .
> Furthermore, I am at present so distracted by some most unpleasant
> business affairs that I can no longer find sufficient leisure to continue my
> composition of *Parsifal*. Have pity! It will all be over soon, and I shall

find again those beautiful moments of leisure for talking to you about myself. But do not torment yourself about me; my present vexation will soon pass. Be good to Cosima and write to her kindly and at length. I shall then always share your news. Love me for ever. Thus you will often see me in your mind, and perhaps we shall really meet again one day.

(JG 193–4: 10.(?)2.1878)

What has occurred at Bayreuth, that Wagner will never write another letter to Judith? Circumstances point to a domestic crisis which was threatening the peace of Haus Wahnfried. Perhaps confessions were heard, perhaps letters were discovered, perhaps Schnappauf had omitted to snap up a letter or two. At any rate, Cosima confides to her diary:

The sorrow I was fearing has caught up with me; it has encroached from outside! May God help me! Grief, my old companion, be with me and live with me. We know each other well – how long will you be staying this time, truest and most dependable of friends? (CWT II 45: 12.2.1878)

Judith remains faithful to Wagner, at least to that which is most real in him – that which makes him immortal. In September 1881 she visits the Wagners, and in 1882 she attends the Festspiele:

He receives us with that touching cordiality which is so characteristic of him, whenever he finds himself in the company of people who truly love him. There is no trace in him of the egotistic insensitivity which great men frequently show, after they have attained some degree of public acclaim. He is, if anything, too sensitive, he allows his mood to lead him into momentary bouts of severity. . . . Sometimes he can forget and completely change his opinion. He can love what a short while ago he did not, and always with the same sincerity. (JG 87–8: 1882)

Judith must have written this with a heavy heart. 'Sometimes he can forget'. 'He can love what a short while ago he did not'. She conceals that he can also not love what a short while ago he did. It is good that she does not know what Cosima tells the diary about her:

At midday our friend Judith Gautier. I do not yet know whether R. is pleased or just embarrassed, as he says. (CWT II 798: 26.9.1881)

On the next day:

Yesterday I avoided responding to R.'s remarks concerning Judith's demeanour which he finds embarrassing. . . . Today he is sad about that and says it would be the end of him, if any obstacle arose between us. (CWT II 799: 27.9.1881)

Finally:

Judith visits us after our meal. I receive her myself, since R. is a little tired. (CWT II 984: 25.7.1882)

Minna, Jessie, both Mathildes, Judith – he discharges them all when their duty is done. Their suffering must have been keen, as the enchanted became disenchanted. One is almost tempted to think of potions of love and of forgetfulness which have a way of materialising at those turning points in Wagner's and in their lives. His cool comments on those he once loved probably conceal his own grief – 'everything is tragic'. If the potion of forgetfulness brings sadness, the potion of love can engender ecstasy and terror. Tristan sings:

Den furchtbaren Trank,	*The draught that we drank,*
der der Qual mich vertraut,	*To what torment it led –*
ich selbst – ich selbst,	*Myself, I brewed*
ich hab' ihn gebraut!	*The drink and its dread!*
Aus Vaters Not	*From grief which sire*
und Mutterweh,	*And mother bore,*
aus Liebestränen	*From love's own tear drops*
eh und je –	*Evermore,*
aus Lachen und Weinen,	*From gloom and from gladness,*
Wonnen und Wunden	*From death and devotion,*
hab' ich des Trankes	*Have I devised*
Gifte gefunden	*This poisonous potion.*
	(Tristan und Isolde, Act 3, Scene 1)

From Therese Ringelmann to Judith Gautier – every one of Wagner's loves tasted the poisonous potion. They experienced ecstasy and emptiness, and the world received the *Ring, Tristan und Isolde, Meistersinger* and *Parsifal*.

IV

CREDIT IS DUE

The present-day value of the various nineteenth-century denominations mentioned in this chapter is, very approximately, as follows:

1 franc	= £1
1 florin	= £3
1 gulden	= £3
1 thaler	= £4
1 ducat	= £11
1 louisdor	= £18
1 friedrichsdor	= £19

*What makes you think I could ever have enough money?**

Wagner needs a constant supply of cash for his home comforts, his comprehensive library, his extensive travels and, above all, for wooing his inspiration. He explains this to Franz Liszt, his friend and helper:

> If I am once again to submerge myself in the current of artistic creativity, in order to thrive in a world of my imagination, then this imagination needs a good deal of support, my fancy needs sustenance. I cannot live like a dog when I am working, nor can I sleep on straw and swig cheap liquor. I must be coaxed one way or another if I am to accomplish the horribly difficult task of creating a non-existent world. (BWL II 4: 15.1.1854)

To conjure up this non-existent world, he must be able to forget the existing one. No external light or sound is allowed to find its way into the study, which must be heavily perfumed and equipped with costly cushions, coverlets, carpets and wall hangings, in order to trap the inspiration. He commissions the Viennese seamstress and milliner Bertha Goldwag to supply:

1. One Dressing Gown, pink with starched insets.
   One ditto blue.
   One ditto green.
   One quilted Dressing Gown, dark green.
2. Jackets: One pink.
   One very pale yellow.
   One light grey.
3. Trousers: One pink.
   One pale yellow.
   One light grey.
   One dark green, as the quilted Dressing Gown.
4. Boots: White – Pink – Blue – Yellow – Grey – Green.
5. Covers: One white, embroidered, trimmed pink, lined with heavy pink satin.
   One blue, trimmed blue, white lining.
   One pink, trimmed pink, pink lining.
   One blue Bed Cover, white lining.

* UFH 222, letter to Uhlig, 1852

6. Cushions: Two large white, embroidered, fully decorated, one pink, the other yellow.
   Two smaller ones, embroidered but undecorated.
7. Ribbons: As many and as beautiful as possible, and also approximately 10 yards of the white embroidered ribbon.
8. Supply a large quantity, say 20 to 30 yards of the lovely heavy pink satin material.

In addition, beautiful floral lace. Money is ready for you; if you need it immediately I will send it. Now see that everything turns out nicely and let me know soon when you can come, together with a skilled dressmaker. (KWP 119–21: 15.11.1865)

One may shake one's head in disbelief, but one should also consider the possible reasons for this extraordinary commission. Wagner was plagued through much of his life by a highly sensitive skin which reacted badly to most ordinary fabrics. An authentic need for supple, soft materials might account for, say, ten per cent of his craving for luxury. A desire for warmth for another ten: Italy, the sun, were a magnet to him. Long after his death, Bertha Goldwag remembers:

He wore satin trousers. . . . His main reason was that he needed an inordinate amount of warmth if he was to feel well. All his clothes which I made for him had to be heavily padded with cotton wool, for he was always complaining of the cold. (KWP 30–1)

Rather more significant, however, is the fact that Wagner was a man of the theatre, both in the theatre and at home. To those colossal stage characters, Wotan, Tristan, Sachs, Gurnemanz, Brünnhilde, Isolde, he adds one more, Richard Wagner. Not that he is consciously playing a part. The true artist *is* Wotan, *is* Wagner. Quilted dressing gowns, yellow fur boots and velvet beret are stage properties, as are Tarnhelm, ring and spear. They help the artist to realise his role. To create such miracles as the *Ring, Meistersinger* and *Parsifal*, Wagner can seldom permit himself to step outside his part. His creative genius gives him little peace. There is no need to begrudge him his heavy pink satins and floral lace if these are what the process of creation required. Were one to calculate another thirty per cent for the trappings that facilitate the process, one would have assembled at least half an explanation for Wagner's odd commissions from Fräulein Bertha. May the other half rest in its deserved obscurity.

Inside and outside the theatre, Wagner is his own poet, composer, producer

Wagner contemplating his operas in the comfort of his home

and costume designer. Minna's daughter Natalie describes his apparel:

> Snow-white pantaloons, sky-blue tail coat with huge gold buttons, cuffs, an immensely tall top hat with a narrow brim, a walking stick as high as himself, with a huge gold knob, and very bright, sulphur yellow kid gloves. (SB 416)

In May 1863, the fifty-year-old Wagner moves into his new home in Penzing, near Vienna. He furnishes each room as though he were designing for the stage. In his own words:

> Dining Room: dark brown, with small rosebuds (very plain).
> Salon Study: plain purple, monochrome, the corners decorated with garnet velvet borders and gold trim.
> Study: pale brown-grey, with purple flowers. Dark brown velvet borders.
> Tea Room: plain green with violet velvet borders and gold trim in the corners.
> Bedroom: plain purple with green velvet borders and gold trim, purple bed curtains.
> Dressing Room: pale green with dark red flowers.
> Music Salon: brown woollen curtains with Persian pattern, sofa ditto, garnet plush for armchairs. (MM 101–2)

145

The reassuring sense of abundance, warding off all memories of privation, provides the peace of mind he needs for his work. But his desire for luxury extends beyond his own needs. There must be more of everything, not only for him but for his friends as well, for Wagner has an unbridled instinct for giving, as Peter Cornelius, his composer friend,* learns one Christmas:

> The crazy Wagner had lit a huge Christmas tree, with a royally opulent table beneath it for me! Just think: a wonderful heavy overcoat, an elegant grey dressing gown, a red scarf, a blue cigar case and lighter, fine silk handkerchiefs, magnificent gold cuff links, the *Struwwelpeter*,† a stylish pen wiper with a gold motto, several fine cravats, a meerschaum cigar holder with his initials – in short, presents such as only an oriental imagination could devise. It made my heart heavy, so next day I gave half of them away. At last I was happy. (MM 138: 11.1.1864)

Without luxury Wagner cannot work, cannot live. It would be exceptional for a nineteenth-century composer to make a regular – let alone a considerable – income from his works, so Wagner sets about discovering hidden sources of supply. He studies the art of raising money as painstakingly and systematically as he had once studied composition. He detects hitherto uncharted paths to the hearts and wallets of benefactors who prove unable to resist the virtuoso cashier. To such a degree of perfection does he bring the art that one is tempted to compare the richness and variety of his ideas in this field to those displayed in his writings and compositions.

The relationship between Wagner and his friend Ernst Benedikt Kietz provides a model of the borrower's methods and of the creditor's inevitable fate. Kietz, painter and draughtsman, shares Wagner's years of penury in Paris, from 1839 to 1842. He lives in the city, Richard and Minna in the suburb of Meudon. In the letter that follows, Wagner is not asking his friend for money, far from it, he is merely asking for postage stamps. It may, in fact, amount to the same thing, but it sounds less demanding:

> Once again take up the trusted sword and slash through the knot of my adversity! The enclosed letters are of great importance to me, as you may well imagine. They must catch the next post, but at present I cannot

---

* Peter Cornelius (1824–74) was a pupil of Liszt. His operas include *The Barber of Bagdad* and *Le Cid*.
† Popular children's classic.

afford the postage. Dip into your magic sack and clear them for me.
(WSB I 522–3: 13.10.1841)

Having aroused his friend's sympathy, he comes to the main point:

> Look at the enclosed pawn ticket. Strictly speaking, the redemption or
> renewal period expired on the 15th of last month, but when I queried
> this they granted me a four-weeks extension without any trouble. . . .
> Since you have a real passion for holding forth eloquently in French, do
> me a favour and go to the address on the ticket, Rue St Honoré, and talk
> to the people.

As Kietz can see, he is not being asked for money but is being entrusted with an
ennobling assignment.

Six months later Wagner is to leave Paris, to await the fate of his *Rienzi* in
Dresden. The debts he has left behind are considerable. He informs Kietz:

> I enclose a note for your uncle Fechner which you can send to him.
> Risking that gentleman's contempt, I must state that I *cannot* pay him
> anything before the autumn. I *cannot*. . . . People who have suffered as
> I have, care little about conventions which are dear to your uncle and
> his kind. All the same, it vexes me having to say this. (WSB II 89:
> 12.5.1842)

Wagner's creditors do not take long to learn that it would be profitless to count
on his gratitude. Strictly speaking, a money lender is less interested in gratitude
than in receiving his money. It is only when both fail to arrive that he gets
alarmed. He might consider, of course, that his involuntary donation will
contribute to the progress of *Tristan* or *Lohengrin*, but that would be asking too
much.

Wagner's next letter to Kietz comes from Teplitz, unstamped:

> If it were possible to pay postage for this letter to Paris, I would have done
> so with the money from Schleifstein.* (WSB II 124: 13.6.1842)

Over the years, Wagner has borrowed considerable amounts from Kietz.
Solicitously, he now enquires how much he owes him:

> The Devrient woman has lent me 1,000 thaler, to enable me to pay as
> many debts as possible, but above all to help you. I am no longer sure

---

* Possibly one of Wagner's many little-known patrons.

what sum I owe you, so I am sending you 600 fr. through Avenarius.*
You will let me know whether that covers the total amount. I would not
presume to advise you what to do with this money, firstly because I know
that you do not want my advice, and secondly because I am only too well
aware that you would not follow it, anyway. Besides, your long silence

*One of Kietz's many drawings of Wagner:
portrayed here as an orphan of the storm, sharing his boots
with his half-sister Cäcilie*

makes it quite impossible for me to judge your present circumstances.
From all I hear you have made no progress in your art. (SB 244:
5.1.1843)

Evidently, repaying a debt, albeit with borrowed money, comes as such a shock
to Wagner that he stoops to abusing his friend. What is more, his left hand takes
what the right has given:

* Eduard Avenarius (1809–85) was married to Wagner's half-sister, Cäcilie, and
became the head of a large publishing house.

The 100 fr. I owe to your uncle Fechner I shall also remit through Avenarius. If you think he would accept some small compensation for his loss of interest, offer it to him and lay it out for me. Thank him in my name and tell him that I am very glad to be able to repay him. Everything that happened between him and me is, after all, but foolery which annoyed me only so long as I was unable to fulfil my obligations. Now that I can do so, I only remember his willingness to help me out of trouble. That I can and shall never forget! (SB 245: 5.1.1843)

Here speaks a Wagner who, for once, is untroubled in mind and purse. In such a case he too can be grateful. Kietz, however, is still waiting for full restitution of the debt Wagner owes him. Two years pass, then he receives some payment:

Forgive me for being so late in sending your money, but I have to reproach you for omitting to let me have an account when, some time ago, I let you have those 800 fr. I never wrote anything down and I really had no idea of the total amount owing to you. It was up to you to keep me informed. (SB 249: 18.12.1844)

Wagner is to make frequent use of this multiple device: (1) play for time; (2) forget; (3) rebuke creditor for negligence. His letter to Kietz continues with another *ennobling assignment*:

Loizeau [Wagner's former tailor in Paris] has recently sent me several reminders and now demands 278 fr. . . . I am sending you today as much as I can, namely 300 fr. Be good enough to let Loizeau have the balance after retaining the 159 fr. belonging to you, that is 141 fr. which constitutes the greater half of my debt to him. Tell him that for the present I am unable to manage any more, but at least he can see my good intentions. He may safely count on receiving the outstanding 137 fr. at the latest by Easter next year. (SB 250: 18.12.1844)

The letter ends with a promise which makes Kietz forget his troubles:

Miracles do happen, as you will see. He who cannot give you a hundred today, will find ways and means to give you thousands. *I* am that he. Adieu, honest old fellow, whom I love very dearly. (SB 251: 18.12.1844)

A time will come when the 'honest old fellow' will remind Wagner of this undertaking. But first there are more *assignments*:

Receive the bearer of these lines kindly. He is a young Pole, Heimberger by name (from Lemberg). I like him very much and he is in a bad way

149

just now. Allow him to stay with you for the present, and you will prove a true friend to me. (SB 253: 2.5.1851)

Only seven months later:

The bearer of this letter is Hermann Müller, former Saxon Army Guard Officer. You probably have already heard of him. Take him in and look after him with care; it is his first visit to Paris. (SB 256: 5.12.1851)

Sixteen months later Kietz finds himself in trouble and now reminds his friend of his former promise. Wagner replies:

You have recently read a good deal about my successes in Germany and thus assume that I am earning a lot of money. You take it for granted that I am in clover and, since I have not written for some time, that I no longer care about you who are in the mire. On this assumption you write to me of your wretched, undeserved bad luck, that you had to prostitute your art for lack of money, and all this you blame on me, with reproaches and insults – though indirectly – of the most odious kind. . . . When I find myself in the situation in which you suppose me to be, you need not doubt that I shall think of you too, you old rascal. Ready money, however, will always be a great problem. You know that I am unable to live frugally, and my weakness for spending more than I earn is a permanent one. . . . All I can offer you with any confidence is and always will be, therefore, the following: come and stay with me, if this appeals to you, for as long as you like, even permanently. You shall have a comfortable room for yourself and everything you need. . . . Any substantial sums of money, however, will always be out of the question. (SB 265–7: 2.4.1853)

Kietz will have to accept the fact that neither repayment of Wagner's outstanding debt nor ready financial help will be forthcoming, but at least he can be assured of his bed and board, and much later he is to take up that offer. Five years pass, before Wagner honours him with another errand:

Will you do me a great favour and get me some snuff? Can you afford to pay for three pounds? I cannot enclose cash in a letter to France, and nobody will give me a bill of exchange for 12 to 14 fr. If you can do this, please buy two pounds of the ordinary and one pound of the special kind *à la divette*, and send them via Marseilles, *par mer*. (SB 276: 18.10.1858)

The 'honest old fellow' does what he can. He is happy to be Wagner's friend and to bask in his friend's ever-increasing fame, but his own wretched circumstances cannot always be forgotten and it is not surprising that he should occasionally give expression to a grievous sense of neglect:

With this letter I draw your attention to my address and to myself. . . . Your new address has been forwarded to me. You are always everywhere – and nowhere, nowhere at least for me! . . . I have been preparing this

Ernst Benedikt Kietz,
Wagner's 'old comrade'

letter for a long time, as one prepares a trial sermon, to gain readmittance to the temple of friendship. . . . You have not written for years and that seems to prove that, oblivious of our old friendship and my loyal love, you are angry with me and wish to break off. With these lines I am making one last desperate effort! . . . It is three years now since I embraced you here and saw you for the last time. You made me many beautiful promises then, by word of mouth and in writing. Now I get contempt and indifference. . . . So I vegetate like a plant growing among ruins. The one thing that lives fresh in my heart is the memory of our former friendship. Do not destroy that for me. (SB 279–80: 18.1.1861)

Has Wagner forgotten his old comrade? Hardly, but their relationship has changed. In his works for the stage Wagner explores the most secret places of his characters' hearts. In his private life he is less keen to consider his friends' and acquaintances' feelings. The friends suffer and cannot understand why he often treats them like strangers. Wagner's development as an artist and as a man is so unpredictable that all his relationships are precarious and subject to modification. Kietz probably realised that friendship with a genius entailed more than financial sacrifices. In one of his poems Friedrich Nietzsche, himself a temporary friend and disciple, writes:

Ich muss weg über hundert Stufen,	A hundred steps above me rising.
Ich muss empor und hör euch rufen:	Up then! I hear you agonising:
'Hart bist du. Sind wir denn von Stein?'	'We are not stones! Leave us alone!'
Ich muss weg über hundert Stufen,	A hundred steps above me rising;
und niemand möchte Stufe sein.	And none will be a stepping stone.

(Nietzsche, *Gedichte*: Leipzig, undated: 9)

During the next nine years, Wagner and Kietz write intermittently. Wagner even repeats his offer to take Kietz into his home:

Your journey from Zurich to us in Lucerne and back again I shall be able to finance. . . . So, come and see us in Tribschen where we will put you up. (SB 293: 21.5.1870)

Kietz remains in Zurich for the time being and after a few months receives another letter from Tribschen, but not written by his friend this time:

Dear Herr Kietz,
Richard is overworked and asks me to tell you that he greatly regrets your present calamitous situation. He hopes the war will soon be over and that you will be able to return to your home, but that in the meantime you may find employment in Zurich. If we have not asked you to visit him in Tribschen, it is because our guest room is occupied by Kapellmeister Richter, and because immediately after completing some urgent work in hand, my husband and I shall be going on a short journey.

Cosima Wagner.   (SB 294: 6.9.1870)

Thus is the 'honest old fellow' cast into perpetual darkness.

Looking back at Wagner's early attempts at borrowing, one finds his technique still traditionally based, much like his earliest compositions. He turns for assistance to the friend of his youth, the poet and dramatist Theodor Apel:

> My financial affairs, you rescuing angel, are not yet completely straightened out, God knows! . . . To achieve that and to take care of my immediate needs, I would require 200 thaler. Be not alarmed, but that is how it is! (WSB I 202: 19.4.1835)

A crude move, in need of refining. During the next five years he will develop the technique.

Here is a sample of his progress at the end of that period. He writes to his brother-in-law, Eduard Avenarius:

> My dear friend and patron,
> Please answer simply yes or no, whether I may count on your ability (I wish to God I need only appeal to your good will) to add another 50 fr. to the sum I already owe you. (WSB I 375: 4.1.1840)

The significant phrase is the one in brackets. He takes Eduard's good will for granted, thus making it easier for him to say yes or, conversely, harder to say no. The letter continues:

> Necessity not only teaches us to pray, it also forces on us a certain measure of impertinence which you, more than anyone else, will understand and forgive.

Again, he takes his brother-in-law's good will for granted, and in so doing he announces his main theme, Eduard's moral uprightness and mental alertness, for a second time in close succession. In his compositions he bases his so-called leitmotiv technique on the same principle, which demands early repeats of a new motif, to impress it upon the listener. Following his own precept, he sounds his theme for a third time in Eduard's ear. He continues:

> In order to pay my rent and various other items, I visited the pawnbroker yesterday with my last non-essentials, but without obtaining the sum I need. Since this amounts to no more than 50 fr., you are once more (and for the *last* time) my only refuge.

Is it not inconceivable that his brother-in-law could refuse such a paltry sum, especially 'for the last time'? Avenarius obliges, but seven weeks later he receives Wagner's request for a tenfold sum:

> If the state of your business allows it, could you advance me 500 fr. till Easter? (WSB I 444–5: 22.2.1841)

A more conventional method of borrowing, developed by Wagner in a rather original manner, is the *wail of woe*. Many a victim of cash flow problems has failed to make the grade, because he does not moan loudly enough. When Wagner lets out a wail, it takes the prospective donor's breath away, and his ability to say 'No' along with it. And when one begs not for oneself but for one's starving wife, would not a 'No' almost amount to a crime? Here is an early exercise in this method. The letter is addressed to Theodor Apel:

> I am turning once again to you, friend of my youth which, alas, has vanished; to you who has himself experienced the hardest blows of fate.* . . . I live in desperate penury and you must help me! You will probably feel resentful but, O my God, why am I driven to ignore your resentment? Why? Because for a whole year I have been living here with my wife in utter poverty, without a penny to call my own.
> (WSB I 405–6: 20.9.1840)

A later sample of the *hungry wife* method shows considerable progress and refinement. Being heavily implicated in the Dresden uprising of May 1849,† Wagner has escaped and is in Paris, prior to settling in Switzerland, while Minna is still in Dresden. He appeals to Liszt:

> With the confidence of one who is *completely* helpless, I beg of you – provide me with money quickly, to enable me to travel to Zurich and exist there until I receive the desired salary. You will be the best judge of what amount is required for this. Unfortunately I do not know whether my wife will comply with my ardent entreaty and join me in Zurich, since she may be unable to raise the necessary funds. Be so good as to ask her whether she needs anything. . . . My God, how hard I always try not to weep! My poor wife!! (WSB III 83: 18.6.1849)

How can Liszt refuse to ask Minna? Once he takes that first step, the second –

---

* Apel had lost his eyesight in 1836.

† In April 1849 the King of Saxony dissolved both chambers of deputies, provoking an armed revolt in which Wagner took a prominent part, though as a non-combatant. The uprising was put down and its leaders were condemned to death. Wagner obtained a false passport and escaped to Switzerland.

providing her with the means to join her husband – will have to follow, especially since Wagner now reinforces his request in a second letter (repeat appearance of original motif):

> Are you in a good mood? Probably not, as you have just opened a letter from your thorn-in-the-flesh. And yet, it is absolutely vital that you should be in a good mood today – now – at this very moment. Recall the most wonderful hour of your life, lodge yourself right in it, and from that position look upon me, serenely and benevolently, for I come to you as a sincere petitioner. Today I have received a letter from my wife which touches me more than words can tell. She wishes to come to me, to stay with me and share with me once more all the ills of life . . . but the fulfilment of her desire to join me is impossible, for neither of us has any money at all. . . . So I implore you by all that is dear to you, try and raise whatever you can, and send it – no, not to me, but to my wife. . . . You see what sort of person I am – I can beg, I could steal, to bring happiness to my wife, be it ever so brief! (WSB III 97–9: 19.7.1849)

Liszt replies:

> I have sent 100 thaler to your wife in Dresden. (BWL I 36: 29.7.1849)

Thanks to his friend's generosity, set in motion by Wagner's technical prowess, Minna joins him in Zurich, accompanied by Natalie, their dog Peps, and Papo the parrot.

A variation of the *wail of woe* method of securing funds is the *jester's plea*. Here the donor is treated to some witty banter which puts him in a propitious mood. Wagner sends a messenger to Avenarius:

> My wife beseeches you most humbly to give the bearer of this note 10,000 fr. for her. Should it prove impossible to meet this sudden request, she would be satisfied with the loan, for twelve hours, of your gracious coffee-grinder ['*gütige Kaffeemühle*']. (WSB I 372: *December 1839*)

During his stay in Paris Wagner earns a little money by making arrangements of popular music of the day for the publisher Maurice Schlesinger, to whom he writes:

> I cannot possibly go to sleep before impressing upon you the significance of the visit which I intend to pay you tomorrow morning, namely the

'*Wagner earns a little money by making arrangements of popular music*': Kietz caricature of Wagner and Minna in Paris

settling of our account and 100 fr. in advance. . . . My dearest Herr Schlesinger, these 100 fr. you simply must let me have, otherwise I can take no responsibility for your appearance before the judgement seat of posterity, when it might be said that Moritz Schlesinger, the generous, the acute Moritz Schlesinger had refused an advance of 100 fr. to the subsequently far-famed Richard Wagner. . . . The prospect of this eventuality will of course make you shudder, and the fortunate result of that shudder is that you will let me have the requested advance without delay. I am counting on this with the most amazing confidence! . . . I cannot go on – my poetic flights have exhausted me – and all that for 100 fr. (WSB I 478–80: 27.4.1841)

After his return to Germany he finds a new publisher, C. F. Meser, to whom he writes from the Bohemian health resort Marienbad, where he is drinking the waters:

Highly esteemed friend, comrade of all sorrows and joys of this life! If you will lend or otherwise procure for me 100 thaler, at any rate of interest whatever, which I herewith solemnly declare to repay by the first of September of this year, you would immensely oblige your devoted servant Richard Wagner, who is unable to make ends meet in this very expensive spa, Marienbad. (WSB II 444: 20.7.1845)

In his letter to his friend Wilhelm Baumgartner, a pianist and composer who lives in Zurich, we find a successful combination of the *jester's plea* and the *hungry wife* methods:

Dear brother, I worry about your future. In winter you have a steady income which you use up as you go, while in summer you earn very little and have to go short. I herewith offer you to open a credit account with me. My position is the opposite to yours: from next summer onwards I shall be receiving considerable sums of money from Bordeaux (definitely 3,000 fr. per annum), but just now I am not so well supplied. . . . If you will send me 300 fr. now, I shall undertake to return that amount without fail at the beginning of July. Just think how pleasant it will be for you to receive, all of a sudden, an unexpected windfall of 300 fr., and in the heat of summer! You see how I care for the future of all my friends, while at the same time caring for my dear wife's comfort. (WSB III 254–5: 13.3.1850)

One should not overlook a variation of the *jester's plea*, in which the wives of both writer and addressee are allotted prominent parts. Wagner writes to his friend Josef Tichatschek, the principal tenor at the Dresden opera and his first Rienzi and Tannhäuser:

> Do you know anyone who would be able to advance me 5,000 fr.? I am sure such a person does exist, only I do not know him. Please find him for me! . . . But, most important, *my wife* must not come to hear of it, for to find out about my embarrassing situation would greatly upset her. Consequently *your wife* must not know either. (SB 221: 19.10.1859)

Wagner's aversion to postage stamps has already been mentioned. The following selection indicates the extent of his phobia and the efficacy of this method of saving, i.e. borrowing money:

> I am sitting here in a dubious Berlin inn, while the residue of my Parisian cash looks even more dubious, therefore forgive me if this letter bears no postage. (WSB II 73, to Herr and Frau Avenarius, Paris 21.4.1842)

> Be so kind as to share the postage between you. I find it impossible to stamp the letter, and I am anxious it should reach you soon. (WSB II 95, to Anders and Kietz, Paris 13.5.1842)

> It is a calamity that packets like this cannot be pre-paid from here to England. (RWF 185, to Klindworth, 10.1.1856)

> I shall not put postage stamps on this letter, as I intend to post it after vainly enquiring at the post office for a letter from you. It will then be 7 o'clock, too late for stamping my letter. (WSB IV 62, to Uhlig, 3.6.1851)

Where did Wagner learn the art? His mother writes to him:

> It will be eight days before I get my money, and this letter would have to wait until then for me to buy postage stamps, therefore I send it now, unstamped. You are a rich man and I am a poor woman. (*Bayreuther Festspielführer* 1933, 23: *undated*)

Now we know.

Closely related to the saving of postage, only more lucrative, is the *camouflage* technique. Here, Wagner asks someone a seemingly innocent favour. By the time he or she has realised that this really amounts to a request for money, it is usually too late. Richard and Minna return from Paris to Dresden (April 1842), leaving Natalie, then seventeen, behind. After a year they want her to join them, but that costs money. So Richard writes to his sister Cäcilie – not to her husband Eduard! – in Paris:

> Natalie can really only flourish in an atmosphere far removed from the French surroundings, however respectable. Please help her pack her belongings and if you, dear Cäcilie, do not wish to travel with her, your husband need not feel anxious for her. All you have to do is to entrust her to the guard. She will not be staying overnight in Frankfurt but take the evening train from there, and arrive safe and sound in Leipzig. Eduard will be so good as to give her the money for the journey.
>
> (WSB II 237: 8.4.1843)

Quite another method of raising money or obtaining goods which Wagner has perfected can be called the *divine inspiration*, after his letter to Liszt:

> Listen, Franz! I had a divine inspiration! *You must get me an Erard grand piano!* Write to the widow and tell her that you visit me three

Franz Liszt

times (!) every year, and you definitely require a better grand piano than my old lame one. Tell her a hundred thousand tall stories and make her believe it will add to the firm's prestige when an Erard stands in my house. In short, do not give it another thought, but act with brilliant impertinence. *I must have an Erard.* (BWL II 137: 21.7.1856)

Two years before, he had finished *Das Rheingold*, and possibly his memory is still haunted by Wotan's divine inspiration:

Den Ring muss ich haben! – I must have that ring!

(Scene 2)

Wotan obtains the ring from Alberich, and Erard's widow hands over the grand piano.

Several years later Wagner hears of one of his acquaintances' sudden access to unexpected wealth. This gives him another *divine inspiration*, and he writes to the young composer Baron von Hornstein:

I hear you have become rich. . . . In order to rid myself of the most pressing obligations, worries and wants which rob me of my peace of mind, I require an immediate loan of ten thousand francs. With this I can put my life in order and start working again. You may find it hard to provide me with this amount, but if you really *wish* it and do not shrink from sacrifices, then I am sure you will find it possible. . . . Now let us see what sort of man you are! If you prove yourself to me, – and why should one not expect such a thing? – the assistance you give me will bring you into close contact with me, and you will allow me to stay next summer for approximately three months on one of your estates, preferably by the Rhine. (ZH 15–16: 12.12.1861)

The Baron replies:

Dear Herr Wagner,
You should turn your attention to *really* wealthy persons whom you will surely find among your numerous patrons and patronesses all over Europe. I regret that I am unable to be of service to you. As to your extended visit to 'one of my estates', I am not at present prepared for a lengthy visit, but if this should become possible at some future time I will let you know. I have read in the newspapers, with great regret, that the production of *Tristan und Isolde* will not take place this winter.

(ZH 15–16: *December 1861*)

This is one of the rare cases where the victim turns aggressor, provoking a reply to grace the baronial mantelpiece.

> Dear Herr von Hornstein,
> I would be wrong not to rebuke you for your answer to my letter. It will probably not happen again that a man like me will have contact with you, but it should be a wholesome lesson to you to be made aware of the impropriety of your lines. It is not your place to advise me in any way whatever, not even as to the relative wealth of individuals. You should have left it to me to decide why I have not approached any of the patrons or patronesses you have mentioned. If you are not prepared to receive me at one of your estates, you should have grasped the singular opportunity I offered you, by making appropriate arrangements at a place of my own choice. Your promise, therefore, to let me know when it will be convenient to you to receive me is an insult. You would also have been wise to suppress your sentiments concerning my *Tristan*.
>
> (ZH 20–1: 27.12.1861)

Occasionally Wagner makes use of his divine inspirations to assist a friend in need. Elisabeth, the sister of the philosopher Friedrich Nietzsche, had deposited her stocks and shares with a bank whose manager, an amateur composer, had begged Wagner to peruse an opera he had just written. Wagner immediately advised Elisabeth to withdraw her custom: 'Child, a bank manager who finds the time to compose operas, has not enough time to look after his bank!' The bank crashed, of course. Elisabeth lost her stocks and shares, but Wagner's inspiration had demonstrated its divine provenance.

Whenever Wagner is thwarted, his reaction is apt to be rash and somewhat irrational, no matter whether the sum involved is ten thousand francs or the price of a travel ticket, as in the early years of his married life with Minna. The first matrimonial crisis, in May 1837, was caused by Wagner's growing debts and his inability to furnish his wife with sufficient household money. Depressed by the prospects of a bleak future, Minna elopes with a Herr Dietrich. In *Mein Leben* Wagner describes his pursuit, starting at Königsberg but ending prematurely, and how he did not *take* but *carried* his travelling expenses with him:

> With death in my heart I stormed out of the house to investigate Minna's disappearance. . . . My purpose was to overtake the runaways, which seemed possible with the help of a considerable amount of money, the

lack of which had to be laboriously remedied, at least in part. On old Möller's* advice I packed the silver which we had received as wedding presents, for possible use on the journey, and after a delay of several terrible hours I started on my journey by fast mail coach, together with my distressed old friend Möller. It was our aim to catch up with the earlier mail coach. . . . This proved impossible, and when we reached Elbing early next morning, we found there was no more money left, thanks to our extravagance in travelling by fast coach. So we were forced to turn back, but not before selling a sugar bowl and a cake basket, a transaction made necessary by the need for purchasing tickets for the return journey by slow coach. I still remember this journey back to Königsberg as one of the saddest events of my early days. (ML I 148–9)

With less impetuosity he might have realised that without old Möller for company he could have afforded an extra fast coach and returned with Minna, sugar bowl and cake basket. But the impetuosity sprang from his love – at that time – for his wife.

The couple are soon to be reunited, but the unpleasant experience makes him work even harder at perfecting his techniques of securing funds. He determines that it is more economical to make people come to him, rather than travelling to them. In June 1849 Wagner is in Paris, Minna in Dresden:

Minna, I beg you, by all that is dear to you, say yes and come. You shall be comfortable, that I promise you. . . . Scrape together whatever you can, or borrow money for which I shall soon reimburse you. . . . I have made quite a few preparations and I also expect money from Frankfurt, as well as from Switzerland. In short, I am utterly confident, but only if my dear Minna is with me again. Yes, then all will be well, all will be well! (WSB III 80: 8.6.1849)

Just as he needs Minna for his domestic contentment, so he is anxious to have his friends around him on such occasions as his own readings of the recently completed texts of his operas. He invites Peter Cornelius:

Peter, listen! On the evening of Wednesday, the fifth of February, I shall be reading *Die Meistersinger* at Schott's in Mainz. You can have no idea what this is to me and what it will be to my friends. You must be there that night! Ask Standhartner immediately for the money, in my

* Abraham Möller, merchant and avid theatre-goer, befriended Wagner in Königsberg and helped him and Minna escape across the Russian border in 1839.

name. . . . It will be a sacred evening, believe me; it will make you forget the world. (RWF 294–5: *late January 1862*)

It was not a trifling affair to travel, in the nineteenth century, from Vienna to Mainz, but countless guests would hasten from Tokyo, San Francisco and Melbourne, were they to receive such an invitation today.

One of Wagner's chief ambitions in the sphere of finance was to obtain regular subventions, such as a monthly pension which would permit him to switch some of his powers of invention from the monetary to the artistic plane. Subsidies of that kind are unlikely to be offered by any one person, but they might be obtained from a number of like-minded individuals. He writes to his Dresden friend, Ferdinand Heine:*

> Unfortunately, I have learned no trade which would enable me to earn my daily bread. As things stand, my livelihood must be provided for me, if I am to remain an artist. . . . You could make a start by asking one or two sympathetic people to form some kind of committee. . . . You should then disclose your intentions to a much larger number of men and women who have your confidence and who share our objectives, without involving my own person in any way, and invite them to join with you. You might consider a discreet circular to that end. (WSB III 150–1: *19.11.1849*)

In Bordeaux, Wagner gets to know the wine merchant Eugène Laussot and his wife Jessie. Jessie's mother, Mrs Taylor, has formed a small family council, with the object of remitting a regular quarterly subsidy to – Minna Wagner. She approaches her thus:

> I hope you will forgive me for addressing these lines to you, but since the matter I wish to raise concerns only you and me, I thought it best to discuss it with you directly. My daughter, Madame Laussot, has already written to you about the warm sympathy which we feel for you, and that it is our sincere desire to contribute to your livelihood, until your husband will be successful enough not to be forced to sacrifice his art by using it for earning a living. . . . I do not pretend to understand your husband's works sufficiently well, but I am so infected by my daughter's

---

* Ferdinand Heine (1798–1872) was a producer, costume designer and actor at the Dresden Court Theatre.

enthusiasm that it is my dearest wish to see his genius freed from his fetters, so that he need no longer encounter financial problems. I was therefore extremely happy when you accepted my offer of an annual grant of 2,500 francs for two years, beginning on August the first, payable in quarterly instalments. . . . I should be most relieved if the worthy companion of a man whose talent I admire were to honour me with the gratifying name to which I aspire – that of your friend. (SB 393: 8.5.1850)

Frau Julie Ritter, who had helped Wagner by listening to the outpourings of his wounded heart after the Jessie Laussot affair, now helps again. She grants Wagner an annual pension which she discontinues only after eight years. In April 1856, Wagner introduces Otto and Mathilde Wesendonck to the first act of *Die Walküre*. With a soprano friend as Sieglinde, he himself sings Siegmund and Hunding. Two days later Otto writes to him:

It is my heartfelt desire to see you conclude your great work, unaffected by worries about your material existence. . . . You have told me that in order to find the necessary peace for completing the *Nibelungen*, you need – in addition to the Ritter annuity of 3,000 fr. – an identical sum from another source, without having to rely on fees for performances of your operas. I will undertake this. . . . Forgive my moralising; it is a bad habit, though well-intentioned, and since I am preaching wise self-denial to you, I shall practise it myself. . . . Now let us see who will keep his word best. (FZ II 38: 28.4.1856)

Two annuities are to prove little more helpful than one. Wagner analyses his situation, which he has long learned to regard as the inevitable outcome of his own nature, in a letter to Franz Liszt:

Anybody who knows what my works are really about, sensing and respecting what is different and special in them, will understand that I, of all people, ought to be entirely relieved from having to peddle my works to such institutions as our theatres. . . . The only way to achieve this is through a lavish and regular pension granted by several German princes in partnership. (BWL II 230–1: 2.1.1859)

This desirable state of affairs is to materialise, some five years after this letter, and it takes just one German prince, the newly crowned King Ludwig II of Bavaria, to make reality of what must have seemed, to everybody except Wagner himself, a wild dream.

If one looks at things through Wagner's eyes, his demands seem reasonable. If one understands his works as manifestations of the search for the hidden interrelations of human striving and the divine spirit, then one should excuse him from turning such works into merchandise. On the other hand, these works constitute, in his lifetime, an appreciable section of the repertoire of Europe's opera houses. Should Wagner not be expected to take an interest in securing an income from their performances and, like most of his fellow composers, try to live on it? One's point of view here will determine one's judgement of Wagner's works and nature.

From the very beginning, Wagner has been aware of his worth. We have already seen him as a teenager bartering his piano arrangement of Beethoven's Ninth Symphony for several other Beethoven scores. It is this self-assurance which enables him, early in his career, to reject disadvantageous offers for his works. Breitkopf & Härtel have accepted *Der fliegende Holländer*, but Wagner dislikes the proposed fee. He tells his friend Ferdinand Heine:

> The publication of the *Holländer* has been put off for the present. I have asked for 1,000 thaler and that is too much for them. I have written that I shall wait until it is no longer too much for them. (WSB II 313: 2.8.1843)

Breitkopf & Härtel lose the opera, and Wagner has it printed privately, losing money instead of making it. His relations with the publishers continue on a friendly basis, however, so much so that they offer him one of their concert grand pianos, to be paid for by instalments. The inevitable happens, Wagner falls into arrears, and eventually – eight years later – he proposes a straight exchange, his *Lohengrin* for their concert grand:

> It would be handsome of you and worthy of your cultural standing, as well as of your upright character, if you were to venture on an undertaking which at present would require sacrifices on your part, while a future successful outcome must be questionable, or might only gradually be realisable. . . . At the same time you would be acting in a neighbourly and humane manner, if you acceded to my request and provided me with the longed-for opportunity of paying a regrettably long overdue debt to you. . . . The cancellation of that debt I would regard as my sole fee for the publication of the full score and the already completed piano arrangement of my *Lohengrin*. (WSB III 539: 8.4.1851)

What happens next is a rarity in Wagner's life: his conscience is beginning to trouble him. Breitkopf & Härtel accept his offer, but Wagner sees little hope of the publishers recouping their outlay for engraving the score, since with the exception of Weimar, no theatre shows any interest in the opera. He writes to Liszt:

> Härtels have written today to say they accept my proposal, and they are going to *engrave the full score as well.* How has that come about? Now that they have granted my request, it seems almost incredible to me: *the score of an opera which only Weimar performs!!* What is your opinion? Can I really expect this of them? In my view, they are so magnanimous that I feel quite ashamed! I am almost tempted to decline Härtel's offer for *Lohengrin*, provided they would engrave the full score of *Der junge Siegfried* instead. This child of mine, engendered but not yet brought forth, is of course closer to my heart than *Lohengrin*. (BWL I 136–7: 29.6.1851)

Breitkopf & Härtel say yes to *Lohengrin*, but no to *Der junge Siegfried*, which will only be completed twenty years later, entitled *Siegfried*.

In eight years' time Wagner is to offer the first half of the *Ring*, namely *Das Rheingold* and *Die Walküre*, to Otto Wesendonck:

> Can we do business together? . . . In return for my assigning to you the permanent copyright, I would require 300 louisdor or, preferably 6,000 francs for each score. (OW 54–7: 28.8.1859)

Otto accepts. This does not stop Wagner from selling the scores for a second time to the publishing house of Schott, and from making a present of the *Rheingold* manuscript to King Ludwig. The score is, strictly speaking, not his to give, belonging as it does to its original purchaser, Otto Wesendonck. Mathilde's husband, however, remains a generous friend and parts with his property, an act of generosity which touches the King:

> My dear Herr von Wesendonck,
> I am moved to express my warmest gratitude to you for so kindly handing over Wagner's manuscript score of *Das Rheingold*. Rest assured that I would never have made any claim on the manuscript, since the idea of presenting the precious score of that wonderful work was Wagner's own. I am aware of your kindness in offering hospitality to the artist at a time when he was struggling against adversity and incredible ill fortune, and I wish to express my heartfelt gratitude to you, my dear sir. It is thanks to

*'This child of mine': young Siegfried Wagner as Young Siegfried
in Wagner's* Siegfried

your generous support that the world possesses Wagner's immortal
works which he created in Switzerland, and it is incumbent upon me to
convey these my feelings to you. (OW 121: 28.8.1865)

Meanwhile, Wagner has been working at his *Meistersinger* score. Schott* wants to publish the opera and has made the customary advance payments. But not enough:

> You are wrong, my dear Herr Schott! You are quite wrong in your manner of handling a man like me. Much may be extorted by the threat of hunger, but not lofty works of art. Or do you believe that after a night made sleepless by worries, I should find the necessary serenity of mind and good ideas for my work by day? . . . Since the end of August – nearly two months now – you have practically left me in the position of a drowning man. . . . You complain about your lack of peace and quiet, but I am wondering whether or not you contribute to your own peace by robbing me of mine. . . . For the sake of the eternal laws of justice I could not spare you this end result of a sleepless night. (LS 132: 20.10.1862)

Schott replies by return of post:

> I prefer to pass over in silence what you call the end result of one of your sleepless nights, for knowing full well how to conduct myself towards artists, I should not like to tell you what I expect from them. . . . I cannot possibly supply you with the considerable amount you ask for. Indeed, a mere music publisher will never be able to meet your needs. Only someone like an enormously rich banker or a prince who has millions at his disposal could do that. If such a person cannot be found, one should consider an appeal to the German nation. (LS 132–3: 21.10.1862)

It takes Wagner another five years to complete *Die Meistersinger von Nürnberg*, which Schott is to publish and whose first performance takes place in Munich, in June 1868, with Wagner sharing King Ludwig's royal box.

The next decade sees the Master, as he likes to be called, in his newly built Haus Wahnfried in Bayreuth. At last he is in a position to dictate his terms without fear of a rebuff. He writes to Franz Schott:

* Franz Schott (1803–75) was the director of one of the world's leading music publishers, based in Mainz. He published the *Ring*, *Meistersinger*, *Parsifal* and the *Wesendonck Lieder*, and it was to him that the young Wagner had offered his piano arrangement of Beethoven's Ninth Symphony. Schott's wife, Betty, was also to become one of Wagner's most generous patrons.

Haus Wahnfried

I need ten thousand gulden for putting the finishing touches to house and garden. If you will advance me this sum immediately for forthcoming compositions, I would undertake the delivery of six larger orchestral works, each comparable in extent and substance to a grand overture. . . . Should my proposition, my wish be somewhat unusual, remember it is *Franz Schott* who is appealed to, and he who appeals is none other than *Richard Wagner*. (LS 245: 1.10.1873)

What are those orchestral works? Cosima tells us. Her diary names the planned pieces:

Dirge: Romeo and Juliet	*Lohengrin's Sea Voyage*
Epilogue to Romeo and Juliet	*Tristan the Hero*
Brünnhilde	
Wieland the Smith (CWT I 785, 792: 24.1 *and* 14.2.1874)	

Schott pays the requested ten thousand gulden. It is a pity that the six works were never written.

In the opening year of the Bayreuth Festspiele, 1876, Wagner receives a commission from the United States, on which Cosima comments in her diary:

R. always at work, complains he is unable to visualise anything for this composition. It had been different with the *Kaisermarsch*, or even with the *Rule Britannia Overture*, where he had imagined a great ship, but here he can think of nothing but the 5,000 dollars he had demanded and might not even get. (CWT I 970: 14.2.1876)

But he does get his 5,000 dollars for the *Grand Festival March for the Hundred Years Jubilee of American Independence.*

At last, after nearly fifty years of striving, Wagner's money worries are almost over. Now he is able to negotiate from a position of great strength. They want to perform the *Ring* in Prague and ask for Wagner's permission. He replies:

> I can only assign performance rights for the four parts of the cycle *Der Ring des Nibelungen*, if I can be assured that the theatre in question will make special efforts in connection with the staging of the tetralogy. . . .
> 1. The four parts will be performed in sequence. . . .
> 2. This procedure is to be guaranteed by an immediate advance payment of 5,000 marks.
> 3. Ten per cent of all gross takings are payable from the day of the first performance of each work until thirty years after the author's death. . . .
> 4. All scores etc. to be obtained from the publishers, J. B. Schott's Sons in Mainz. (KM 181–2: 10.9.1878)

None of the women in Wagner's life were able to offer him lasting contentment, not even Cosima. None of his wealthy patrons could ever supply all his needs, not even a King. Why? Perhaps his early childhood provides a clue:

> The worries and irritations caused by a large family (I was the seventh surviving member), the problem of providing the necessities of life, and my mother's anxiety to keep up appearances in spite of our very limited means, prevented her from showing us much tenderness or motherly comfort. I can hardly remember ever being caressed by her.
> (ML I 17–18)

In a letter to Minna, Wagner reflects:

> The time will come when the world will survey a life like mine and will be ashamed when it realises how thoughtlessly I was exposed to perpetual unrest and insecurity, and what a *miracle* it is that my works were created under such conditions. (SB 537: 14.2.1862)

V

THE PURE
FOOL?

Strange and numerous are the foolish thoughts and actions that punctuate Wagner's life. He was well aware of them, and yet he could not live without them.

> The world has my works,
> let the world put up with my follies.
> (WR 15, letter to Standhartner: 12.4.1864)

Mindless pronouncements and oafish behaviour relaxed his restless mind. They were his Tarnhelm which hid his real self from the world and, at times, even from himself. Many were the occasions when the ecstasy of his creative endeavour had to be eased by the palliative of sheer nonsense.

From Paris, Wagner writes to Mathilde Wesendonck:

> I do not expect people to understand me. Let us hope they will understand my works. I tell you, the feeling of my own integrity provides my strength. I feel pure. (RWW 239: 22.7.1860)

'Today I can write this way about Wagner, tomorrow that way,' says Thomas Mann. Understandably, for Wagner revelled in contradictions and contrariness. He spoke, he wrote, this way today, that way tomorrow. Such behaviour creates consternation, pain and anger, even in the perpetrator. He says so himself, in his letter to Otto Wesendonck:

> You dear, good fellow! Believe me, I fully appreciate your extraordinary, sympathetic response. But I am practically certain that I am beyond help. My life is an ocean of contradictions, from which I can only hope to emerge when I die. (OW 37: 10.9.1856)

Contradictions, frequently in the shape of personal proclamations, have been preserved in Cosima's diaries:

> Shakespeare is the truest image of the world. (CWT I 849: 3.9.1874)

Five years later:

> A brute such as Shakespeare. (CWT II 442: 13.11.1879)

The word 'brute' was later obliterated, probably by their daughter, Eva, and changed to 'poet'.

> There are people who stand above fate: they *make* fate. Such a rare genius was Frederick the Great. (CWT I 347: 26.1.1871)

173

Richard says he has come to detest Frederick the Great. (CWT II 377: 6.7.1879)

Again, this entry was later inked over and made illegible.

Goethe showed his great genius in the way he observed life. (CWT I 246: 16.6.1870)

He [Goethe] played about with his genius like a blockhead. (CWT II 362: 7.6.1879)

The unknown hand (Eva?) has once more inked over the last sentence, possibly to assure posterity that the great man was incapable of errors of judgement. On the French, Wagner pronounced:

At the outbreak of hostilities between Germany and France, I would take refuge in the capital of the enemy. Believe me, I fear I shall lose all my patriotism, and secretly I might rejoice if the Germans received a proper beating. (RWW 132: 30.4.1859)

Richard says there is nobody as stupid as the French. He has come to loathe them more and more. (CWT II 896: 23.2.1882)

In *Lohengrin*, we hear:

> *Defend our soil with fist of mail,*
> *Thus shall our German might prevail!*
> (Act 3, Scene 3)

Yet, to Franz Liszt he says:

It is with horror that I contemplate Germany and my plans for the future there. May God forgive me, but all I can see in Germany is small-mindedness, boorish behaviour, pretence and arrogance. . . . Believe me, Franz, we have no fatherland! If I am a German, it is because Germany lives within me. (BWL II 280: 13.9.1860)

How does he rate his fellow composers? Occasionally he alters his opinion:

Mendelssohn, the gnat. (CWT I 123: 6.7.1869)

[Mendelssohn] that fine musician. (CWT II 275: 27.12.1878)

But generally not. He once said, 'I believe in God, Mozart and Beethoven.' About God it was conceivable that he might change his mind, but never about the other two. Otherwise, he admired Bach and valued Handel and Haydn. His pronouncements on 'lesser' composers are usually acid.

Brahms
R. plays four-handed with Rubinstein on the piano, a symphony by Brahms. Once again, it makes us feel sick. (CWT II 303: *3.2.1879*)

Chopin
Herr Rubinstein plays Chopin for us. R. expresses his dislike of the modern, richly decorated music for the piano. (CWT I 864: *31.10.1874*)

Saint-Saëns
Such a wretched musician. (CWT II 955: *5.6.1882*)

Schumann
In the evening to the theatre. Schumann's *Genoveva*. The crude vulgarity of the work horrifies us. (CWT I 909: *10.4.1875*)

Messrs Lock, Stock and Barrel: I
Mendelssohn had a few ideas, then came Schumann, a brooding fool, and now Brahms who is nobody at all! (CWT II 753: *27.6.1881*)

Messrs Lock, Stock and Barrel: II
Mendelssohn, Schubert, Schumann – second, third and fourth raters.
(CWT I 286: *18.9.1870*)

Messrs Lock, Stock and Barrel: III
Faust, *Le Prophète*, *Les Huguenots*, Bellini, Donizetti, Rossini, Verdi, one after another, I feel physically sick. I seek refuge in Goethe (Paralipomena to *Faust*). R., too, has enough and begs Richter to desist.
(CWT I 356: *12.2.1871*)

With regard to his fellow human beings in general, Wagner is also, on the whole, more contra than pro. On principle he is contra everybody who is not unreservedly pro Wagner. He challenges whatever and whoever crosses his path and inevitably, odd creatures stray into his line of fire, totally unaware of the danger they are in. He opens fire nonetheless, to the detriment of his own blood pressure:

In the evening, a singer, Fräulein Wülfinghoff, calls on us. This drives Richard to distraction. He thinks it is dreadful that one has to put up with such people. (CWT II 767: *21.7.1881*)

He resents unwelcome visitors. He also resents the mountains:

We decide to make our way to Abetone. But on the journey Richard gets so angry with the green mountains, and also with the bare mountains that, playfully grumbling, he decides to turn back. (CWT II 581: 11.8.1880)

Insects:

During lunch he becomes very irritated, and takes offence at the flies. (CWT II 583: 18.8.1880)

Female summer guests:

Richard gives us a delightful account of the ladies drinking the waters. Fat, morose, malicious, and roses sprouting from their hats. He recalls the Spartans who killed off the superfluous. (CWT I 1054: 11.6.1877)

Military uniforms:

The Austrian Emperor's uniform annoys him. Its sleeves are too short, and when the Emperor toasts the Italian royal couple, his bare arm can be seen. (CWT II 826: 15.11.1881)

He would not have tolerated such sartorial shortcomings on his own opera stage. He also resents military service:

Richard is indignant that our good apprentice gardener will be called away from his work, to do his three years army service. He is bound to lose his diligence, and his pride in his labour. Richard also disapproves of the weather. (CWT II 769: 26.7.1881)

And military music:

Richard returns from his walk, infuriated by the marching music he had just heard. 'And my son shall one day march to that?' (CWT II 693: 16.2.1881)

Patriotism, Wagner recognises, is a virtue to be valued more highly on the stage than in everyday life: a father must be allowed to show concern for his young. It would take an exceptional monarch to sympathise with this sentiment. Luckily, Ludwig was one. He writes to Wagner:

I have no doubt you will succeed with your efforts to obtain the very desirable exemption from military service for your little Siegfried. (KL III 226–7: 11.10.1881)

The year before, Cosima had noted:

Next summer he wants to travel to Gräfenberg and then to America, and possibly for good, if only to get Fidi [Siegfried] out of that dreadful playing at soldiers. (CWT II 579: 27.7.1880)

And again:

He is considering how best to free Fidi from military service. Perhaps through naturalisation elsewhere? (CWT II 594: (6.9.1880)

Wagner with Siegfried (Fidi)

A year later he expresses himself quite plainly, causing distress to all those who regard Wagner as a national hero:

He talks about the army and how much he hopes for Siegfried's exemption from service. When a visitor remarks that soldiers will die for glory, he exclaims, 'Yes, because they fear the sergeant major more than the bullet. Bullets at least can be merciful.' (CWT II 845: 10.12.1881)

> *Defend our soil with fist of mail,*
> *Thus shall our German might prevail!*

But that was some time ago. It is a long way from *Lohengrin* to the *Meistersinger*. Here, Hans Sachs proclaims the sanctity of ART, and affirms its precedence over the sanctity of the NATION:

> *Though should depart*
> *The might of Holy Rome,*
> *Still thrives at home*
> *Our holy German art!*
> (*Meistersinger*, Act 3, Scene 5)

Less folly here than integrity.

Quite terrifying, however one looks at it, is Wagner's attitude towards the Jews. True, antisemitism was commonplace in the nineteenth century. True, Wagner surrounded himself with Jewish admirers, Jewish financiers and Jewish associates. Heinrich Porges was one of his chief assistants at the Bayreuth Festivals in 1876 and 1882.* Hermann Levi conducted the first performances of *Parsifal*. Opera director Angelo Neumann toured extensively with Wagner's operas, spreading their fame in Germany and abroad.† The virtuoso Joseph Rubinstein was Wagner's semi-permanent house guest, combining the functions of official pianist and official listener. Karl Tausig, who made a piano arrangement of *Die Meistersinger*, was one of his few intimate friends.‡ All these were Jews, though Felix Mottl (1856–1911), the first Bayreuth *Tristan*

---

* Heinrich Porges (1837–1900), a Prague choral conductor and writer on music, became Wagner's musical assistant at the Bayreuth Festivals of 1876 and 1882. Later he was chorus master at Bayreuth.
† Angelo Neumann (1838–1910) gave up a career as an opera singer in Vienna to become opera director in Leipzig. His *Personal Recollections of Wagner* were published in 1907.
‡ Karl Tausig (1841–71), a very fine pianist, Liszt's best pupil, stayed with Wagner in Zurich. He instituted an association of patrons for the Bayreuth Festival. His early death was the result of typhoid fever.

conductor, was not: Fischer-Dieskau, in his book *Wagner and Nietzsche*, does him an injury when he circumcises him posthumously.

Porges, Rubinstein, Neumann, Levi, Tausig – they all had to endure his constant reproaches concerning their Jewishness, yet they all continued to love him with self-effacing devotion.

Occasionally, Wagner is capable of a kind of magnanimity:

> Visit by Kapellmeister Levi, who moves Richard to pity, because he regards himself as an anachronism, being a Jew. Richard assures him that the Catholics may think themselves more aristocratic than the Protestants, but that the Jews were, after all, the oldest, the most aristocratic race. (CWT II 129: 2.7.1878)

Could the sad dog's eyes of the Kapellmeister have coaxed those words from Wagner's lips? But he was also capable of this:

> Richard deplores the stupidity of the public who reserve their enthusiasm for *Die Walküre*, whereas Herr Neumann was putting *all* his works before the public. 'How strange', Richard says, 'that it has to be a Jew.' (CWT II 1026: 17.10.1882)

And, when the mood takes him, he can be brutally irrational:

> Richard tells me that, while he was drinking his beer at Angermann's, a Jewish piano teacher had tripped over Russ. Richard apologised to the man on the dog's behalf, but Karpeles replied, 'Oh, your dogs are sacred to me. I know Fips and Peps, too.' We marvel at the ways of the Jews who, like the Jesuits, can sniff out anything. (CWT I 856: 4.10.1874)

Could it be that Wagner's abusive behaviour towards Jews is just another manifestation of the irrational side of his nature? Cosima notes:

> Playfully grumbling, he says all Jews ought to burn to death at a performance of *Nathan the Wise*. (CWT II 852: 18.12.1881)

Again he grumbles playfully when he loses a manuscript in the post. He writes to Karl Klindworth:*

> This could only have happened to me. I am positive the Jews caused my manuscript to be stolen. (RWF 511: 4.2.1870)

On another occasion:

* Karl Klindworth (1830–1916), a pupil of Liszt, lived in London from 1854 to 1868. He made piano arrangements of several Wagner operas. His adopted daughter, Winifred Williams, later married Siegfried Wagner.

I had a letter from Präger* today, in which he tells me that three medallions which I had sent him to London, had arrived in pieces. This is really too bad. They were my last ones. . . . A Jewish fanatic must be responsible for this. (RWF 176: 4.10.1855)

But the Jews are not always to blame. He writes to Frau Ritter:

Give my best regards to Julie and tell her that *Siegfried* is progressing well. Alas, a blot of ink has found its way on to the beautiful portfolio – probably Mime's fault. (RWF 208–9: 6.5.1857)

Is it possible that Wagner's antisemitic spleen, which is predominantly theoretical, is just another means for achieving a mental and physical equilibrium? Where others spit, scratch, or blow their noses, Wagner curses the Jews, the French, the Germans, the mountains, the flies, and large ladies with roses on their hats. And then he feels better.

Occasionally, neither the Jews nor any one else are to blame for the strokes of misfortune, but that little nocturnal creature, the *Fledermaus*, the bat. In the following episode it is not Richard's but Cosima's irrational response which is provoked, but it demonstrates how, from time to time, the Wagner household was ready to follow his lead into the realms of the absurd.

In her diary, Cosima broods:

A Fledermaus terrifies me. (CWT I 436: 8.9.1871)

Next day:

The Fledermaus was a bad omen. Richard is unwell and melancholic.
(CWT I 436: 9.9.1871)

Again, on the same day:

An impertinent letter from Müller-Meser, the Dresden publisher. This is another gift of the Fledermaus. (CWT I 437: 9.9.1871)

And the following day:

Still the Fledermaus. Loulou [Cosima's daughter, Daniela] is suddenly taken ill. Violent fever and a headache. . . . And then Richard – I find him suffering from a pain in his foot. (CWT I 437: 10.9.1871)

---

* Ferdinand Praeger or Präger (1815–91), pianist and writer who had made London his home. He admired Wagner but his claim of close friendship with him devalues his book *Wagner as I Knew Him*, which contains much wishful thinking.

It must have been a Jewish Fledermaus!

It was left to Siegfried, Wagner's son, to make amends for this, the most considerable of his father's follies. When in charge of the Bayreuth Festival, he was asked to bar Jewish patrons and artists from Bayreuth. He replied, in 1921:

Dear Herr Püringer,
In reply to your letter which I read on my return here, I must tell you that I cannot share your views at all. We have a great number of loyal, honest and unselfish Jewish friends. They have frequently given us proof of their devotion. You demand that we should turn all these people from our doors for no other reason than that they are Jews? Is that human? Is that Christian? Is that German? Oh no! If we were really to consider such action, we Germans would first of all have to turn into quite different people. Our consciences would have to be as clear as a mountain stream. But that is not our way at all. The lives of all great Germans show that the German people treated them meanly, apathetically, with malice and with stupidity. The Festivals from 1876 to 1889 bear me out. My father, who had been ill at that time, was forced to travel to England, in order to make up for the Festival deficit, by conducting concerts. Even so, it was impossible to scrape together the paltry sum of 150,000 Marks. Thank God for the English, the French, the Americans and other friends, who later undertook the pilgrimage to Bayreuth, for they helped us over our financial crisis. And what did the Germans do? They complained that the foreigners were receiving preferential treatment in Bayreuth. . . .

If the Jews are willing to support us, they deserve our particular appreciation, for my father attacked and offended them in his writings. They are entitled to hate Bayreuth, and yet, many of them revere my father's works with genuine enthusiasm, in spite of his attacks on them. . . .

If among a hundred thousand Jews there should be no more than a single one who loved my father's works with his whole heart and his whole soul, I would feel ashamed to turn my back on him, just because he is a Jew. It is a matter of complete indifference to us whether a human being is a Chinese, a Negro, an American, a Red Indian or a Jew. But we could well take a lesson from the Jews in solidarity and in helping one another. . . . I hope you will understand me. Bayreuth must be a true abode of peace. (Richard-Wagner-Gedenstätte, Bayreuth)

*   *   *

Some of Wagner's lesser follies are so incredible that they take one's breath away. Cosima notes in her diary:

> Richard tells me of a dog who was sold to an English master. In Dover, the dog escaped and swam and then trotted back to his first owner in Aschaffenburg. (CWT II 551: 23.6.1880)

Swam? Across the Channel? And then trotted 550 miles to Aschaffenburg? If Wagner could really believe this, then he could believe anything. Does the extent of his credulity make his less savoury thoughts any less disturbing? His daughter Eva thought not. The following few lines were inked over, in an attempt to make them illegible:

> Richard notices that Fidi frequently keeps his mouth open, so he tells him that Beethoven would have composed much more, if he had kept his mouth closed. (CWT II 597: 9.9.1880)

One can sympathise, if not with the deed, then at least with the motive. Daughter Eva* was used to her father making a fool of himself in front of his family. But not in front of the twentieth century!

The next example of Wagner 'playing the clown' is positively attractive. He gives his servant girl written instructions to search for one of his manuscripts. One wonders whether she managed to find it:

> Dear Anna,
> Ask Herr Mathieu to open the big desk in my downstairs study. Then unlock the upper right hand drawer with the enclosed key. In that drawer, or possibly in the middle one, you will find another, smaller key. Take it out and ask Herr Mathieu again to open the bookcase for you. Now take the key which you have just found in the right hand or middle drawer, and with it you open the top left hand drawer. In this drawer there is a music manuscript portfolio, that is sheets of music paper with written music. This portfolio consists of a music note book with a cover of dark blue maroquin. On the spine of this cover is the title, *Das Rheingold*. Now, it is possible that this portfolio is not in the left hand drawer after all. In that case, it must be in the right hand one. You will have to open that drawer with a key which you will find in the left hand drawer. You must open both doors and pull out the left hand drawer. If the portfolio is not there either, then the * * * must have taken it.

* It is not, in fact, certain that Eva is the culprit, but she remains the chief suspect.

Now see if you can find it. (SB 723: *undated, probably early 1866*)

This is a unique performance. His friends' health and ill health, however, are topics which recur again and again, providing many examples of his eccentricities and obsessions. One of his chief correspondents, Theodor Uhlig, feels unwell. Wagner, recently converted to hydrotherapy, counsels his friend:

> When our health is unnaturally impaired, then only a radical water cure can bring relief, and that's for sure. (WSB III 458: 22.10.1850)

Yes, perhaps. But can water perform miracles? Friedrich Brockhaus, his brother-in-law, had an accident and lost the sight of one eye. Wagner advises Friedrich's daughter:

> I have heard of your father's mishap. To repay him for his former kind actions and good wishes I now advise him . . . to take himself to a hydropathic clinic and undertake a strict water cure, under intelligent guidance. Above all, let him spare no expense of time or patience, and I prophesy he will gradually recover completely. What is more, he will very probably regain his lost eye. (WSB IV 145–6: 23.10.1851)

A miracle indeed! Maybe Wotan himself could have regained his lost eye, 'under intelligent guidance' from the Rhinemaidens? Does not Flosshilde sing in praise of the sun's power:

> *It kisses the eye to open.*
> (*Rheingold*, Scene 1)

Wagner writes his first detailed, enthusiastic water letter to Uhlig:

> This is my daily programme: early in the morning a cold pack, from 5.30 to 7, followed by a cold bath and a walk. At 8 I have breakfast which consists of dry bread, with milk or water. This is followed by a first and a second enema. Then another walk, then a cold compress on the abdomen. At about midday I get a cold massage, short walk and another compress. Then lunch in my room. . . . One hour's lazing, then a long two-hours walk, alone. Approximately 5 o'clock another wet massage and a short walk. At 6 a hip-bath of fifteen minutes, followed by a short walk, to get warm. Then another compress. Dinner at 7 consists of dry bread and water. Then two more enemas, and then I play Whist till 9. After that I get another compress, and then bedtime at 10. I have grown quite accustomed to the regime and I am considering taking less food and more baths. . . . On my return to Zurich I shall continue the

Thus he resumes the way of life to which he had been accustomed, although he could have saved himself much time, trouble and expense.

How can we make sense of Wagner's nonsense, of his foibles and inconsistencies? He was aware of them, and attributed them to his delight in the nonsensical:

> O, this is my salvation, this ability to transform sense into nonsense. This way I escape the danger of plunging into an abyss. For instance, today I almost wrote into the composition sketch [of *Parsifal*], 'Here comes Dame Kundry.' (CWT II 155: 6.8.1878)

So hectic was the process of artistic creation that frequent periods of mental indiscipline became a necessary part of it. So Kundry, the rose from hell, becomes Dame Kundry, and of his work on *Siegfrieds Tod* he can joke, 'Today I have killed him off.' The knife that cuts into 'the nerves of his brain' is always nearby when he works. His ravings, his irrationality, his follies are often no more than an escape from the knife, a retreat from the abyss. Acting the madman – like Hamlet – is his way of not becoming one. How well Cosima knew this:

> What he says is often quite different from what he means. He merely airs his vexation. (CWT II 867: 5.1.1882)

To his step-sister Cäcilie he confided:

> I simply have a hard, hard time of it. Let all those who cannot understand me consider this. (FW 253: 27.11.1863)

VI

WAGNER'S
COSIMA

Richard Wagner ~ Minna Planer
born 22nd May 1813   born 5th September 1809
died 13th February 1883   died 25th January 1866

Hans von Bülow ~ Cosima Liszt
born 8th January 1830   born 25th December 1837
died 12th February 1894   died 1st April 1930

Daniela   Blandine
born 12th October 1860   born 20th March 1863
died 28th July 1940   died 4th December 1941

Richard Wagner ~ Cosima (Bülow)

Isolde   Eva   Siegfried
born 10th April 1865   born 17th February 1867 born 6th June 1869
died 7th February 1919 died 26th May 1942   died 4th August 1930

Hans von Bülow ~ Marie Schanzer
                        born 12th February 1857
                        died 20th August 1941

Cosima survives her husband by forty-seven years. She dies in 1930, aged ninety-two. Some of the near-blind old lady's utterances were recorded by Eva and Daniela, her two surviving daughters:

> Superstition is the poetry of the people.

> Living for art is like living for God. No room for half measures.

> Germany is my fatherland and music my motherland.

> Every day one ought to read a poem by Goethe.

(CWZ 752, 754, 763, 765)

Here is the residue of the intellectual capacity which had attracted Wagner and which she had placed entirely at his disposal.

Her way to Wagner was convoluted. Her first marriage, to Hans von Bülow, seems to have been prompted by a characteristic desire 'to be of service'. At the time she felt that Bülow's personal happiness as well as his artistic progress depended upon their union. Bülow's letter in which he begs Franz Liszt for his daughter's hand is ominous:

> As the bearer of your name Cosima Liszt surpasses in my heart all other women. . . . Since she has permitted me to love her, I can be certain that my admiration for her is not based on wishful thinking. . . . I give you my word that, however much I feel attached to her in my love, I would never hesitate to make a sacrifice of myself, should her happiness require this, and to relinquish her, if she ever feels she has married the wrong man. (MB 67–8: 20.4.1856)

On their honeymoon, in 1857, Cosima and Bülow visit the revered composer of *Rienzi*, *Der fliegende Holländer*, *Tannhäuser* and *Lohengrin*. Wagner recalls:

> The two acts of *Siegfried*, which then existed only as composition sketches, were mastered by Hans to such an extent that he was able to play them as though he was reading an actual piano score. As usual, I sang all the parts. . . . Cosima listened with her head lowered and kept quiet. When spoken to, she began to cry. (ML II 567)

Why the tears, one wonders. For *Siegfried*? For *Siegfried*'s composer? For herself?

*   *   *

Cosima begins to turn away from her husband. The genius of Wagner is overwhelming, and she sees it as her mission to be of service to him. Her diaries contain a significant clue:

> He [Bülow] would never have lost me, if fate had not led me to the one man whom it became my purpose in life to live or die for.
>
> (CWT 1 28: 8.1.1869)

Cosima's desertion of her first husband will torment her throughout her long life. Only at the age of ninety will she be able to look with detached affection at her pre-Wagner period. Here she speaks openly to Daniela:

> You know about my engagement to your father. It was after the *Tannhäuser* Overture. He had conducted it magnificently. I had never heard this music before, and you can imagine how it *overwhelmed* me. They all went home to bed, but I could not go to sleep without having spoken to him. After quite some time he came home. He thanked me very warmly and said he was dreading the moment when I would leave the house. I said that was nothing to worry about – I would stay. So we became engaged. The stars then smiled on us. (CWZ 756: 1928)

So Cosima becomes engaged to Bülow, who had conducted Wagner's music so magnificently, and Bülow marries the young woman who bears the name of his beloved teacher, Liszt. The stars, however, do not smile down for long, for Cosima leaves Bülow and goes to live with Wagner, and now her conscience will haunt her days and her nights:

> At breakfast R. read me a letter which he had just received from Hans who is living there [in Munich] all alone, in the midst of the most abominable intrigues. It made my heart bleed. (CWT 1 83: 10.4.1869)

> My melancholic mood will not leave me – at night it makes me wake up with a start, and in the evenings I wonder how poor Hans might be. I was so little to him – yet, how hard it is to take even this little away from him! . . . My heart will probably never shed this burden, and I know of no other remedy than to bear it patiently and not let my children or my beloved husband feel how troubled my soul can be. (CWT 1 86: 16.4.1869)

> Good night, my glorious, good and great one whom I love, whom I serve; good night, my children; good night, Hans, whom I have made so unhappy. I dream of a world in which we shall all be united and love one another! (CWT 1 124: 8.7.1869)

Lenbach portrait of Cosima aged 42

> Yesterday, after I had written this, Hans [Cosima means Richard!]
> brought me a letter from the cook in Munich who reports that Hans
> has gone away in a very bad mood, without saying where. I am
> overwhelmed with terrible grief. . . . Children, my children, remem-
> ber your mother's words – there is no burden harder to bear than the
> wrong we do to others. (CWT I 145: 28.8.1869)

The sad spectre of betrayal and of the betrayed will not leave her in peace.
What sustains her is the conviction that Wagner needs her more than Bülow
ever did. She is the mother of Bülow's two children, but she is Wagner's angel of
peace, his elixir of life and midwife to *Parsifal*. Bülow's shadow, however,
continues to darken her nights:

> I dreamed of the death of Napoleon III, and it was Hans who called to
> me, 'Cosima, Cosima, I am going to die this night.' (CWT I 846:
> 22.8.1874)

Here Richard cannot help. In any case, it is better for his peace of mind if he
knows nothing of Cosima's grief.

> A letter from Hans, thanking me for mine. I say nothing to R., neither
> about Hans's letter nor about my reply, and I weep quietly to myself.
> (CWT I 927: 5.7.1875)

> It is 22 years now since I heard the *Tannhäuser* Overture for the first
> time, my very first experience of R.'s orchestral music. That evening
> sealed my fate, my engagement to Hans and all the happiness and
> sorrows which were our share! (CWT I 1078: 19.10.1877)

She writes to her daughter Daniela, who is not yet twenty-one years old:

> When you experience sorrow or hurt, my beloved darling, accept it as
> atonement for your mother's offence to life; this will give you strength
> and courage. (CWB 171: 16.3.1881)

When Wagner addresses his stepdaughter, his veiled grief over the fate of
Daniela's father can be felt:

> You are your mother's pride and my wonderful joy. My love for you
> has never been subject to any trials, and it is free from sorrow or
> apprehension. You tell me so prettily what I meant and what I mean to
> you. I only regret that I can mean nothing at all to your father. Well,
> everything here is fate! (CWB 345: *probably July 1881*)

A recently published document shows that even after Wagner's death Cosima had not forgotten her first husband: she believes the time is now ripe for establishing artistic relations with him. She makes her plans for future Bayreuth seasons, for she is now the guardian of the Festival. The following conductors are to be invited:

Hans von Bülow

1885	*Parsifal*	Hermann Levi
	Tristan und Isolde	Hans von Bülow
1886	*Parsifal*	Hermann Levi
	Tristan und Isolde	Hans von Bülow
	Der fliegende Holländer	Hans von Bülow
	Lohengrin	Hans von Bülow
1887	*Parsifal*	Hermann Levi
	Tristan und Isolde	Hans von Bülow
	Der fliegende Holländer	Hans von Bülow

1888	Parsifal	Hermann Levi
	Tristan und Isolde	Hans von Bülow
	Der fliegende Holländer	Hans von Bülow
	Tannhäuser	Hans von Bülow
	Lohengrin	Hans von Bülow
1889	Parsifal	Hermann Levi
	Der fliegende Hollander	Hans von Bülow
	Tannhäuser	Hans von Bülow
	Lohengrin	Hans von Bülow
	Die Meistersinger	Hans von Bülow
	Der Ring des Nibelungen	Hans Richter

(CWZ 35)

Cosima intends to let her former husband have the lion's share of the next five years' performances. But her plans do not materialise and Bülow conducts elsewhere.

Cosima's love for her second husband, however, is even stronger than the guilt she feels over her desertion of the first. On their wedding day, 25 August 1870, she presents Wagner with this poem. She calls it 'Litany':

LITANEI	LITANY
Unsündiger,	Sinless one,
Erhaben-Begehrender,	Sublimely striving,
Gross-Entsagender,	Resigning in greatness,
Besonnener, Beharrlicher,	Calm and determined,
Bedächtiger, Geduldiger,	Thoughtful and patient,
Unerschrocken, Sendungstreuer,	Undaunted, true to your task,
Heilig-Unbeständiger,	Hallowed, impermanent,
Weihvoll-Ungeduldiger,	Solemn, impatient,
Hehr-Unbesonnener,	Nobly impetuous,
Wahnflüchtiger!	Shunning delusion,
Schaffend Vernichtender,	Creative destroyer,
Vergeudend Ordnender,	Methodical prodigal,
Volks-Fürstlicher,	Prince among men,
Ruhm-Unbekümmerter,	Indifferent to glory,
Eitelkeits-Barer,	Bereft of vain pride,
Leicht-Sinniger,	Light of heart,
Vor-Sorgender	Foresighted one,

194

Argwohn-Unkundiger,	Free from suspicion,
Gütig-Gibicher,	Kindly provider,
Ganz sich Hingebender,	Wholly devoted,
Tief-Verschlossener,	Alone, aloof,
Begeisterungsgewaltiger,	Potent, impassioned,
Zündend Redender,	Inspiring orator,
Glutvoll Schweigender,	Fervent in silence,
Hoffnungslos Glaubender,	Unhopeful believer,
Unerbittlicher dem Übel,	Foe of all evil,
Eroberer dem Schwachen,	Friend of the helpless,
Wahrheit-Verkündender,	Proclaimer of truth,
Trug-Verscheuchender,	Banishing falsehood,
Kühn-Entlarvender,	Boldly unmasking,
Mild-Verhüllender,	Gently concealing,
Liebe Übender,	Ministering love,
Leben Ausströmender,	Exhaling life,
Welt-Fremder,	World-alien,
Natur-Trauter Heimischer,	Native in nature's home,
Seher des Seins,	Prophet of existence,
Herr des Scheins,	Conqueror of mirages,
Lenker des Wahnes,	Controlling delusion,
Freude des Willens,	Joy of the will,
Erlösung Vollbringender,	Bringing redemption,
Selig-Schaffender,	Creator of bliss,
Alltönender-Schauender-	All-sounding, all-seeing,
Könnender,	all-skilled,
Unbegreiflicher,	Incomprehensible,
Unschuldiger, Freier,	Stainless in freedom,
Kind und Gott.	Child and god.

(MEC I 841)

Not great poetry but a powerful love which combines mystic veneration with unquestioning surrender, a mixture on which Wagner thrives.

Cosima presents Wagner with three children, Isolde, Eva and Siegfried, all born before their parents' wedding, companions to Bülow's and Cosima's daughters, Daniela and Blandine. In her diaries she gives an account of what was possibly the most important event in her life with Wagner, knowing that her children would one day read what their mother had written, and hoping that it would help them to understand the irregular pattern of their dual paternity.

Wagner has composed the *Siegfried Idyll*, which he now presents to Cosima on her thirty-third birthday, on Christmas Day 1870. She notes:

> I can tell you nothing about this day, my children, nothing about my feelings, nothing about my mood, nothing, nothing. I shall merely inform you, plainly and simply, of what took place. A sound awoke me which grew ever stronger; I knew I was no longer dreaming, there was music, and what music! When it had died away, R. come into my room with the five children and gave me the score of his 'Symphonic Birthday Greeting', – I was in tears, so was everybody in the house. R. had placed his orchestra on the staircase, and thus our Tribschen is consecrated for all time! (CWT I 329: 25.12.1870)

So private are the themes which Wagner had woven into the fabric of the *Idyll*, so intimately connected with their courtship, that Cosima flinches from its publication. In August 1877 she writes to Schott's:

> I must confess that I have urged my husband not to divest this work of its personal character, and I now ask you most cordially, dear Herr Doctor, not to be angry with me and not to appeal to my husband again. (LS 289: 21.8.1877)

'Do not be angry', 'do not appeal' – the diaries provide a clue to Cosima's role as guardian of the *Siegfried Idyll*:

> After lunch the musicians played the *Idyll* for us, in an arrangement by Richter; great emotion. R. said it seemed strange to him that originally he had intended to use only one theme for my morning music, the one which had come to him in Starnberg (where we were living together) and which he had promised me to work into a quartet, but then he had unconsciously put our whole life into it, Fidi's [Siegfried's] birth, my restoration to health, Fidi's bird etc. As Schopenhauer observes, the musician depicts life in a language which reason cannot comprehend.
> (CWT I 350: 30.1.1871)

There are times when their love, and their close family life, produces odd examples of domestic behaviour. When Cosima describes how they all celebrate Wagner's sixtieth birthday, one does not doubt the sincerity of the emotions, but even allowing for the difference of the nineteenth century's customs on such occasions the ritual was somewhat bizarre:

> At midday the Three Cheers. I ask, 'Long live who, Daniela?' 'Our most

faithful guardian.' I rise, the glass in my hand, 'Long live who, Blandine?' 'Our dearest friend.' 'Long live who, Isolde?' 'Our kindest father.' 'Long live who, Fidi?' 'My papa.' Whereupon the military band intones the Prelude to the third act of *Lohengrin*. We are all reduced to tears. (CWT I 686: 22.5.1873)

Family festivities prompt Wagner to poetise. His verses for Cosima's thirty-sixth birthday hardly reveal the poet of *Tristan* or *Meistersinger*:

The Holy Family: Joukovsky's painting shows Siegfried as the Boy Christ; Daniela as Mary; Blandine, Eva and Isolde as Angels, and the artist himself as Joseph

Herr Siegfried kommt: nehmt euch in Acht!	*Here Master Siegfried comes, beware!*
Von keinem sei er ausgelacht!	*Be disrespectful if you dare.*
Denn er ist dick, wenn auch noch klein;	*Though little, he is stout and strong,*
und, wird er gross, dem Mütterlein	*His mother's champion before long.*
wird er ein Sohn und Helde sein,	*No greater hero far and wide,*
der ihr und allen Freude macht.	*Mama's and everybody's pride.*

(Richard-Wagner-Gedenkstätte, Bayreuth)

There can be little doubt of Cosima's indispensability for Wagner's life and work. When they are apart, as in the days of her intermittent reunions with her first husband, he frets:

> The time will come when you shall inspire my soul to bring forth its future works. But do give me the peace I need. Stay with me, do not leave me again. Tell poor Hans openly that I can no longer live without you. O heavens! if only you could be my wife in the eyes of the world! This constant coming and going, this returning and having to leave again and being at the disposal of others – it is terrible! . . . I will go to sleep! Good night! Come what may, *you are my wife!* (DB 46–7: 20.8.1865)

There are frequent soliloquies in his diary, *Das braune Buch* (The Brown Book). In an illuminating passage he calls his private life 'artificial', his contacts with the world 'not really in earnest', while he prefers his social intercourse to be 'rather light-hearted'. All this for the sake of his work and for Cosima's sake, for she is his reality, she prompts his work:

> I can only live reasonably by acknowledging reality and by coming to terms with it, i.e. by placing myself completely outside its sphere of influence. I can and must live only in some kind of cloud. Since I am wholly an artist, I can only lead an artificial life. That entails having as little to do with others as possible, no conversations with people at all, or only in jest, never seriously, for that always leads to trouble and triviality. If the King agrees to my proposals and if, as a result, my life becomes pleasantly secure and free from all worry, then I shall think of my creative work only, and never again of mere activity. I shall set up my kind of court. Hans must take over all 'activity', music school, performances, etc. My dealings with the world will be through him, and

rather light-hearted. I shall no longer attend to anything myself. Once a week I shall hold court, when I receive the reports of my general and his adjutants. I shall be pleased with any successful achievements and shall not grieve over failures, for I had no expectations of either. That is how things shall be. But I must work out a sensible diet with the doctor, to enable me to arrange my days to the greatest possible advantage for my work. That will have to be artfully contrived, and the ritual will be in the style of Versailles and Louis XIV, stiff and formal, chapter and verse. Ill health must never bother me again. Cosima must always be with me – ever present, there is no other way. But we shall never speak, and especially not in earnest. Then, I believe, I shall still be able to bring to life my serious artistic works. But seriousness will be reserved for my art, everything else must be light and cheerful. Cosima, though, will secretly be serious with me, that goes without saying, but she will not show it. Only Brünnhilde and all the others, whatever their names are, shall demonstrate the seriousness of it all. (DB 42: 18.8.1865)

If that is indeed so, if for Wagner Art is reality and Life is artificial, then much of his aberrant behaviour becomes more comprehensible.

So stark is the *reality* which he uncovers in his art that he occasionally approaches it with utmost reluctance. For where there is reality there must also be inadequacy, and the artist will have to face the unpleasant task of reconciling the concept of his perfect vision with the imperfect realisation of his creativity. He informs King Ludwig:

Nobody but myself can appreciate the extent of my labour. When I arrived at the Norns scene, at the beginning of *Götterdämmerung*, I actually contemplated it with horror, and for a long time I felt myself unable to tackle it. . . . And yet, it had to be, and from my own terror I wove the rope of the Norns. . . . And a few days ago I found it possible at last to overcome my dread of Brünnhilde's confrontation with her sister Waltraute, which had tormented me for a long time. But now I have begun that scene. (KL II 306–7: 5.5.1870)

When he is sick with longing for Cosima, he even loses interest in the performances of his works. The King commissions the architect Gottfried Semper to build him a Wagner Theatre in Munich, but Wagner moans:

I am unable and unwilling to see anyone, not even the dearest and brightest, when Cos is not here. Anything that happens in her absence is painful to me. How I hate this theatre project, indeed how childish the King seems to me when he insists so passionately on that idea. Semper is here now, and I am supposed to discuss things with him and to talk about this absurd project! I cannot imagine a greater torment than that facing me now. You see, that is how I am! (DB 83: 9.9.1865)

Daughter Eva, who received Wagner's diary from her mother Cosima in 1908, was so shocked by this entry that she tried to render it illegible. But neither her attempts at pasting over nor at crossing out were skilful enough to prevent the eventual deciphering of Wagner's and also of Cosima's diaries.

When Cosima is obliged to leave Tribschen once again, their grief at parting is great. Her telegram of 16 April 1867 is in verse:

> *It is decreed by God above*
> *That we must leave what most we love.*
>
> (KL II xxi)

On the same evening he notes in his diary:

> I do not think I have ever in my whole life been as sad as I am now!! How easily that is spoken, yet how unspeakable it is! I walked home and sank down exhausted. A brief sleep, heavy as lead, such as often drives out a cold, made me aware – as from the depth of my soul – of the utter misery of my life. I long for a severe illness and death. I do not want to go on, – I have had enough!
> Let there be an end, an end!
> Today she left me. What an eloquent leaving!
> What use can future unions be?
> The leaving is real! O sorrow! (DB 105–6)

The last lines are written as a four-lined unrhymed stanza, perhaps a healthy sign – he has not forgotten his métier.

They frequently correspond by telegraph, but the postman must not know their identity, otherwise the press would have a field day. So he calls himself *Will*, while her name is *Vorstel*, derived from Schopenhauer's *Wille und Vorstellung* (The World as Will and Idea):

> Lucerne, 11.4.1866, 9.05 am
> Why today no letter from Vorstel? Little Will crying, please comfort child quickly. (KL V 27)

The telegram reaches Cosima three hours later in Munich (those were the days), and she wires back:

Vorstel wrote daily. Little Will must not cry but scold post office. Vorstel sends love, bright sunny day. (KL V 28)

Cosima returns to him for good, and now he is ready to face living and working with renewed interest. It is a different Wagner who writes to her from Bayreuth, while she is busy closing down Tribschen prior to joining him:

What bliss when I can show everything here to the children! . . . How they will love the opera house! O, if only you were here, but let the mama not overtax herself! . . . O, now kiss our children and love, love, love me! I breathe with you and foresee great blessings in you, with you! I shall work my magic and I know how, but only for you! . . . O my love, my love! How lovely you are! . . . Blessings on our Fidi! Blessings on all the loved ones so full of life! But – their mother! O that mother! I sense her blessing and I am blissfully happy! (BRC: 24.4.1872)

Happiness and wedded bliss attend their move from Tribschen into their Haus Wahnfried in Bayreuth. They hold their Festival seasons there in 1876 and 1882, and their love abides in spite of those late entanglements of his heart with Judith Gautier and, possibly, with Carrie Pringle from England, one of his flower maidens in *Parsifal*. Cosima records:

'You are my all,' he says to me, and when I show my pleasure he adds, 'you are the whole of Wahnfried and I am your Wahnfritz.' (CWT II 64: 19.3.1878)

We are left alone in the drawing room and become engrossed in each other. 'O my treasure, you bring out everything that is good in me! There will only be badness left inside me.' 'My only one.' 'No, you are the only one!' After a silent embrace we part and R. exclaims, 'If people only knew – we are the world to each other, we need no more!'
(CWT II 102: 29.5.1878)

When R. is in bed he says, 'This century has performed one good deed, it has created you.' At first this makes me laugh, but then the solemnity of it strikes me and turns me to prayer. (CWT II 765: 17.7.1881)

In the evenings he reads to her. Together they assimilate the literature of two and a half millennia. Cosima names the books in her diaries. They read:
Homer – Sophocles – Aeschylus – Xenophon – Sappho – Plato – Aristophanes – Euripides – Thucydides – Plutarch – Herodotus – Demosthenes – Ovid – Lucretius – The Edda – The Volsunga Saga –

Unfortunately, R.'s craving for silk materials provokes me to an observation which I should have suppressed, as it caused some ill feeling. (CWT I 42: 24.1.1869)

This is a minor discord, but there are major ones:

In the evening R. talks to me about the *Odyssey* and the *Iliad*, while smoking, and drinking his beer. In the next room the carpenter had been varnishing, and all these smells mingle and cause me to feel more and more dizzy, while a headache deprives me entirely of my vision and finally of my hearing too. When I informed R. of my condition, he became very aggressive and saw a reproach in what was merely an explanation. He then said a number of things that should better be left unsaid, and I went upstairs to my room, upset and crying. Now I am wondering what is best to be done. Should I wait for his anger to abate or should I go down to him and quietly explain the whole thing once more, and calm his temper? I had hardly finished writing this when R. came in to say good night. I then went down with him and dispelled the mist in his mind. (CWT I 80: 1.4.1869)

The woman suffers, but the wife proves herself. On occasions when she does not succeed in 'dispelling the mist in his mind', she seeks comfort in her purdah philosophy of life:

R. dealt harshly with me today, when he more or less accused me of not loving Eva, because I could not take the child with me on a late walk. That was hard indeed, and although many hours have passed, I still must weep bitterly as I write this down. But I am certain that all this is my just desert. (CWT I 88: 23.4.1869)

Cosima has learnt to value obedience and she surrenders her own judgement in all things to Wagner:

Today, my children, I have done a great wrong; I have offended the friend, and since I never want to do that again – it is the blackest of sins –, I recognise in this the pitiful condition of our human nature. We were talking about Beethoven's Symphony in C minor, and I obstinately insisted on a tempo which I felt was right. R. was taken aback and hurt, and now both of us suffer, I because I have done this, and he because he has seen me self-willed. (CWT I 200: 18.2.1870)

Eleven years later:

> I have committed a grave error. In handing the pages of the score to Herr Humperdinck, I wrap them in a prepared sheet. R. is quite beside himself. Although we retrieve the sheet immediately, R. has lost half an hour and is very indignant. But afterwards he is extremely kind and regrets having been so vehement towards me, while I am disconsolate about my misfortune. (CWT II 773: 2.8.1881)

After more than a century it may seem ludicrous that such trivialities could cause such uproar, but they did. When the storm clouds have passed, he is all love again, and he ends a letter to her:

> Now I want to dream my way to you. . . . Are the children good? Has Fidi wet himself again? You remember we have a son! A son! And such good daughters, one of whom – at last, at last – resembles her mother. Kiss them all from me, the children nurtured by such a good mother! I love you as I am sure no woman has ever been loved. Blessed one, my beloved, wonderful woman! Farewell, sleep well, be serenely divine as always when you abide in your soul's domain! My greetings and love! Be kissed, be adored! (BRC: 10.12.1871)

The artist who dares to plunge into the awesome chasm where the myths of the world have their being in order to create from them a new mythology for our time, who suffers the terror and the heartbreak of his own creations, needs solace and security at home. Wagner's appreciation of what Cosima means to him is perfectly expressed in one sentence:

> You are the hook which keeps me from falling into the abyss.
> (CWT I 580: 13.10.1872)

Such is his life with her.

> In the morning the two older children to church, the two smaller ones with us, playing very prettily. As I am writing this, R. calls to me from the salon upstairs, where he is at work. 'Cosima, where are you?' 'Down here, I am writing my diary.' 'Are you writing good things?' 'Of course, but why are you thinking of me now?' 'Foolish woman, what else can I ever think? What makes me persevere with my work? Thinking of you! I would like to know what would have become of me if I had not found

you. Useless and worn out, after committing one folly after another. Miserably wasted away!' Then he turns back to his work. (CWT I 420: 23.7.1871)

Such is her life with him.

VII

WAGNER IN
ENGLAND
AND
ALMOST IN
AMERICA

In March 1839 Wagner loses his position as director of music at the theatre in Riga. His unending financial problems sour his zest for work and living. Minna has already escaped from him on two occasions, and he searches for a new beginning elsewhere. Paris seems to offer real prospects to a young German composer. If he can conquer the French, his fame will be assured and Germany will be taught a lesson, while German opera directors will rue the day they allowed him to leave the country of his birth. They set sail. Their boat, the *Thetis*, breaks its journey after twenty-four days and docks in London, allowing Richard, Minna and Robber, their Newfoundland companion, to disembark. *Mein Leben* reports:

> So we reached London Bridge, the unique centre of this immense, densely packed universe. After our dreadful three weeks at sea, we were at last on solid ground again, and we yielded to a state of giddiness – still used to the pitching motion of the ship – which also affected Robber. The dog whisked round every corner and threatened to lose his way every minute. So the three of us sought refuge in a cab which took us to the Horseshoe Tavern, a sailors' pub recommended to us by our captain. Here we contemplated how to conquer this monster of a town. . . . The narrow cabs then in use were meant to carry two people facing each other, so we had to lay our huge dog crosswise, his head through one window and the tail through the other. (ML I 175–6)

The English connection had been established somewhat earlier, when Wagner performed his *Rule Britannia* Overture in Riga. The motley programme also offered an anonymous Concertino for Double Bass, the first act finale of Weber's *Oberon* with Minna Wagner in the cast, and sundry recitations of Schiller's poetry and drama.

In 1837 Wagner had sent the *Rule Britannia* score to Sir George T. Smart, president of the Philharmonic Society in London. Now he calls at his house, where he learns that Sir George is not in town. He leaves a note, enquiring after the fate of his Overture. This prompts the president, on his return, to send the score – twenty-four months after receiving it – to William Watts, secretary of the Philharmonic Society, asking him to 'have the goodness to give this Score to the Directors'. By that time – it is now the second half of September – Wagner has already left for Paris. There the saga continues. *Mein Leben* takes up the story:

> One morning, when we had been anxiously debating how to find

the money for our first quarter's rent, a postman arrived with a parcel for me from London. I took this for a signal of imminent divine intervention and broke the seal, while the postman asked me to receipt the package and to pay seven francs for carriage. To my horror I discovered inside my *Rule Britannia* Overture, returned by the Philharmonic Society. Furiously I refused to accept the package, whereupon the postman

Poster for the Riga Concert

argued, with some heat, that I had opened it. He argued in vain. I informed him I did not possess seven francs and, anyway, he should not have let me open the package before requesting payment. So I made him return the only copy of my Overture . . . and I have never summoned up enough interest to find out what became of it. (ML I 194)

What became of it? The *Rule Britannia* Overture reposes in the archives of the British Library, which is a pity, for had Wagner paid the postman, he would have read Mr Watts's enclosed letter, which might have taught him something about British patriotism:

20.4.1840

Sir,

In returning the Score of your overture I am desired by the Directors of the Philharmonic Society to apologize for their having detained it so long without a reply. They beg me to add that they should have had much pleasure in the performance of it, but that being written on a Theme which is here considered common place prevents its being admissible at their Concerts.

    I am Sir, Your Obed. Servant
      W. Watts
      Secretary (British Library, draft letter, Loan MS.48.13/35, f.48)

Back to the first half of September 1839 in London. Having failed to get hold of Smart, Wagner tries his luck with Sir Edward George Bulwer-Lytton, whose *Cola Rienzi* he had used for his own libretto of his opera. Bulwer is a member of Parliament. Wagner has only a few words of English, but he makes his way to Westminster:

None of the subordinates in the vast Houses of Parliament could make out what I wanted, so I was handed from official to official, in ever ascending order of rank, until at last I was introduced to a distinguished-looking gentleman who had just come out of one of the larger chambers. He was informed that I was an utterly unintelligible individual. . . . He was very polite and asked me in a friendly manner, in French, what my business was. When I told him I was looking for Bulwer, the celebrated author, he seemed suitably impressed, but said Sir Edward was not in London. I then asked him whether I could come in and watch a debate. He told me that they were using temporary premises, with very limited space for a few privileged spectators only, with special admission tickets, since the old Houses of Parliament had burnt down. I pressed him further, intimating my confidence in him, and my guardian angel who must have been a true peer of the realm – we were standing by the upper chamber – soon opened a door to the restricted area in the House of Lords. This I found tremendously interesting . . . (ML I 177)

Doors will open for Wagner, in England today, and in France tomorrow, though in that country some are also to be slammed in his face. *Mein Leben* continues:

I was able to hear, amongst others, the Bishop of London, who was the only one whose voice and bearing struck me as artificial and unsympathetic, though this may have been due to my dislike of all clergymen. (ML I 178)

Next day the Wagners travel to France. No, Paris will not be conquered, but Wagner's two and a half years on French soil yield the birth of two operas, his *Rienzi* and *Der fliegende Holländer*. In 1842 they return to Germany. The Dresden uprising of 1849 will drive him into exile in Switzerland, and fifteen and a half years after the first brief stay in England, he prepares for a second visit.

Mr Anderson, treasurer of the Philharmonic Society, visits him in January 1855 and invites him, on behalf of his society, to conduct eight concerts in London. Wagner cannot make up his mind. He is busy with the instrumentation of his *Walküre*, but the opportunity to conduct a first-rate orchestra persuades him no longer to resist 'the stupidly friendly English face of Mr Anderson'. The official invitation reads as follows:

22.1.1855

Dear Sir,

I beg leave to inform you, on the part of the Directors of the Philharmonic Society, that their Colleague Mr Anderson has reported the gratifying result of his Conference with you. They desire me to express their entire satisfaction with the arrangements which Mr Anderson has made and which they have confirmed; and I am directed, therefore, to state, that they agree to pay you the sum of Five Thousand francs (Two Hundred pounds Sterling) for conducting the Eight Concerts & Rehearsals of the ensuing season, the dates of which are subjoined. They have now publicly announced your appointment to the Office, and expect that you will, in conformity with your arrangement with Mr Anderson, arrive in London at least a week before the date of the first Concert.

I am further desired to convey to you the friendly assurances of the Directors, and to offer you their best assistance in engaging apartments for you, should you wish it.

I have the Honour to be, etc.

I have to add, that the Directors will be gratified by your having the kindness to bring with you any Orchestral pieces (Symphonies or Overtures) of your own Composition, which you may think suitable for the Society's Concerts. (Dates of the Concerts & Rehearsals subjoined)

Have the goodness to write to me, acknowledging the receipt of this Letter. (Archives of the Royal Philharmonic Society)

Wagner arrives in London on 2 March 1855, this time without Minna. He has ten days before he will conduct his first concert, which gives him leisure to observe:

In Paris, the businessmen look like people going for a walk. In London, people going for a walk look like businessmen. (CWT I 726)

He rents an apartment in Portland Terrace, in the vicinity of Regent's Park where he takes regular walks. He also goes to concerts:

. . . which I attended in the large auditorium of Exeter Hall. The oratorios which they give there almost every week, are indeed presented with great confidence, the result of so many repeat performances. The chorus of 700 voices earned my approval for their precision, which several times reached a respectable standard in Handel's *Messiah*. It was here that I learned about the true spirit of the musical life of the English, which is actually closely related to English Protestantism, and therefore the oratorio attracts the public to a far greater extent than the opera. The audience appreciates the dual privilege of experiencing the simultaneous offerings of both oratorio and church. As the churchgoers sit with their prayer books in their hands, all concertgoers can be seen with Handel's piano scores, which are available at the box office in the popular shilling editions. These they follow most diligently, so as not to miss – as it appeared to me – certain celebrated passages, such as the beginning of the Hallelujah Chorus, where custom requires everybody to rise from their seats. Originally, this had probably been a spontaneous expression of enthusiasm which is now repeated with painstaking precision at every performance of the *Messiah*. (ML II 538–9)

On 12 March he conducts his first concert. The programme is ambitious:

PART I

Sinfonia No. 7 (Grand)	Haydn
Terzetto, 'Soave sia il vento'	Mozart
(Clara Novello, Mr and Mrs Weiss)	
Dramatic Concerto (Violin, Herr Ernst)	Spohr
Scena, 'Ocean, thou mighty monster!' (Clara Novello)	Weber
Overture, 'The Isles of Fingal'	Mendelssohn

Sinfonia Eroica	Beethoven
Duet, 'O my Father' (Mr and Mrs Weiss)	Marschner
Overture, 'Zauberflöte'	Mozart
	(EL V 167)

Next day the *Morning Post* reports:

> The performance of last night sufficiently proved that the committee have made a wise selection; for, taking into consideration the unhappy fact that the new conductor had been allowed but one rehearsal, with a band to whom his readings and style of beat were utterly strange, the general result was most honourable both to him and to them. Many portions of the great symphonies, Haydn's No. 7 (Grand) and Beethoven's 'Eroica', and the whole of Mendelssohn's Overture to the 'Isles of Fingal', have never, in our recollection, been so well played in this country; and we are consequently justified in thinking, that the truly poetical feeling which animated these would have been apparent throughout but for the disadvantages to which we have already alluded.
>
> That there is a deeply conceived purpose, emanating from conscientious study of the score, in all Herr Wagner's readings, it were impossible to doubt; for, although he displays a perfect command over the orchestra, by frequently hurrying or slackening the time at will (too frequently, perhaps, to satisfy the strictly orthodox, who consider a conductor's duty to be purely metronomic), such deviations are never the offspring of mere caprice, or a silly desire to parade practical skill; . . . Herr Wagner was most flatteringly received both by the band and audience, which included, as usual, all the most distinguished artists in London. His success, therefore, was complete. (EL V 167–8)

The following seven concerts include Beethoven's Fourth, Fifth, Sixth, Seventh, Eighth and Ninth Symphonies, excerpts from *Lohengrin*, twice the *Tannhäuser* Overture, but also such items as Cipriano Potter's Symphony in G minor, an Overture by Onslow, and the Third Symphony by Charles Lucas.

What does Wagner think of his orchestra? He reports to Minna, after the fourth concert:

> London, 8.5.1855, I think.
> Alas, the orchestra of the Philharmonic Society which also plays for the Italian Opera here, consists almost entirely of Englishmen. There are three Germans – a trumpet, a trombone and one other – as well as three

Frenchmen. All the others are brave Englishmen. . . . Now these gentlemen are quite good players. They have mastered their instruments and they can play everything that is required of them, but they play so mechanically – just like Geneva musical boxes. They actually perform everything at the same dynamic level, and find it difficult to play softer or louder. The Parisian orchestra is far superior. These Englishmen are crude fellows. I would rather try to breathe life into a German dance band musician than stir the feelings of these dull creatures. It also irks me that I find it difficult to make myself understood. French is of course no use here, and when I have to be explicit, I ask Sainton to translate for me. I have acquired a few short phrases as my standby, such as 'Once more, please!' (RWM I 183)

So much for his assessment of English musicians. How do the English assess the German conductor and composer? The *Daily News* enthuses:

13.5.1855

Beethoven's sublime sinfonia *Eroica* was magnificently executed from beginning to end. We never heard the band play more evidently *con amore*, nor ever observed a better understanding or more complete sympathy between them and their conductor; and we felt as much gratified as surprised that such a result could have been effected by a single rehearsal. The funeral march was taken a good deal slower than usual; and the effect (as it struck us) was to heighten the solemnity and pathos of the movement. . . .

Whatever differences and controversies may exist as to the doctrines and tenets of the musical school to which Herr Wagner is said to belong, and as to his own character as a composer – disputes into which we do not enter, because we are as yet unacquainted with their merits – on one point he has left no room for question – his consummate excellence as an orchestral chief. He has all the requisite qualities: thorough knowledge, firmness, energy, self-possession, and the happy art of making his meaning clear to the performers. (EL V 169–70)

The Times begs to differ:

Herr Wagner was kindly received by the audience, and the symphony of Haydn, one of the finest of the twelve 'Grand', was executed with amazing spirit. Such a familiar work, however, in the hands of such a company of players, would fare well even without a conductor. It was in the concerto of Spohr (magnificently played by Herr Ernst), the overture of Mendelssohn, and the symphony of Beethoven, that the qualities of the new conductor were put to the test. The result, on the whole, was by no means satisfactory; but this may be accounted for in more ways than one. Herr Wagner's method of using the *bâton* (like that of some other German musicians) must be very perplexing, at first, to those unacquainted with it. The confusion between the 'up' and 'down' beat, which he appears to employ indiscriminately – so unlike the clear and decided measure of his predecessor – requires a long time to get accustomed to. Moreover, Herr Wagner conducts without a score before him, which says more for his memory, we think, than for his judgement. (EL V 173)

Conducting without a score is not his only faux pas. He is horrified when he learns that kid gloves are to be worn on the rostrum. He reacts with characteristic panache, turning the absurd demand to his own advantage: he now procures kid gloves, wears them on the way to the rostrum and then discards them. But for Mendelssohn's music he puts them on again, allowing the audience to guess why.

On the whole, he dislikes London heartily. He had originally planned to use much of his spare time for working at the *Walküre* score, but his present dejected mood prevents progress. He complains to Liszt:

> 16.5.1855
>
> I live here like one of the damned in hell. I never imagined that I could sink so low again. I cannot describe the misery I feel in being forced to live in this wretched condition. I now realise that it was quite sinful, quite criminal to accept this invitation to London which at best would have led me far away from my real business. . . . I am stuck up to my ears in a morass of customs and conventionalities, without hope of refreshing myself with a single drop of fresh water. 'Mein Herr, we are not accustomed to that!' – this is the constant echo I am forced to hear. . . . Everyone assures me that the public is favourably inclined towards me, but that same public can never be really roused. They receive the sublime and the trite without ever revealing whether they have been touched or not. (BWL II 72)

Then he discloses his main predicament:

> Gradually, all pleasure in my work is evaporating. I was going to complete the score of *Die Walküre* during my four months here, but that is now out of the question. I am so depressed by this awfully dreary

and wicked situation, that I shall not even finish the second act. It was my intention to begin *Der junge Siegfried* at Seelisberg on Lake Lucerne, but I think this will have to wait till next spring. I am hit hardest by this disinclination to work; it makes me feel that everlasting darkness is closing in. Really, what is there for me to do in this world, if I cannot work? (BWL II 73)

There follows the most telling passage of this remarkable letter:

My companion in this hell is Dante, whose study I have hitherto neglected. I have passed through his Inferno, and just now I am at the gates of Purgatory. Oh, I am in need of this purgatory, for come to think of it, it was my truly sinful stupidity which tempted me to London and which I now repent most keenly. I must, I must admit defeat. My past experiences have already convinced me that resignation – in the widest sense of the word – is a necessity, and now I have to subdue altogether this terrible, untamed zest for life which again and again disturbs my judgement and throws me into a chaos of contradictions. I only hope that one day I may pass through Purgatory and enter into Paradise'.

(BWL II 73)

As always, he will find release from the contrariness of life in his art. Many times will he make the crossing from purgatory to paradise. The purgatory, of course, is often of his own devising – when he marries the wrong wife, when he lobbies the wrong people in Paris, when he mounts the barricades in Dresden, when he wastes his time with foolish pursuits such as trying to raise funds by conducting in London.

Franz Liszt probably understands his friend better than anyone else and knows how to cheer him. A few weeks earlier he has sent these wise and encouraging words:

2.5.1855

It may cost you some effort, but since we cannot alter what is inevitable, we must try to bear it. Of course, to accommodate ourselves with it would be hypocrisy. The English philistine is just as unpleasant as the German, and the chasm between the public and ourselves yawns wide wherever we go. (BWL II 70)

Now he replies to Wagner's purgatory letter:

2.6.1855

So you are reading Dante? He is splendid company for you. . . . A plan for a Dante Symphony has long occupied my mind, and I intend to finish it by the end of the year. Its three movements will be called Hell, Purgatory and Paradise – the first two purely instrumental, the third with chorus. When I see you in the autumn, I shall probably be able to show it to you, and if you do not dislike it, you must allow me to dedicate it to you . . . Let come what will, I implore you *to be patient and to persevere*. . . . All this nonsense cannot touch you. Just write your *Nibelungen*, and be content to live as an immortal! (BWL II 76–7)

For the present, the enthusiasm of his London public fails to give Wagner much pleasure. He grumbles to Minna:

15.5.1855

This much is certain – yesterday there was a great rush for tickets, and for the first time the place was overcrowded. Everybody maintains this was due to my compositions being included in the programme. Maybe so, but really these concerts with all their fuss and bother are a penance for me, and I shall refrain from telling you how bitter I am and how absolutely sick of it all. Enough said – I shall conduct a further three concerts, and in six weeks I shall have left this place. May God grant that I shall find all well in Zurich, and that your fretting and agonising will no longer undermine your constitution. To worry myself to death over your own worries would be all I need. (RWM I 189–90)

His inability to work makes him unreasonable, makes him loathe his surroundings, makes him castigate Minna.

The London press carries detailed reviews of all his concerts, but neither *The Times* nor the equally respected *Morning Post* can raise his spirits, especially since neither critic allows his judgement to be affected by overmuch expertise:

The Times, 12.6.1855

The overture to *Tannhäuser* – repeated for the advantage of his Royal Highness Prince Albert (instead of the March, which had been announced, from the same opera) – does not improve on closer acquaintance. So much incessant noise, so uninterrupted and singular an exhibition of pure cacophony, was never heard before. . . . Such a wonderful performance, however, as that of the Philharmonic band last night would, had it been possible, have made even *Tannhäuser* acceptable; but it was not possible, and we sincerely hope that no execution, however superb, will ever make such senseless discord pass, in England, for a manifestation of art and genius. (EL V 309)

218

Morning Post, 13.6.1855

Herr Wagner is a necessary evil. We believe him to be quite in earnest, and perfectly conscientious. He feels inwardly impelled to act as he does, feels that he has a mission, which is to destroy and not to complete. He is the chosen instrument and we look upon him with a kind of superstitious reverence. Germany, however, and not England,

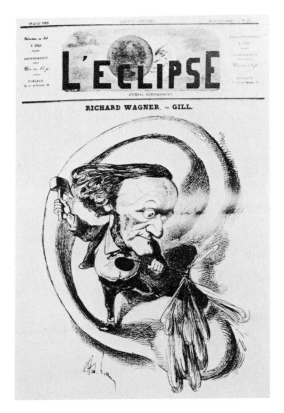

Contemporary caricature

is the proper arena for his exploits. There he is at home and natural – one of the last links in a chain which will soon end where it began, in artistic nothingness; the necessary expression of something, which if he did not, somebody else must express; but here he is out of his element. England – young and fresh in musical feeling, full of reverence for those great masters whom she is only now beginning fully to understand and appreciate, deriving all her ideas of excellence from them and striving to found a national school upon the sure foundation which such models afford – cannot possibly relish corruption. . . . The rooms were well attended. (EL V 311)

Wagner celebrates his forty-second birthday, 22 May 1855, with this greeting to himself:

> *Im wunderschönen Monat Mai*
> *kroch Richard Wagner aus dem Ei:*
> *ihm wünschen, die zumeist ihn lieben,*
> *er wäre besser drin geblieben.*
>
> *A maytime chick, we know it well,*
> *Was Wagner when he burst his shell.*
> *Today it cannot be denied,*
> *He might as well have stayed inside.*
>
> (RWM I 191)

Neither the press nor Wagner himself excel in unbiased observations. He informs Otto Wesendonck as to the true nature of the English:

> 21.3.1855
>
> The Queen's taste is quite trivial. . . . I cannot conceive anything more unpleasant than the typical Englishman. Your typical Englishman is your typical sheep. They both have a practical mind which makes them find their fodder in the meadow. Yes, he will find his fodder, but alas, the beautiful meadow and the blue sky above do not exist for his peculiar organs of perception. Bad luck for him who can see both sky and meadow, but can't get at the fodder! (OW 12–16)

He finds solace in the animals in the Zoological Gardens, and writes to Minna:

> 7.4.1855
>
> I have been to the Zoo again. This time I visited mainly the lions and tigers who gave me a splendid roar at feeding time. Two lion cubs had chosen a mastiff for their playmate. The birds are fabulous. A wonderful ostrich variety with pink plumage has quite entranced me. This is all very beautiful, I must say. (RWM I 161)

The dumb creatures touch his heart and help him forget – for a time – his fellow men. Later he will say to Cosima:

> The worst and sometimes the ugliest of beasts is man. (CWT I 155: 28.9.1869)

From his London Inferno he writes to Minna:

17.4.1855

> Unfortunately I have had several sleepless nights again. Once, when I woke from a restless doze, I suddenly heard a nightingale in the park. This brought floods of tears to my eyes, and now I often hear this dear bird in the evening and in the early morning. Oh, if nature could move me no longer, I would not want to live among people. You feel like this, too, and your love of animals pleases me much. Yes, they are our only comfort . . . (RWM I 168)

Gradually he gets to know a good number of pleasant specimens, and some of them are two-legged: for instance, and unexpectedly, the Queen of England. He writes to Liszt:

5.7.1855

> I suppose you have heard that Queen Victoria has received me most handsomely? She and Prince Albert attended the seventh concert, and since they wanted to hear a sample of my works, I had the *Tannhäuser* Overture repeated. This gave me some fleeting satisfaction. The Queen really did take to me. She asked to have a conversation with me after the first part of the concert, and she was so cordial and kind that I was quite moved. These two are indeed the first people in England who dared to speak up for me, openly and fearlessly. Considering that they were dealing with a political outlaw, with a traitor on the 'Wanted' list, one will understand that I am deeply grateful to them both. (BWL II 85)

The warrant for his arrest really did exist:

Steckbrief.

Der unten etwas näher bezeichnete Königl. Capellmeister

Richard Wagner von hier ist wegen wesentlicher Theilnahme an der in hiesiger Stadt stattgefundenen aufrührerischen Bewegung zur Untersuchung zu ziehen, zur Zeit aber nicht zu erlangen gewesen. Es werden daher alle Polizeibehörden auf denselben aufmerksam gemacht und ersucht, Wagnern im Betretungsfalle zu verhaften und davon uns schleunigst Nachricht zu ertheilen.

Dresden, den 16. Mai 1849.

Die Stadt-Polizei-Deputation.

von Oppell.

Wagner ist 37—38 Jahre alt, mittler Statur, hat braunes Haar und trägt eine Brille.

WANTED

Richard Wagner, Court Kapellmeister, in connection with the recent riots in this city in which he is known to have taken an active part. A warrant for his arrest has been issued, but Wagner has not yet been apprehended. All police authorities are requested to look out for the said Wagner and to arrest him, if found in their neighbourhood, and to inform us immediately.

Dresden, 16.5.1849.

Wagner is aged 37 or 38, of medium height, has brown hair and wears spectacles.

His mood mellows. It is June, he has a delightful audience with the Queen, and at the end of the month he will be back in Switzerland, where the feverish entanglement with Mathilde Wesendonck awaits him. With rare euphoria he reports to Minna:

12.6.1855

My God, dearest Mienel, I am completely hoarse after talking so long with the Queen. First she asked me how Peps [their dog] was; then, whether Knackerchen [their parrot] was being good; then, whether I had bought any presents for my wife. . . . Do not think this is a joke, it really happened. The Queen of England has had a long conversation with me. I can now inform you that she is not fat, but rather short and not at all pretty, and alas, she has a somewhat red nose. But she is uncommonly friendly and affable, and though she may not be an eminent thinker, she is decidedly pleasant and kind. She has no love for orchestral music, and when she attends a full-length concert, she does so to please her husband who is fond of music and who likes German orchestral pieces. This time, though, she seems to have been really impressed. Sainton kept her under observation from his desk and assures me that she followed my conducting and the performance of the orchestra with quite an unusual and ever-growing interest. The *Tannhäuser* Overture in particular went down extremely well with her and with the Prince. Anyway, at the end of the Overture I turned round to them, and *both* applauded most cordially, giving me several friendly smiles. The audience, of course, backed them up, and this time they honoured me with a lot of unanimous, prolonged applause. . . . In Germany, I am hounded by the police like a highway robber; in France, they vex me with passport problems; but the Queen of England is not embarrassed to receive me before the most aristocratic gathering in the world, with the utmost friendliness. That really is something! . . . Greetings to all dear friends,

from your

Knight of the Garter.   (RWM I 213–15)

The end of his series of concerts is approaching, and now he cares even less about the critics. Let the *Sunday Times* proclaim:

6.5.1855

The more we see and hear of Herr Richard Wagner, the more are we convinced of the soundness of our first opinion, that, however extraordinary a man he may be in other things, to whatever extent he may possess the general impulse of the artist, music is not his special birthgift . . . either Richard Wagner is a desperate charlatan, endowed with worldly skill and vigorous purpose enough to persuade a gaping crowd that the nauseous compound he manufactures has some precious inner virtue, that they must live and ponder yet more ere they perceive; or else he is a self-deceived enthusiast, who thoroughly believes his own apostolic mission, and is too utterly destitute of any perception of musical beauty to recognise the worthlessness of his credentials.

(EL V 266–7)

In case Minna has got hold of this or any other adverse reports, he advises her:

19.6.1855

Do not let the lies and the brutal ill-treatment of the newspapers get you down. As a rule, the writers are money-grubbing blackguards. No decent person will ever write for a newspaper, unless he is driven to it by shameless lies which need a rebuttal. (RWM I 221)

Although he never stopped fretting, he has made progress with the instrumentation of *Die Walküre*. The final concert must have made up for at least some of his past agonies. He informs Minna:

26.6.1855

They want to make it hard for me to leave them. Last night the orchestra and the whole packed hall showed me their very gratifying appreciation. First, they received my appearance on the platform with warm applause, then the Beethoven [Fourth] Symphony created a sensation, and at the end, after the *Oberon* Overture, the orchestra rose and gave me one round of vociferous applause after another. At the same time the whole audience began to clap and refused to stop their ovations, so that I did not know whether to acknowledge the orchestra's ever-growing applause or the public's furious acclaim. Finally I gestured to them all, fairly begging them to let be and go home. At last, and with great difficulty, I succeeded. But now I had to shake hands. The entire orchestra, about 100 players, lined up to shake my hand, and there were several moving scenes. Even members of the audience crowded around me, and there was no end to further shaking of hands, men, women, everybody. In a word, I was moved, for at long last I was able to feel everybody's strong affection for me. Naturally, my little Queen's attitude towards me contributed a great deal to this unconcealed demonstration of approval which was quite spontaneous. I take this as a tremendous rejection on their part of *The Times* and the other critics, which is quite unprecedented, for no audience has ever shown such a degree of independent thinking. So, I am about to leave London as a conqueror, after all, as a much acclaimed conqueror. (SB 478)

All's well . . . ? Perhaps. But critics, more often than not malignant or incompetent, continue to bother him. True, the *Tannhäuser* Overture is quite avant-garde, especially to the ears of the then conservative London audiences, but the critics show little inclination to learn and understand.

How differently did Robert Schumann behave when, ten years previously, he encountered *Tannhäuser* for the first time. He was a critic, too, but in a different class. At first he disapproves and says so to Mendelssohn:

> Dresden, 22.10.1845
>
> Another opera by Wagner. . . . but honestly, he is unable to write four consecutive bars of decent, let alone beautiful music. . . . This opera is not a whit better than *Rienzi*, only more tedious and artificial. But if one pronounces on this, people will say one is jealous. That is why I confide in you, for I know that you are fully aware of it. (SBNF 252)

Three weeks later:

> Dresden, 12.11.1845
>
> I must take back a good deal of what I had told you after reading the score. On the stage everything appears in a different light. Much of it has moved me greatly. (SBNF 254)

After another fortnight – this time to Heinrich Dorn – he acknowledges, ungrudgingly, Wagner's achievement:

Tannhäuser . . . contains much profound and original music and is a hundred times better than his previous operas. (SBNF 256)

On the last day of June 1855 Wagner leaves London for Zurich. There Minna awaits him, and he is drawn to Mathilde. The English venture has yielded a profit of approximately £40, and 100 pages of the instrumentation of *Die Walküre*.

Wagner will visit London for a third time twenty-two years later, and this time with Cosima. The opening of the Bayreuth Festspiele in 1876 had resulted in an appalling deficit, and in order to raise funds he must once more shoulder the unloved burden of conducting. Again, there will be eight concerts, this time in the Albert Hall, and he will share the rostrum with Hans Richter.

The first performance of *Der Ring des Nibelungen* in 1876 was a memorable event in the history of music. Wagner wrote the words, composed the music and produced the performances. To expect him to discharge the debt as well is, surely, asking too much. He writes to his old Mannheim friend, Emil Heckel, founder of the first Richard Wagner Society:

11.2.1877

Get to know Germany and the German public! Everything, but everything is lost there. What we have accomplished last year is a miracle and will remain one, as long as anyone remembers it. . . . For now, I have to concern myself with paying off the deficit. To that end I intend to give concerts in England for several months. If I return alive, I hope nobody will ask me to do anything other than look after myself, recover and forget. (BB 259)

He will return from his English expedition with just one tenth of the total Festival debt, but his concerts, with some of the Bayreuth soloists, are an immense success, and London audiences are ecstatic. The critics rejoice that Wagner has profited from their predecessors' advice, and that he is no longer 'a desperate charlatan'.

Musical Times, June 1877

Nothing like this can be found in the entire range of music. Wagner uses the orchestra with as much ease as a child plays with a little toy, and can make it do almost everything but speak. Its expression of the varying sentiments of the text is marvellous in directness and fidelity, while the constant play of colour, managed with all an artist's eye to effect, is a source of continual wonder and delight.

George Bernard Shaw, at a very tender age, reports in *The Hornet*:

6.6.1877

At each concert Herr Wagner was received with tempestuous applause. On the 19th May he was presented with an address, and a laurel wreath was placed on his brow, which latter distinction was probably more gratifying to his feelings than favorable to the dignity of his appearance. (G. B. Shaw: *How to Become a Musical Critic*, London 1960: 24)

Queen Victoria receives him at Windsor, and Cosima keeps a detailed diary of all events of note:

1.5.1877

Dover impresses us greatly, as does the first drive through London which is very pleasant. On the platform at Charing Cross we find practically the whole orchestra assembled. . . . We visit the Albert Hall which we like very much, in spite of its vast dimensions. Our singers have already arrived. I drive with R. in a hansom cab [Cosima writes *handsom-cab*]; the fog makes everything look eerie. . . . The detached houses with their large gardens make one feel independent and comfortable. If I had to choose a large town, it would be London.

6.5.1877

Wrote letters, visited Zoo, met the famous lady novelist George Eliot; her dignity makes a pleasant impression.

7.5.1877

Full rehearsal. R. exhausted, not by the rehearsal, but by the indiscipline. . . . Concert in the evening at 8. I sit in the *grand tier* with the Leweses [George Eliot and husband G. Lewes] and am horrified by the acoustics, double echo which invalidates any impression. Also, our singers rather feeble. Sad feelings, in spite of R.'s splendid reception.

12.5.1877

Cristal Palace [sic], flower show, then our 3rd concert, in the afternoon. Materna splendid in *Walküre*; *Ride of the Walküren* encored; R. received by Prince of Wales who tells him that he had attended the Philharmonic concerts 20 years ago.

13.5.1877

We think of America, never to return to Germany.

(CWT I 1049–51)

(Can she mean this? Can he mean this? The answer, six weeks later, is Yes.)

14.5.1877

Rehearsal till one, then to Mr and Mrs Lewes for lunch [she writes 'Frühstück' = breakfast, or elevenses], and then with them to the studio of Burne-Jones, the Pre-Raphaelite. Lovely, delicate paintings, he himself rather pleasant. At 8 in the evening the concert, many members of the royal family and a fairly full house. Herr Unger is already hoarse in the *Lohengrin* duet and declares he will be unable to sing the *Forging Songs*. We decide to repeat *Wotan's Farewell*, but find Herr Hill had already gone home – utter confusion.

15.5.1877

Rehearsal; calamity, the Court complains about the programme alterations, but we cannot possibly adhere to it, since Herr Unger will hardly recover in time.

16.5.1877

Rehearsal from 10 to 1, concert in the evening, *Götterdämmerung* with Materna, *Ride of the Walküren* and Prelude to *Meistersinger* all make great impact.

17.5.1877

To the British Museum, to view the drawings, then rendezvous with R. at the station, on our way to Windsor. There he is received by the Queen and Prince Leopold who mentions Rus [their dog], whom he once saw in Lucerne.

19.5.1877

Today I am indisposed and have to force myself to go to the concert. It is superb. £1,600 proceeds, and a very excited audience; quite un-English, we are told. R. crowned with a laurel wreath, an address on behalf of the orchestra, and endless high spirits.

22.5.1877

R.'s birthday! Very nice letters from all the children and many other congratulations. A banquet in the evening. . . . R. speaks very movingly, thanks for his reception and, quoting Semper, compares moments and years – it is such moments, he says, that make him forget his years. Otherwise, the festivities are rather noisy, rather German.

23.5.1877

I visit Westminster Abbey . . . at the end of the service the organ played 'Elisabeth's Prayer' [from *Tannhäuser*]; I found this very moving.

25.5.1877

I visit the British Museum again and am delighted with the marvellous drawings. Then rendezvous with R. at Charing Cross and fish dinner in Greenwich. Return journey by steam boat, very successful, weather mild and grey, powerful impression. R. says, this is Alberich's dream fulfilled, Nibelheim, world dominion, bustle, labour, oppression by steam and fog everywhere. In the evening *Tannhäuser* in Italian! Oh! – all dreadful, only the orchestra wonderful, but unfortunately not at all well conducted.

26.5.1877

Visit the Tower with R., we like the warders, Beefeaters; lunch with R. in the aquarium. Paid several calls. In the evening *Don Giovanni*.

29.5.1877

Concert in the evening, Herr Unger cannot manage a single note, does not offer an apology and just stands there unperturbed, watches poor Materna struggle through the Awakening Scene [*Siegfried*], still stands by while Richter remonstrates and while R. glares at him with murder in his eyes, without making the slightest effort. . . . The audience very good-natured.

(CWT I 1049–52)

The 'good nature' of the London audiences impressed him now as it had towards the end of his earlier visit, in 1855, when he became aware that the English are perfectly capable of scenes of frenzied enthusiasm. Audiences elsewhere may hiss at a hoarse singer, the English remain 'good-natured'.

And now the reckoning:

30.5.1877

We find that after paying all expenses, R. will have realised £700 for Bayreuth. This is some relief to me, for I was prepared for the worst, but R. is very depressed.

4.6.1877

London goodbye! (CWT I 1053)

Nine tenths of the deficit remains unpaid. The idea first given expression in Cosima's diary on 13 May now grows in substance. If Europe does not care about

Bayreuth, perhaps America will care about Wagner. He writes to Hans von Wolzogen, his young friend and disciple:

2.7.1877

I do not wish to mention the trials I had to endure, when I learned that none of my appeals and requests for sharing the responsibility for last year's festival deficit had elicited any kind of response. I now struggle with this load of care, having sacrificed my last savings, and – have become totally uninterested in this whole business of patronage and societies. I now intend to make a final attempt to talk the Munich Court Theatre into taking over the whole affair, and then I shall – for the present, anyway – wash my hands of my creation, the 'Bühnenfest-spiele', the stage festivals. If nothing comes of it, I shall go to America to protect my family, and shall never dream of returning to Germany.

(KRW 364)

America as a sanctuary, America as the promised land – it is not a new thought after all. Thirty years earlier Wagner had written thus to Franz Löbmann, an acquaintance in Riga:

Dresden, 5.7.1848

Dearest Friend,

Your brother has disclosed to me his intention to take the military band which he has formed for that purpose, to the United States of North America. He tells me, however, that he needs your financial assistance, and he asks me to support his plea for help. Speaking for myself, I tell you quite frankly that as a poor band player I would not go to America, for the simple reason that I would have been over there long ago. Our wretched musicians have nothing to look forward to but slavery. I cannot understand why one should advise a person against seeking his good fortune over there, where I would surely find it faster and better than here. . . . I therefore support your brother's appeal whole-heartedly. (WSB II 607)

The prospect of finding deliverance from financial strain in the New World is reassuring, and he will take care neither to cross that utopian bridge nor to burn it. He is well aware that going to America for material gain may harm his creative powers, and he elaborates this point in his letter to the actor and producer Ferdinand Heine, his old Dresden friend:

19.11.1849

For the present and for all future, America can only have financial attractions for me. If conditions here remain as they are now, I might well feel so stifled that I would have to consider going to America, though only as a craftsman, with batons for tools, and with a fatter wage packet than is obtainable at home. The difference between us two is that *I have no children.* As the *head of a family,* you would begin a new, incalculably long life in the new world, while my line would be extinguished with my death. There would be a future for you, but none for me. My creative art is my family. (WSB III 153)

Contemporary German caricature depicting the lure of the dollar

The thought that settling in America might have a detrimental effect on his art does not deter him from further transatlantic flirtations, but when he escapes from the Dresden police in 1849, it is to Switzerland and not to America. He consults Liszt:

January 1854
While I am practically starving, I hear from America that they are

actually giving 'Wagner Nights' in Boston. They urge me to come over and inform me that the interest in my works is growing, and that I could make a good deal of money with concert performances. 'Make money', my God, I need not make money, were I to go the way which I long to go. But if I really were to consider such an undertaking, how could I terminate my obligations here with any decency, in order to go where I could make money? And how should I feel over there? Dear me, all this is as impossible as it is ludicrous, for I would have sunk very low, if I were forced to brood over the feasibilities of such a project. My work, my *Nibelungen*, would then certainly be out of the question. (BWL II 7–8)

But America continues to haunt him, and he soliloquises thus in a letter to Liszt eighteen months later:

> 13.9.1855
>
> What can I say about this offer from New York? I heard of it while I was still in London – they were considering sending me an invitation. Truly, it is a blessing they are not offering me a great deal of money. If they did, then the prospect of earning, say, ten thousand dollars in a brief space of time, would force me to undertake an American expedition, particularly in view of my hopeless financial position. On the other hand, would it not be foolish to sacrifice my vital powers to so miserable a purpose? . . . so will you please thank those gentlemen in New York very kindly, in my name, for their consideration which I do not really deserve, and say that 'for the present' I felt unable to accept their invitation.
>
> (BWL II 97)

The next communication to Liszt on the American topic seems to have been dictated by his guardian angel:

> 3.10.1855
>
> If the people in New York should ever decide to offer me a considerable sum, I should find myself in the most awful predicament. If I refused, I should have to keep it a secret from everybody, for they would look at my precarious position and they would charge me with recklessness. Ten years ago I might have considered such an undertaking, but it would be callous to make such detours for a living, especially now, when I am fit for one pursuit only, to devote myself to my very own affair, my *Nibelungen* which, in other circumstances, I should never finish in my lifetime. (BWL II 101)

The guardian angel has done her duty and on the very next day in this letter to

Klindworth he provides himself with more ammunition for saying No:

> 4.10.1855
>
> The Americans press me and want to persuade me to come to New York for six months. I do not think they will succeed, for while I show great stupidity in making money, I possess unique gifts for spending it. A pity that nobody appreciates these gifts. (RWF 176)

Composing the *Ring* is now his main objective and three years go by until his thoughts turn once more to America. Hartenfels, the Frankfurt concert agent, conveys to him an invitation to New York. Wagner has left his Asyl at the Wesendoncks and has retreated to Venice, where he has to learn how to live without Mathilde – or, at least, without her actual presence. Is this the right moment for transatlantic temptations? He answers Hartenfels:

> 24.12.1858
>
> As far as I am concerned, this matter could be seriously considered only if it were a definite offer, and if the terms would be particularly advantageous. I am somewhat indifferent as to the fate of my operas in America. . . . I am without any private means and receive no regular income. It might therefore be advisable for me to avail myself of an opportunity for earning a considerable sum of money through artistic activities and endeavours which, though somewhat uncongenial, would be of a limited duration and would secure me the material requirements for my work. That would be my sole purpose (RWF 243–4)

It would be a shame to allow such fiscal sources to go untapped. If he should decide against the offer, perhaps friend Klindworth – his foster daughter Winifred will marry Siegfried Wagner one day – could do with the money?

> 1.2.1859
>
> I have a recent offer from New York, to conduct my operas there next winter. I am playing for time, but I intend to propose you as my deputy.
> (RWF 247)

Meanwhile, the New York offer begins to seem more and more attractive and he succumbs in style – naming his own terms and proposing Klindworth (whom he had already nominated to take his place) as second conductor:

> 4.3.1859
>
> My dear Klindworth,
> Next winter I shall go to New York for 5 months. German 'Elite-Oper'. Performances of my operas. They seem to pay well. I am considering the

affair more and more seriously and have sent them my terms which include, as a main condition, your appointment as second conductor, for a fee of 10,000 francs, i.e. 2,000 dollars, for five months, while I would conduct my operas only. . . . I would be glad of your company; the journey, too, would be less tedious. I really look forward to accepting, provided agreement can be reached on the main condition.

(RWF 248)

Several thousand dollars and a travelling companion – an agreeable prospect. Wagner hates being alone when he is not working. He needs love and admiration. He likes to have people around him who can provide these. But now he must disappoint Klindworth:

28.4.1859

My dearest Klindworth,
I have to tell you that the Americans have turned me down. Although they have made a counter-proposal which can still be talked and thought over, this would only concern myself, as they already have their permanent conductor, Anschütz. He would direct the other operas, as my second conductor, so they could not possibly appoint a third one. I would be very sorry indeed if you should have counted too seriously on their readiness to fulfil my wish, and I hope that this negative decision will not cause you too much disappointment. I myself shall probably drop the whole affair. It reminds me rather too much of London!

(RWF 249)

His Dantesque experience of 1855 makes a timely reappearance in his memory and mutes any disappointment he might otherwise have felt. On 18 June he writes to Klindworth:

No further news from America. The whole thing seems to be evaporating. I hope fate will have spared me that calamity, otherwise I might have yielded to the lure of the lucre. (RWF 251)

His own misgivings, moreover, have been compounded by his friend Liszt, who advises him to stop toying with overseas projects:

14.5.1859

Quite honestly, I do not think much of your American ideas, and I would fear New York might prove even more nightmarish to you than London. (BWL II 253)

Fifteen years pass before his thoughts turn seriously to America again. There is insufficient capital for the Festspielhaus. Dexter Smith, editor of the New York *Staatszeitung*, is interested in Wagner, who now submits a request:

> Bayreuth, August 1874
>
> I am obliged to you for the interest which, as I learn from your newspaper, you accord my works, and I am glad to be able to explain my ideas to you. Our German theatres show at present every type of opera, Italian, French and German, which they perform every night of the week. I am convinced that under those circumstances the development of a genuine style and of a real dramatic art is an impossibility, and it is for that reason that I undertook the building of an opera house where singers and orchestral players meet once a year, for the specific purpose of presenting to German audiences a series of performances whose standard of excellence would show what German art can be like. . . . I do not think that Germany can take particular pride in the fact that America has to support me. . . . I would be most obliged to you and to the American public, if your widely read newspaper succeeded in establishing an American fund for supporting my undertaking.
>
> (Bayreuther Festspielführer 1924, 222–3)

America reacts like Germany, negatively. They leave it to the King of Bavaria to safeguard the Festspielhaus. After the 1876 opening, however, even the King's generosity is unlikely to cope with the accumulated debts, and Wagner asks Friedrich Feustel, prominent member of the Festspiel council, to solicit subscriptions from likely supporters all over the world, to save the Bayreuth undertaking:

> 13.5.1877
>
> If this, too, should fail, I am determined to accept Ullmann's American offer. That would mean the sale of my property in Bayreuth; I would then cross the ocean, with my whole family, and Germany will have seen the last of me. (BB 262)

King Ludwig is informed of Wagner's plan to emigrate and is flabbergasted:

> June 1877
>
> O those tiresome money matters! I was grieved when Düfflipp reported to me that you were intending to sell your Bayreuth property and to emigrate to America! I implore you, by the love and friendship which has united us all these years, to abandon this *dreadful* plan. All Germans would be indelibly stained, were they to allow the departure of their

greatest man, and were they not prepared to starve, in order to sustain their supreme genius in their fatherland. For myself, my grief would be so great, so overwhelming as to poison, indeed to extinguish for ever all my joy in living! . . . Your roses will not grow on America's sterile soil, where selfishness, lovelessness and Mammon hold sway. I wish and hope with all my heart that you will return from Bad Ems to my Bavaria, invigorated and with fresh hope for a sunny future. (KL III 103–4)

The royal prostration suits Wagner well. Will Ludwig rescue Bayreuth for a second time, and therewith ransom his friend for the greater glory of the fatherland? He hurries to inform the King:

22.6.1877

I am sorry, my dearly beloved friend, that this report has reached you prematurely. I have to confirm, however, that after the London disappointment – which I had foreseen – the only feasible last resort is emigration to America. I fail to see how I can satisfy my festival creditors, other than by liquidating all my Bayreuth assets. In any case, this would be the first step; the next entails giving over one gruelling year – in the winter of my troubled life – to obtaining an adequate income; and nobody should expect me to return to a country which has sapped my mental vitality, which has withheld from its fellow countryman all means of existence, and which at the end has let me go with total indifference. (KL III 105)

Ludwig guarantees Bayreuth's survival, and Wagner is able to sacrifice his American dream to the birth of *Parsifal*. He presents the King with the completed Poem and assures him:

23.8.1877

If I should succeed in cheating my stubborn fate out of sufficient leisure for finishing my *Parsifal*, I would celebrate my final victory over life. No consideration for external circumstances impels me towards this goal, for it goes without saying that this 'Bühnenweihfestspiel' [stage consecration festival] will not be handed over to our well-endowed Court and Municipal theatres. Only a few will see this work; its joyous destiny will be to please him who once was gracious enough to reawaken in me its slumbering seeds. (KL III 108)

Parsifal must be composed, and that can be accomplished only in Europe, the continent of Chrétien de Troyes and of Wolfram von Eschenbach, the original creators of the medieval *Parzival* poem. As it turns out, it will be accomplished in that little town in northern Franconia, Bayreuth, where a farsighted town council has donated the plot for his future Festspielhaus. It is there, Wagner now knows, that his *Parsifal* belongs. King Ludwig appreciates this:

> 9.8.1878
> I fully understand and sympathise with your decision to safeguard the spiritual character of *Parsifal*, your Bühnenweihfestspiel, whose words alone are heavenly, this profound work which you will never wish to leave to the mercy and profanation of the ordinary stage. (KL III 132)

One year later, Wagner again insists on the unique character of this work and its exclusive reservation for Bayreuth, when he advises the King:

Stage set for Metropolitan Opera production of Parsifal. *This was almost identical to that used in the 'exclusive' Bayreuth production 21 years earlier*

> 25.8.1879
> I must say it again and again that handing over *this* work to our municipal theatre audiences, with their late comers, early leavers, with their banging of seats and their air of boredom, would be as sinful as the desecration of the Eleusinian mysteries. (KL III 159)

The *Parsifal* score is making fine progress and America seems forgotten. In January 1880 he moves with his family to Naples, and suddenly we read in Cosima's diary:

1.2.80

> . . . after a tolerable night. He wants to go to America (Minnesota), to establish a stage school and settle in a house, for the asking price of one million dollars. He would dedicate *Parsifal* to them and perform it over there; his present position in Germany has become intolerable. I have not seen him for years as I saw him yesterday. Today his eye infection has got worse and troubles him. Again and again he talks of America, calls it the only continent on the map of the world which he would be pleased to see; 'That part of the world is to other countries what the ancient Greeks were to other races.' He calculates the whole enterprise, while we sit in the dark because of his eyes. (CWT II 486–7)

So, is *Parsifal* no longer to be reserved for Bayreuth alone? For one million dollars it will be dedicated to the Americans? Is this a sudden caprice? No, this time he is quite serious, and a few days later he makes a detailed report to Dr Newell S. Jenkins, his American dentist who had treated him in Bayreuth:

8.2.1880

> I do not think it impossible that I shall decide to emigrate to America, together with my whole family and with my last work. Since I am no longer young, it would require a very substantial offer from across the ocean. An association would have to be formed which would endow me with a capital sum of one million dollars, to reimburse me for my settling in America and for all related expenses. One half of that sum would be used for purchasing a house and grounds in a climatically suitable part of the United States, the other half would be invested in a state bank, with an annual yield of five per cent. With that, America would have bought me for all time. This association would also have to raise the funds for the annual festivals which would present all my works, one by one, in model performances, beginning with the first showing of *Parsifal*, my latest work which I shall not allow to be given elsewhere until then. The aforementioned capital sum would also be regarded as remuneration for all my future enterprises, whether as producer, conductor or as creative artist, and any future compositions would belong, without further fees, to the American nation, for all time.

(Die Welt: 14.12.1975)

*　　　*　　　*

This epilogue to the American saga ends as abruptly as it began. The price is too high even for the Americans, and Wagner resolves to give Germany another chance. In his next letter to the King he says nothing about the United States, but reiterates his maxim, *Parsifal* for Bayreuth:

> 28.9.1880
> I really could not blame our church authorities, if they raised their quite legitimate objections to spectacles which showed the most sacred mysteries upon the same boards on which, the day before and the day after, frivolity reigns supreme, to please a public which is attracted only by frivolity. I have accordingly entitled my *Parsifal* a 'Bühnen*weih*fest-spiel', a stage consecration festival drama. Therefore a stage must be consecrated for this work, and this can only be the stage in the unique Festspielhaus in Bayreuth. There and there alone may *Parsifal* be performed. Never shall *Parsifal* be offered to any other stage for the public's entertainment. (KL III 182–3)

Wagner completes the score of *Parsifal* in January 1882, its first performance takes place in the Bayreuth Festspielhaus on 26 July of that year, and seven months later he is fated to die, not in Minnesota, but in Venice.

VIII

BOUNTEOUS PROTECTOR AND BELOVED FRIEND

PROLOGUE

King Ludwig I 1786–1868

After a series of financial disasters, Lola Montez, the Irish dancer, arrives destitute in Bavaria.

The King receives Lola Montez in his Munich residence.

She becomes the King's favourite and is showered with valuable presents.

The King puts an imposing Munich house at her disposal.

Lola Montez provokes the resentment of the cabinet, the press and the population.

The King refuses to give her up.

Ministers advocating the dancer's banishment are dismissed.

The King sends her passionate poems.

The press satirises their relationship.

The King bestows a title on her, Countess von Landsfeld.

The people are so incensed at Lola Montez' privileged position that the King fears an insurrection. She has to leave Munich.

Lola settles in Switzerland.

The King consoles himself by building magnificent castles.

1848: The King abdicates.

King Ludwig II 1845–1886

After a series of financial disasters, Richard Wagner, Saxon composer, arrives destitute in Bavaria.

The King receives Richard Wagner in his Munich residence.

He becomes the King's favourite and is showered with valuable presents.

The King puts an imposing Munich house at his disposal.

Richard Wagner provokes the resentment of the cabinet, the press and the population.

The King refuses to give him up.

Ministers advocating the composer's banishment are dismissed.

The King sends him passionate poems.

The press satirises their relationship.

The King bestows the Maximilian Order for the Arts and Sciences on Wagner.

The people are so incensed at Richard Wagner's privileged position that the King fears an insurrection. He has to leave Munich.

Wagner settles in Switzerland.

The King consoles himself by building magnificent castles.

1886: The King abdicates.

It is spring 1864, and Wagner is at the end of his tether. The sumptuous house at Penzing, near Vienna, is costing him immense sums of money which he does not have. His cheques are being returned to him, and for the second time in his life – the first was twenty-five years ago, in Paris – he seems to be heading for the debtors' prison. He escapes from his creditors to Munich where he pens his epitaph:

Hier liegt Wagner, der nichts geworden,	*Here lies he whom the world forsook.*
Nicht einmal Ritter vom lumpigsten Orden;	*Universities forswear him,*
nicht einen Hund hinter'm Ofen entlockt' er,	*Bestowers of titles cannot bear him.*
Universitäten nicht mal 'nen Dokter.	*In short, he tempted no dog from his nook.*
	(GW 36: 25.3.1864)

His creditors trace him to Munich and he finds temporary shelter in Switzerland, with Frau Eliza Wille in Mariafeld. On 5 April 1864 he has a strange premonition. He writes to Mathilde Maier:

> Last night I had a feverish dream. Frederick the Great summoned me to his court to join Voltaire. (MM 149)

Wagner waits for the dream to become reality. Frederick the Great is dead, but other princes live. Nothing happens. On 8 April Peter Cornelius receives Wagner's distress signal:

> *One light* must arise. *One man* must reveal himself to me, one who will *help* resolutely, and *help* now. (RWF 372)

The hunters are catching up. Wagner assures Dr Josef Standhartner, a Viennese friend:

> I shall pay for everything in full and with interest. I shall pay in twelve months' time. But – the last penny will also be my last breath. . . . From the Germans I cannot hope for a single florin to improve my present position. . . . One person only could help now – one, and not several – the right one. He does exist, that I know. But where shall I find him? (KL I xxvii–xxviii)

Switzerland is no longer safe, and he moves on to Stuttgart. On 5 May a letter is handed to him:

Honoured Sir,

I have instructed Court Councillor Pfistermeister to discuss a suitable residence with you. Rest assured that I will do everything in my power to make amends for your adverse circumstances; they are now a thing of the past. The demeaning cares of everyday life I will banish from your soul for ever, and I will procure for you the peace you must have, so that your genius may be free to spread its mighty pinions in the ethereal regions of your heavenly art! You are not aware of this, but from my tenderest youth onwards you have been *the sole source of all my joys*, my friend who spoke to my heart in a way no other person could, my best

King Ludwig II, aged 18

teacher and guide. I shall show you my gratitude for all this to the best of my ability. O how I have looked forward to the day when I could do this! . . .

> Your Friend Ludwig, King of Bavaria.   (KL I 11)

Written twenty-four hours after the first meeting between Wagner and the King.

The miracle has happened, 'the right one', not yet nineteen years old, has revealed himself. Wagner returns from the palace and regales Frau Wille with the royal news:

> I should be the most ungrateful person alive, were I not to tell you immediately of my infinite good fortune! You know that the young King of Bavaria has sent for me. Today I was taken to him. Alas, he is so fair and intelligent, so sensitive and noble, that I must fear his life may be doomed to fade away in this coarse world, like some brief dream of celestial existence. He loves me with the intensity and ardour of first love. He knows everything about me and understands me like my own soul. He wants me always to be near him, to work, to rest, to perform my works, and he will give me all I need for that. I am to complete the *Nibelungen*, and he will have it performed the way I want it performed. I am to be entirely my own master, not his Kapellmeister, nothing but myself and his friend. . . . I am to have whatever I need, so long as I stay with him. What do you say to that? What do you say? Is it not beyond belief? Can it be anything but a dream? (WB 489–90: 4.5.1864)

It is much more. More even than Wagner's dream in which he was summoned to join Voltaire at the court of Frederick the Great. At Ludwig's court Wagner is to be the King's sole companion and mentor.

The young man – he has been King for two months – listens enraptured, as his new friend guides him through his works and acquaints him with the adversities of his life. Ludwig could well have felt as Desdemona had when wooed by Othello:

> *My story being done,*
> *She gave me for my pains a world of sighs.*
> *She swore in faith 'twas strange: 'twas passing strange,*
> *'Twas pitiful: 'twas wondrous pitiful.*
> . . .
> *She lov'd me for the dangers I had pass'd,*
> *And I lov'd her, that she did pity them.*
>
> (*Othello*, Act 1, Scene 3)

For Ludwig who sees himself as the divine agent of salvation, the step from Desdemona to Parsifal is inevitable:

Be whole, be stainless, be redeemed. (Act 3)

Henceforth it will be Ludwig's mission to bestow material riches on Wagner, so that Wagner may bestow spiritual riches upon the world. He pays his debts, puts a comfortable town house at his disposal, places him on his salary list and he gives him royal presents:

1864	Diamond ring
	Portrait of King Ludwig II
	Grandfather clock with Minnesinger*
1865	Chalice with *Lohengrin* decoration
	Tannhäuser water colour painting
	Lohengrin statuette
	Hohenschwangau† water colour painting
1866	Chalice with *Tannhäuser* painting
	Walther von Stolzing‡ marble statuette
1867	Chalice with *Fliegender Holländer* painting
	Bechstein grand piano with built-in writing desk
	Siegfried marble statuette
1868	*Tristan* marble statuette
	Lohengrin marble statuette
1869	*Tannhäuser* marble statuette
	Fliegender Holländer marble statuette
1870	A horse
	Water colour copies of Michael Echter's thirty Nibelungen frescoes
1875	Bronze bust of King Ludwig II
1879	*Parsifal* ivory statuette
	Ornamental centre-piece
1880	Hohenschwangau bronze paperweight
	Renaissance cabinet of ebony and silver
1881	Wall hangings and wall candelabra
1882	Two black swans
	Silken textiles

* Medieval German troubadours.
† The district in which King Ludwig built his castle Neuschwanstein.
‡ Young Franconian knight in *Die Meistersinger von Nürnberg.*

Both giver and receiver have been castigated for giving so generously and for receiving so willingly, but one should remember that the sum total of Ludwig's presents to Wagner over nineteen years fell far short of the cost of decorating and furnishing his own bedroom at Schloss Herrenchiemsee.

The King's cabinet, however, shows little enthusiasm for such munificence. His minister of finance would have seen nothing out of the ordinary in opening an expense account for a royal mistress. But for an artist, and what is more, for an artist from Saxony! As for the Saxon, he too is a liberal donor, and his gifts to the King will probably outlast all the silken textiles, paintings and wall hangings. Wagner gives Ludwig:

1864	Essay, 'On State and Religion'
	Der fliegende Holländer
	Huldigungsmarsch
1865	*Parsifal* (prose sketch)
	Die Feen
	Das Rheingold
1866	*Das Liebesverbot*
	Die Walküre
1867	*Die Meistersinger von Nürnberg*
1868	*Rienzi*

These are his tangible gifts. It is left to their correspondence to reveal Wagner's influence on the King's spirit and intellect.

In the years between 1864 and 1883 they write to each other:

	Letters	Telegrams	Poems
Wagner to Ludwig	262	67	15
Ludwig to Wagner	177	76	2

The effusiveness of their salutations and letter endings is the measure of their reciprocal enthusiasm. For example:

KING LUDWIG II

	Salutation	*Letter ending*
14.8.1865	Basis of my existence, delight of my life, dearly beloved Friend!	For ever and beyond, Your loyal Ludwig.
6.11.1866	My dearly beloved only friend!	Until death, Your loyal Ludwig.
9.3.1867	My only beloved Friend, my redeemer, my god!	Your own Ludwig.

12.8.1876	Great, incomparable, infinitely beloved Friend!	Firm as a rock and eternally Your own true Ludwig.

RICHARD WAGNER

6.10.1866	O my dear, dear wonderful and most beloved of all beings!	Blissfully happy, Your subject Richard Wagner.
22.11.1866	My Champion and Protector! Most beloved Friend! My sweet Lord!	Warmest greetings from my soul to yours! Eternally Your loyal Richard Wagner.
7.3.1867	My dear, most beautiful and final link with the world! My sweet Friend!	With loving loyalty until death, the old magician Richard Wagner.

The present age is out of tune with such outpourings. They even gave Cosima an uncomfortable feeling:

> Richard is writing to the King. . . . He then reads me the letter which really makes my heart ache. I wish he could find a different tone for this correspondence, one which would sound more truthful, without losing its warmth. (CWT I 74: 21/22.3.1869)

The poems in which the King and Wagner pay homage to each other demonstrate that as a versifier Ludwig is the composer's equal. Wagner is a worthier poet in his librettos than on notepaper. He rhymes:

To My King

My royal liege, my patron and my keeper
Whose gentle mildness fills my heart with joy,
O let me plummet deep and ever deeper
In quest for words of praise without alloy!
Then let me mount up where the path grows steeper,
And grant me strength such wisdom to employ
That I may find true words of acclamation,
Expressing my most humble veneration.

Starnberg, 16.9.1864 (KL I 22)

Ludwig reciprocates in like heartbeat and metre:

To My Friend

In times to come the world will sing your praises,
From furthest orient to occident,
And hail the brilliance that within you blazes,
You Master, glorious, omnipotent.
No other name a rival echo raises,
You are yourself your lasting monument.
Your sacred name transcends all other mortals,
For you will enter the celestial portals.

Ludwig. 19.9.1864 (KL I 24)

Wagner's numerous private audiences with the monarch soon begin to displease first the ministers of the crown, then the newspapers and their readers. Wagner is either unaware of the thin ice underfoot, or he chooses to ignore it. He has his portrait painted for the King. The artist is Friedrich Pecht, an old acquaintance from the Paris days. The portrait's strange history begins on 30 January 1865, when Wagner has it delivered at the palace. Ludwig thanks him immediately:

My dear Friend,
I have just returned from my walk and find the glorious picture! What a surprise for me! How wonderfully true to life! Please accept my warmest, most heartfelt gratitude! . . .

Until death, Ludwig.   (KL I 52)

Three weeks later, the *Augsburger Allgemeine Zeitung* publishes an anonymous article – in fact it was by one Oskar von Redwitz – which claims that Wagner was expecting to be paid for his 'present':

Richard Wagner has completely fallen out of favour with the King. Our monarch, so appreciative of the arts, has now decided to make a clear distinction between his love for Wagner's music and the man himself. . . . As for the royal favour, Wagner has tried it sorely with his constant, incredibly excessive demands on the generosity of his illustrious protector. To cap it all, Wagner has now had his portrait painted by his friend Friedrich Pecht, without the Court's instructions, and has left the unbidden picture in the royal antechamber, together with his bill for one thousand gulden. . . . What we are now asking for is just this, that Richard Wagner should not be so misguided as to overstep the limits now clearly set for his demands, that he and *his friends here* should understand that they must open their eyes and stop

247

placing themselves between the people of Bavaria and their beloved monarch. . . . If Wagner disregards our advice, we should have to hail the day when he and his friends will be well and truly *overthrown* and will turn their back on our dear, loyal Munich. For however celebrated Wagner and his music may be, we must proclaim something that is a hundred times more important – our love for our King. (KL IV 48–51)

It would be unwise and indeed out of character for Wagner not to hit back immediately. Three days later, the *Augsburger Allgemeine* publishes his riposte:

His Majesty the King of Bavaria has magnanimously summoned me to Munich, to enable me – after much toil and trouble – to reap and enjoy the fruits of an arduous artistic life, without fear of finding my privacy and working hours disturbed. My only contact with the world in this state of seclusion is my readiness to receive instructions from my illustrious protector. But now my peace is being shattered by a storm of public accusations. . . . It has been my experience in London and Paris that the journals at that time ridiculed my artistic endeavours quite mercilessly. My works were trampled upon and hissed off the stage. It is left to the country which respects my works and credits my writings and other undertakings with seriousness of purpose, and regards them as matters of real significance, it is left to that country to revile in public my own person, my good name, my character as a citizen and my domestic life. . . . As for the Pecht portrait for which I am supposed to have presented a bill for 1,000 gulden, that is pure fantasy and totally untrue, as your correspondent will find on asking the appropriate court authorities. . . . Why did nobody ask for my evidence about the true nature of my relationship with His Majesty and about its circumscribed scope, which is the same today as it has been from the first day onwards? Why attack our beloved Sovereign instead, and threaten him with imminent ill fortune? *It is not I to whom my accuser is answerable – it is to the general public he must reply.*
       Munich, 20.2.1865   Richard Wagner.   (KL IV 52–6)

Who is telling the truth? Wagner had attempted, on 15 February, to acquaint Court Councillor von Pfistermeister with the facts of the case. In that letter he shows his old flair for appearing to explain matters, while clouding the issue with a mare's nest of complex data, and employing the labyrinthine prose which he always brings into play for such contingencies:

From your most recent communication, my dear friend, it has become clear to me that His Majesty means to confer the singular, highly significant distinction upon me of accepting my portrait as a reverential present. . . . It was a misunderstanding, created by my own modesty, which had led me to answer your question as to the portrait painter's remuneration, in what seemed to be the only manner open to me, namely that if our Most Gracious King were desirous of purchasing the picture, this wish would have to be regarded as being tantamount to his

The Pecht portrait of Wagner

request of an earlier date and, that being so, it would be a matter of convenience to advise the cabinet's finance department simply to enter into the usual purchasing negotiations with the artist. It has not been made plain to me that I could nourish the hope of having the portrait accepted as a reverential present. . . . I now see my irresolution happily confounded, for your communication has at long last informed me of our Gracious King's preference for indeed regarding this portrait not as a commissioned purchase, but as a reverential present. This acceptance fills me with truly joyful pride which, alas, has been sorely clouded by the spreading into the wide world of the most odious rumours of shameless demands on my own part. Suffice it for us to recapitulate this course of events, and I can rest assured in the knowledge that you will do all that is necessary to refute these calumnies which are an effrontery not only to me but to my Friend. As I see it, this can only be done by an unequivocal declaration, coming from the appropriate authorities, to the effect that the rumours regarding the presentation of my portrait to His Majesty are completely untrue. (KL IV 43–4)

Attempting to plot a route through this maze, one might arrive at this:
1. Wagner has his portrait painted by Pecht.
2. He discusses the proposed gift to the King with Pfistermeister.
3. Pfistermeister, feeling himself supplanted in Ludwig's confidence by Wagner, senses an opportunity for mischief; he asks what the picture will cost.
4. Wagner is pleasantly surprised. Originally he wanted to present the King with his portrait, but now he is tempted by an unexpected windfall.
5. Pfistermeister has succeeded in tricking him. If Wagner were to accept payment for his 'present', he would fall out of favour with the King, and Bavaria (and Pfistermeister) would be rid of him.
6. Wagner recognises his tactical mistake in time and corrects it, first in his letter to Pfistermeister, then in the *Augsburger Allgemeine*. The result of the contest between fox and snake is a provisional draw.

Wagner receives no payment for his portrait, and in July 1865 he sends Pecht 500 florins. The painter is a generous friend:

I received your cheque yesterday, and I herewith return 100 florins with my thanks. . . . Since we are friends, I regard 400 florins as my fee for the portrait. As I have pointed out to you before, 500 florins would be my fee for any other person. (KL IV 68)

Just as strange are the events that accompany a special gift of 40,000 florins from Ludwig to Wagner. The royal treasurer welcomes the opportunity to land the King's favourite in trouble. He advises Wagner that the money is ready for collection in cash. Wagner sends Cosima. The clerk regrets he has not enough banknotes, so he fills two huge sacks with small silver coins. Cosima is unperturbed. She sends for two hackney-carriages, and escorted by treasury officers she is driven, bag and baggage, through the streets of Munich. Those citizens who missed the spectacle can read about it next morning, while Wagner and Cosima become the most unpopular people in town, a calamity largely offset by two sacksful of silver coinage. The press, though, feeds on the scandal for weeks. In fact, *Der Volksbote* reports a full seven months later:

> Munich, 31.5.1866
>
> 'Allah is Great', say the Mohammedans, and the prophet Richard Wagner has superb digestive organs. It is not a year since the notorious *Madame Hans de Bülow* collected 40,000 florins in those celebrated hansom-cabs for her *friend* (or what?). But what are 40,000 florins? *Madame Hans* can *once again* start hiring cabs, for *the day before yesterday a suit was filed against the selfsame Richard Wagner in connection with unpaid bills to the tune of 26,000 florins*, an affair for which the *Volksbote* has irrefutable evidence. Meanwhile the same *Madame Hans*, who has been known to the public since last December, appropriately enough, as *the carrier pigeon*, resides with her friend (or what?) in Lucerne, where she was also during His Majesty's visit.
>
> (KL IV 146–7)

This is just one sample of the public campaign against Wagner. With the scent of victory in their nostrils, and in the interest of their circulation figures (or what?), the newspapers intensify their coverage. If Wagner keeps quiet now, he will be lost. He had already left Munich in December 1865, when Ludwig had persuaded him to step out of the limelight, and had settled in Tribschen, his new domicile, by Lake Lucerne. Cosima stays alternately with him and with her husband in Munich. These arrangements are of great interest to the press, and its readers have such a detailed knowledge of Wagner's private life that the King is probably the only person who still believes in the myth that the Tribschen couple are merely soul mates. Wagner now requests protection. He writes to his royal friend:

> My King and Beloved Friend,
> In this my hour of need I have one wish only – break your royal silence just for once. Write a letter to my friend Hans von Bülow, expressing your thorough satisfaction with his work, and at the same time voice your royal indignation at the disgraceful treatment accorded him and his

wife by several newspapers of your capital, and give him your permission to publish your letter. . . . Since I must assume that my gracious Friend is far too high above the common hurly-burly of life which we others have to face . . . I have taken it upon myself to write and enclose a suggested draft for such a letter. (KL II 53: 6.6.1866)

Cosima, too, presses her suit and pleads with the King:

> My Royal Lord and Friend,
> I have three children to whom I am in honour bound to convey, untarnished, their father's name. Do not allow the dawning of the day when these children shall revile the love I bear to our friend. For their sake, I beg you, my exalted Friend, write that letter. (KL II 56: 7.6.1866)

Cosima has three children, to be sure, but only the two eldest, Daniela and Blandine, are Bülow's. Isolde is Wagner's child. His 'suggested draft' for the King is a little masterpiece:

> My dear Herr von Bülow,
> Having prevailed upon you, a year and a half ago, to relinquish your post in Berlin for only slight advantages which I was able to offer you at the time, and achieving my desire to see you work, in Munich, side by side with Richard Wagner, towards the realisation of the Master's noble artistic aims which do such honour to the German spirit, nothing could be more distressing to Me to find that My hopes for such developments – which include your own advancement – should have resulted first in hostility towards your person, and more recently in particularly odious and defamatory slanders on the part of a certain section of the Munich press, slanders which make Me fully understand the extent of your rightful indignation. Since I am well aware of your selfless and most honourable conduct and, like the musical citizens of Munich, of your singular artistic achievements, and since I have been able to gain thorough knowledge of your esteemed wife's noble character, – the virtuous lady who with the most sympathetic concern has given cheer and comfort to the man who is her father's friend and her husband's mentor – it is now My responsibility to investigate those inexplicable, libellous accusations and, having established a true picture of the whole disgraceful situation, bring the offenders to justice with ruthless severity.
> (KL II 54: 6.6.1866)

Ludwig accepts the draft and assures Wagner in a telegram:

Cordial thanks for letters received this morning. May we succeed in converting the friend's grief into joy. Letter to B. dispatched today without any amendments. (KL II 60: 11.6.1866)

The draft thus becomes a royal proclamation which Bülow publishes in the Munich *Neueste Nachrichten*. The readers are amused and take waggish delight in their virgin monarch's innocence. *Der Volksbote* bares his teeth:

We cannot, of course, permit ourselves to examine and discuss a letter written by the King's own hand. It is for that reason that we think it best to issue just one straightforward comment – we stand by every word we have printed on Herr Hans von Bülow and Madame Hans von Bülow.

(KL II 55: 22.6.1866)

How much longer can the King remain ignorant? Does he have some inkling of circumstances which he cannot bring himself to contemplate?

In February 1867 Cosima presents Wagner with his second child, Eva. Ten months later King Ludwig writes to Düfflipp, his Court Secretary:

. . . should that sorry rumour be true after all, that report which I could never permit myself to believe, should it really be adultery! – then beware! (KL V 204: 13.12.1867)

Who should beware – Wagner, the King, both? Here, Ludwig stares into the abyss. If his idol has feet of clay, if the King has been deluded, then beware, King and kingdom, for the step from delusion to insanity is a short one for the susceptible monarch whose own leaning towards handsome young men has caused him periodic bouts of mortification which he has been able to counterbalance, until now, only by his faith in Master Richard, his friend and his god. Half a year later he writes to him:

I believe with unshakeable confidence in your faultlessness, but in nobody else's. All attempts to separate me from you have had the opposite effect. My life has become ever more interwoven with yours, so to withdraw from you and from the spirit of your divine creations would mean insanity or death. (KL II 310: 5.6.1870)

It has to be said that Wagner and Cosima manipulate the King. But before one calls such behaviour shameless, one might profitably consider what Gottfried von Strassburg wrote, eight centuries earlier, in his *Tristan*, Wagner's main source for *Tristan und Isolde*. Gottfried tells of Tristan's courtship, on his uncle's behalf, of the Irish princess Isolde, their sea journey to King Marke's court in Cornwall, their sharing of the love potion and the surrender of their minds and bodies to one another. He relates how both of them betray the King who is Tristan's friend and kinsman, because being spellbound they are no longer subject to the laws of loyalty, but to the sway of love. The modern reader may be able to share the reaction of Gottfried's own contemporaries, who endorsed the view that Frau Minne, the manifestation of Love, must and will be served first. True, Isolde deceives her husband, the King. True, Tristan manipulates his royal uncle and loses his honour in the process. All for the love of Love, which is more potent than Honour and Loyalty. As Gottfried puts it:

> *What then can Virtue do or say,*
> *When Minne holds her mighty sway?*
> (Gottfried von Strassburg: *Tristan*, ll. 12,447–8)

In *Tristan und Isolde*, Wagner carries this further. The lovers have been false to King Marke, who reproaches his nephew:

> *Where fled allegiance,*
> *When Tristan can betray?*
> *Where now have faith*
> *And honour gone,*
> *When Tristan let them go?*
> (Act 2, Scene 3)

Tristan does not really evade the answer when he replies:

> *O Sovereign, that*
> *Can I never tell you,*
> *And what you ask*
> *Can never find an answer.*

Everything that can be said about their betrayal and their love has already been heard in the music of the previous scene, which interprets Tristan's words:

> *Live the night of death,*
> *Cherish it too,*
> *Learn as it lisps*
> *Its secrets to you.*

> *Dissembling daylight,*
> *Crown and fame,*
> *Riches and rule,*
> *Bright honour's name –*
> *As dust in sunlight's shimmer,*
> *Must fade without a glimmer.*
>   (Act 2, Scene 2)

One begins to comprehend what is all but incomprehensible, and one hesitates now to call Tristan's conduct by its proper name.

In the thirteenth century Gottfried von Strassburg's contemporaries accepted the shared love potion as explanation and excuse for the lovers' subsequent behaviour. The age of Freud and Jung can perhaps more easily regard the potion as a symbol for a total severance from the prevailing code of conduct; the supremacy of the individual in the face of whose needs the code becomes invalid. Does it make sense to absolve Isolde and Tristan, while condemning Cosima and Wagner? The emphasis has shifted, the need remains the same.

In 1876, Ludwig hears *Der Ring des Nibelungen* at Bayreuth and he confesses:

> I find it impossible to describe to you, my adored friend, the impressions I carried with me from visiting the Bayreuth Festival performances which, together with our fortunate reunion, have made me blissfully happy. I came with high expectations, but the highest of them have been surpassed by a *wide, wide margin*. I was so deeply moved that you must have thought me taciturn or morose! O you know how to convulse the depths of the soul, and your conquering light has thawed the crust of ice which had begun to form around my heart and my mind, as the result of so many sad experiences. (KL III 82: 12.8.1876)

Thus, Ludwig continues to reap the harvest which he had sowed over a decade ago. At that time when his friendship with his adored composer was still young, he was already determined to serve him, and when he writes to Cosima about this, it is as one acolyte communing with another:

> You write, highly esteemed lady, that I have worked a miracle. Rather let us say, it would have been sinful not to have done what I have done. It would have been a crime not to have rescued Wagner, a crime not to love him from the bottom of one's heart. (KL IV 77: 26.8.1865)

Later, he reiterates to Wagner:

It should hardly be necessary to assure you once again that everything I possess is yours also. I always feel that a higher power bestowed all those means on me, so that I could be of service to you, as though you were my feudal lord who is entitled to demand back what is his own. (KL II 229: 2.6.1868)

But even the adoring Ludwig takes mild exception to Wagner's antisemitism:

It is very good, beloved friend, that you are not going to discriminate between Gentiles and Jews when it comes to performing your exalted, sacred work [*Parsifal*]. Nothing is more odious, more disagreeable than such antagonism. Whatever our religions may be, fundamentally we are all human beings and as such we are brothers, are we not?
(KL III 226: 11.10.1881)

The pragmatic nature of Wagner's antisemitism has already been discussed. It is to remain pragmatic, so enabling him to engage Hermann Levi to take charge of the 1882 *Parsifal* performances at Bayreuth, just as, a hundred years later, Wagner's grandson Wolfgang finds it artistically fitting to have the same work conducted by James Levine.

The King's preference for attending performances in an otherwise empty opera house has been a matter of puzzlement. His pained aversion to sharing a room, a theatre or walks in the country, borders on the pathological and has often been seen as an advance symptom of his later insanity. And yet, there must be many perfectly sane people who would prefer not to share a performance of, say, *Tristan und Isolde*, with coughers, programme rustlers, early leavers and eaters of chocolate. In Ludwig's language:

I want to steep myself in your sublime, heavenly work, and I will never consider receiving other royal personages, loathsome as they are, and listening to their empty chatter or doing the honneurs [sic]. I remember only too well the *Lohengrin* performance of last December, when it was impossible to avoid my fellow princes – that was, of course, the end of my evening's delight. For heaven's sake, nothing of that kind in Bayreuth! (KL III 71–2: 11.1.1876)

Seven months later:

I would ask you to have a partition installed, to screen me from other royalty who may be present, and to ensure, if necessary with the help of the police, that they stay away from me in the intervals. Last December I found it unavoidable to share a performance of *Lohengrin* with my mother and with the Archduchess Elisabeth and her children – it was

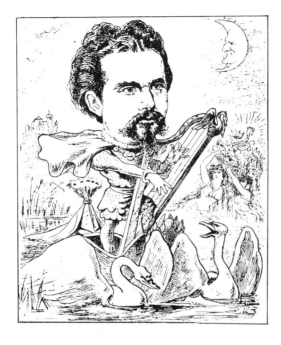

Viennese caricature showing King Ludwig as Lohengrin and Wagner as the Man in the Moon

dreadful. As the *Ring des Nibelungen* surpasses *Lohengrin*, my torture would be proportionately more intolerable, if I had to be with people and make small talk. (KL III 83: *12.8.1876*)

At times, Ludwig's longing for Wagner's works becomes so irresistible that he prefers the creation to the creator. He is, in fact, capable of sacrificing the one for the other. He wishes to have *Das Rheingold* performed, although the *Ring* tetralogy is not yet finished. Wagner's artistic conscience objects to a premature staging – the *Ring* is indivisible – and the King boils with frustrated indignation. He informs Court Secretary von Düfflipp:

> Wagner and the whole theatrical rabble are behaving in a truly criminal and shameless manner. This is an open defiance of my orders which I will not tolerate. On no account must Richter be allowed to conduct another performance and he is to be dismissed immediately; any appeal

257

will be rejected. The theatre folk have to obey My orders and not Wagner's sudden notions. . . . Were Wagner to get away with his abominable intrigues, the whole lot of them would grow ever more impertinent and unscrupulous, until there would be no holding them any longer. This evil must therefore be pulled up by the roots. . . . I have never known such presumption. (KL V 101: 30.8.1869)

Ludwig reinforces this with a telegram to Düfflipp:

An end must be put immediately to the quite unforgivable intrigues by Wagner and his fellows. I herewith give distinct orders for the performance to take place on Sunday. Richter is to be dismissed instantaneously. If W. dares to object once again, his grant is to be revoked for good, and his works are never again to be performed on any Munich stage. (KL V 102: 31.8.1869)

The distraught King hardly notices that he would be the first person to suffer from his rash decree, and in yet another letter to Düfflipp, written immediately after the telegram, he bares his vulnerable heart:

Wagner's wishes should be accommodated as far as possible; on the whole they are justified. Peruse his letter to Me and do everything in your power to deter him from coming to Munich. But there is no need for him to know that this is My wish, otherwise all hell will break loose.
(KL V 102–3: 31.8.1869)

Wagner does not appear in Munich, but hell breaks loose just the same. He addresses a waspish letter to Wüllner, the second choice *Rheingold* conductor (the first choice, Richter, had been dismissed):

Look out and keep your hands off my score, sir, or go to hell! Run along and beat time in glee clubs and choral societies, or if you really must handle opera scores, get yourself one composed by your friend Perfall.* You can tell that fine gentleman to go to the King and make a clean breast of his incompetence, as far as producing my work is concerned. Otherwise I shall light him a bonfire which all his newshound scandalmongers whom he pays from the ill-gotten *Rheingold* profits, will not be able to quench. The two of you need plenty of lessons from me, before you will understand that you understand nothing.
(KL IV 201–2: *September 1869*)

* Karl von Perfall, Intendant of the Munich Court Theatre, composer of several operas.

An artist's impression of Das Rheingold

Wagner is unable to prevent the performance which takes place in September 1869. Ludwig is in his heaven, and Wagner fulminates in Tribschen. Now it is Ludwig's turn to put his own case:

> O God, the craving for your divine work was so strong, so overwhelming! If I have erred, be generous and forgive me. Ah, it was my infinite longing for the first part of the cycle which had already fired me with enthusiasm in my early youth* and which had made me want to die, after drinking in its spirit, its heavenly delights. This made me transgress your command, and I await your rebuke. I detest a lie and I will not try to make excuses, so let me state quite frankly that I admit my error and regret it. . . . My feelings of love and friendship for you are stronger than ever, your ideals are mine, and to be of service to you is my mission on earth. The man does not exist who is capable of wounding me, but when *you* are displeased with me, you deal me a death-blow. O write to me and forgive your friend, for he is aware of his guilt. No, O no! we shall never separate. It would cut me to the quick and I would surrender myself to endless despair. Thoughts of suicide would haunt me. (KL II 290: *November 1869*)

Seventeen years later the King drowns (himself?) in Lake Starnberg. For the present, the friendship survives, but has to face another crisis, for Ludwig can no longer resist his longing for *Die Walküre*. He orders its performance, Wagner objects, and Ludwig cajoles and commands simultaneously:

> Forgive my youthful impetuosity, but I cannot wait until next year for the performance of *Walküre*. O, my longing for it is so irresistible. . . . Very well, find me guilty, condemn me, if you have the heart.
>
> (KL II 305: 2.5.1870)

The first performance takes place, for the King alone, in June 1870, again without the composer's consent. But Wagner swallows his resentment, since his mind is otherwise engaged – two months later he marries Cosima in Lucerne.

As he gets older, Wagner allows Ludwig's munificence to fade from his memory and is able to speak contemptuously of his friend and protector. Cosima notes in her diary:

* He refers to the subject matter, not the music.

[Richard says] It is so humiliating to be dependent on this King; it is a scandal, and I can no longer bear it. (CWT I 422: 27.7.1871)

But what would happen, if the King were to cease being King? Have Wagner and Cosima considered this far more unbearable contingency? They have:

> Visit from Count Bassenheim, who shocks us once again with the news that the King has commissioned a coronation coach with six biblical pictures and six allegories about Louis XIV, for 20,000 gulden. R. says we shall probably soon hear from the Court about sudden insanity or death. We are deeply concerned – we might lose the roof over our heads.
>
> (CWT I 433: 1.9.1871)

There is little profit in analysing the Wagners' lack of any sense of obligation. It was not the Master's gratitude which Ludwig craved but his art.

Wagner does not live to hear the news of Ludwig's insanity, for he dies three years before the King. In the early days of the friendship between the bounteous protector and his beloved friend, Ludwig had composed this epitaph for them both:

> Long after we two will have departed, our achievements will serve as a shining example to posterity. They will delight future centuries, and enthusiasm for God-inspired, immortal art will burn in the hearts of men. (KL I 142: 4.8.1865)

IX

THE BAYREUTH
MIRACLE

*The musicians must not lose a single inch. An orchestra must
not feel cramped, if it is to take pleasure in playing well.
This is more important than anything else.**

Here speaks Wagner, the practical man of the theatre who knows what a
musician needs, and whose Festspielhaus is still a miracle today. The demand
occurs in a letter of April 1872 to Friedrich Feustel, chairman of the Bayreuth
Town Council, and to Theodor Muncker, the mayor, both leading members
of the Festival planning committee. It is doubtful whether any professional
architect could have equalled the amateur's achievement, an acoustically
perfect wooden structure, where the audience is able to concentrate solely on the
action on the stage – the orchestra is invisible and the auditorium is in total
darkness – and can surrender to the ideal blend of voices and instruments,
achieved by architectural features unique to the Festspielhaus. The listener
experiences the aural sensations of a musical fly trapped inside a double bass.

An opera house of his own for his projected *Ring des Nibelungen* and for nothing
else, that is Wagner's ambition at the age of thirty-eight. He is confident that he
will find a stage suitable for his music drama, and if he fails, he will build one.
But will he find a suitable audience?

> A *performance* is unthinkable *before the revolution*. The revolution
> alone can provide me with artists and audiences, for the coming
> revolution is bound to put an end to our *muddled theatrical institutions*.
> It is inevitable that they will all come crashing down. *From the ruins* I
> shall reclaim what I need. I shall erect a theatre by the Rhine, and I shall
> send out invitations to a great dramatic festival. There will be one year's
> preliminary work, and then I shall stage the whole cycle in the course of
> *four* days. With this work I shall acquaint the children of the revolution
> with the meaning of the revolution, with its lofty and great-hearted
> ideals. *Those* audiences will understand me; the present ones cannot.
>
> (SB 783)

This defiant scheme he propounds to Theodor Uhlig, his Dresden friend, on 12
November 1851, only a few years after the abortive Dresden uprising. But twelve
years later he decides that it is within his power to start the revolution in his own

---

* BB 77

music dramas, on his own stage. We read in the *Preface to the Poems of the Stage Festival Play, Der Ring des Nibelungen*:

> It mattered a great deal to me to think of such a performance as being beyond the influence of our established repertoire theatres. I therefore had to consider one of Germany's smaller towns, conveniently situated and capable of accommodating special audiences, a town where there would be no competition with one of the larger permanent theatres, and in which I would not have to rely on a typical city public and its fixed habits. Here I was to build a provisional theatre, as simple as possible, perhaps only a wooden structure, with an interior solely calculated to satisfy artistic needs . . . featuring an amphitheatrical auditorium and enjoying the advantages of an invisible orchestra. In early spring, specially selected eminent dramatic singers from the personnel of German opera houses were to gather there and study my several dramas, without any other artistic activities to distract them. German audiences were to have been invited to assemble on the days appointed for the performances – possibly three in all – which would be open, like our established larger festivals, not to a section of the public of just one town, but to all friends of art from far and near. In midsummer the complete dramatic poem was to be staged, with a preliminary evening for *Rheingold*, and *Walküre*, *Siegfried* and *Götterdämmerung* following on the next three nights. (GS VI 273)

Wagner opts for Bayreuth, a small town, though not really 'conveniently situated', but blessed with shrewd and sympathetic councillors and townspeople who open their hearts and purses to him, confidently expecting – and indeed obtaining – a handsome return in times to come. But where is he to find the 'eminent dramatic singers', prepared to study a work which they might never be required to repeat elsewhere, willing to give up several months' salaries in the process? The *Preface* continues:

> Considering the total lack of operatic style in our German houses, with their almost grotesquely inaccurate performances, there is no hope of finding the essential means for a major undertaking at a single theatre. . . . What no single theatre could offer might, with luck, be realised by a group of artists from various places, who would be summoned to an appointed place for a certain length of time.
>
> (GS VI 274)

This group of artists, together with well over a hundred orchestral players, would require several months' leave of absence from their various establishments. The chances for such a utopian project seem slender, but Wagner succeeds. When the time arrives for calling his singers and players together, some nine years later, they come. Why? Because it is Richard Wagner who calls, and because they feel that what awaits them at Bayreuth will affect their artistic development and will astonish both them and the world. Wagner notifies Feustel:

> 12.4.1872
>
> Singers and orchestral players will *only* get expenses, not 'payment'. Anyone who will not come to me enthusiastically and for the honour of being asked can stay where he is. A singer who will come to me for an absurd *fee*, is of no interest to me. (BB 79)

The building of the Festspielhaus begins, and the invisible orchestra is its key feature. The *Preface*, quoted earlier, states:

> Anyone who intends to gain a true artistic impression from a dramatic performance at one of our opera houses will agree how important this [the invisible orchestra] is, since he is constantly distracted by the activities in the orchestra pit, by the players' motions and the

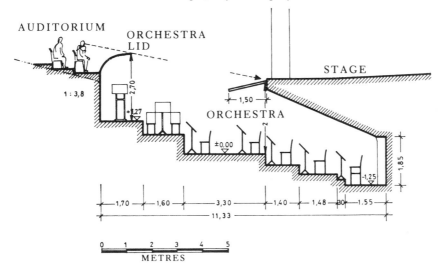

conductor's gestures, which should of course be concealed from view, as are the ropes, cables, framework and boards of the scenery which, as is common knowledge, destroy the illusion when viewed from the wings. Now imagine an orchestra which produces a clear, pure sound, free from those extraneous noises which necessarily accompany the production of an instrumental tone, which is filtered through an acoustic sound screen. Imagine the advantageous position of the singer who can establish personal contact, as it were, with the audience. Imagine also how comfortably the singer will be able to enunciate, and you will agree with the efficiency and superiority of my acoustic-architectonic design. (GS VI 275–6)

Considerable financial backing will be required for translating design into reality. Where is it to come from? The *Preface* provides a prophetic answer:

I can see two possibilities. An association of art lovers, wealthy men and women, could provide the means for the first performance of my work. Considering the notorious small-mindedness of the Germans in such matters, I dare not promise myself that an appeal would succeed. On the other hand, a German prince could easily find the necessary capital, without need for supplementary budgeting. All he has to do is divert the money intended for the upkeep of that wretched public art-institution, his opera house, which only serves to debase and corrupt German musical taste. . . . Will such a prince be found? (GS VI 280–1)

That prince will indeed be found, together with the singers, the orchestra and the audiences.

After laying the foundation stone of his Festspielhaus on his fifty-ninth birthday, 22 May 1872, Wagner undertakes an arduous search for the singers of his *Ring* cycle. The itinerary of the six months between November 1872 and April 1873 is awesome:

Würzburg – Frankfurt – Darmstadt – Mannheim – Darmstadt – Stuttgart – Strasbourg – Wiesbaden – Mainz – Cologne – Düsseldorf – Hanover – Bremen – Dessau – Leipzig – Bayreuth – Dresden – Berlin – Hamburg – Schwerin – Berlin – Bayreuth – Cologne – Kassel – Leipzig – Bayreuth.

In September 1873 Anton Bruckner visits Wagner in Bayreuth and tries to obtain his permission to dedicate one of his symphonies to him. Much later, in 1884, Bruckner – his heart still palpitating with the memory – relates the events of his meetings with Wagner to Hans von Wolzogen. His letter characterises the writer, but possibly to a greater extent the venerated 'Meister', the object of Bruckner's extraordinary devotion. What kind of man is he who commands such adoration and who reduces one of the greatest composers, eleven years after the event, to stammering self-abasement? Bruckner writes to Wolzogen:

My Lord Baron,
It was about the beginning of September 1873 (Crown Prince Friedrich was in Bayreuth at that time), when I begged the Meister to be allowed to show him my Second Symphony in C minor and the Third in D minor. He of Blessed Memory refused, because he was pressed for time (building of the theatre) and said he was unable to scrutinise the scores there and then, since even the *Nibelungen* had had to be put aside. When I replied, 'Meister, I have no right to rob you of even a quarter of an hour, and I only thought that with the Meister's acute discernment, a short glance at the themes would be enough for the Meister to judge the nature of the work,' the Meister patted me on the shoulder and said, 'Come with me.' He took me into the salon and looked at the Second Symphony. 'Good, good,' he said, but he seemed to find it a little unadventurous (for in Vienna they had made me rather nervous about it).* So he turned to the Third Symphony (D minor) and remarked, 'Look at this! Well, well! Well, well!' Then he said, 'Leave the score with me, I will take a closer look after lunch' (it was 12 o'clock). I was considering  whether I should make my request, and Wagner said I could. Very shyly and with a pounding heart I said to my dearly beloved Meister, 'Meister, I have something on my mind, but I dare not say it!' The Meister said, 'Out with it, you know how fond I am of you.' I then made my request, but only in case the Meister should be fairly pleased with my work, since I did not wish to desecrate His Illustrious Name. The Meister said, 'This evening, at 5 o'clock, you are invited to Wahnfried. You will find me there, and by that time I shall have looked carefully over the D minor Symphony. That will be the time for us to discuss this matter.' I had just come from the theatre site and arrived at Wahnfried at 5 o'clock, when the Meister of Meisters hurried towards me with open arms, embraced me and said, 'My dear friend, the

---

* His friends kept urging him to revise, and Bruckner complied rather too readily.

dedication is quite in order, your work gives me immensely great pleasure.' For two and a half hours I was fortunate enough to sit beside the Meister, while he discussed musical affairs in Vienna, offered me beer, took me into the garden and showed me his grave!!! Then, blissfully happy, I was asked, or rather permitted to accompany the Meister into the house. The next day he sent me good wishes for a pleasant journey, with the postscript, 'So – where the trumpet announces the theme' . . .

Anno 1882 the Meister, already ailing, took me by the hand and said, 'Rely upon it, I myself will perform the Symphony and all your other works.' I said, 'Oh Meister!', to which the Meister replied, 'Have you been to *Parsifal* yet? How do you like it?' Since His Highness held my hand, I went down on my knees, pressed His Highness' Hand to my lips, kissed it and said, 'Oh Meister, I worship you!!!' Then the Meister said, 'There, there, Bruckner. Good night!!!' These were the Meister's last words to me . . .

My Lord Baron, I beg you to take great care of this! My most precious bequest!!! Until up there!!!

My Lord Baron,
Your most grateful A. Bruckner.

My stomach!!!

(Anton Bruckner: *Gesammelte Briefe*, Regensburg 1924: 166)

In the summer of 1875 Wagner rehearses the *Ring* in the unfinished Festspielhaus, whose opening is planned for the next year. He invites his singers to the rehearsals:

Bayreuth, 14/15.1.1875

From July 1st to August 15th 1875 initial preparatory rehearsals are to be held in Bayreuth. During this period piano rehearsals of *Rheingold* will take place in the first week of July, *Walküre* in the second, *Siegfried* in the third and *Götterdämmerung* in the fourth. From August 1st to 15th these rehearsals will be repeated in shorter sequence, with the orchestra, so that the players can become acquainted with their task. This will also help the soloists to become familiar with the scoring. . . . June and July of next year, 1876, will be devoted to complete general and dress rehearsals of the whole work. By this I mean that, avoiding pressure and fatigue, the separate dramas will be rehearsed daily, with orchestra and full scenery, so that between June 1st and July 15th *Rheingold*, *Walküre*, *Siegfried* and *Götterdämmerung* will be rehearsed in succession, while the period July 15th to 30th will be devoted to rehearsing all four dramas according to requirements. The first performance of the whole work will take place in the first week of August 1876, as follows:

Sunday	The performance of *Rheingold* will begin at 7 o'clock in the evening.
Monday	*Walküre* first act at 4 o'clock in the afternoon, second act at 6, third act at 8. The lengthy intervals should enable the audience to collect their thoughts, strolling in the pleasant surroundings of the theatre, while allowing the artists to rest in the newly constructed secluded garden spaces which adjoin their own dressing rooms.
Tuesday	Similarly, *Siegfried* will begin at 4 o'clock in the afternoon.
Wednesday	*Götterdämmerung.*

The first repetition will take place, in exactly the same manner, in the second week, and the second repetition in the third week in August. . . . May I now ask for your definite confirmation which will enable me to rely on your participation in the performance of my *Bühnenfestspiel*. Will you also please let me know whether you wish to claim expenses and, if so, to what extent. . . . Please note that all participants will have to give up any thoughts of financial gain, and indeed the will to make sacrifices should be taken for granted. . . . I shall appreciate your reply, so that I may know that you will be numbered one of a truly co-operative association of repute which will be undertaking the realisation of a hitherto undreamt of artistic ideal.

(WK 81–4)

After more than a hundred years, the longer music dramas still begin at 4, and artists and audience still enjoy their one-hour intervals in 'secluded garden spaces' and 'strolling in the pleasant surroundings'.

Having summoned his singers, he now writes to his prospective orchestral players:

Bayreuth, January 1875
I herewith invite you to join the orchestra of my festival which is to be

held at Bayreuth, and I presume that our earlier correspondence has acquainted you with the conditions on which the acceptance of your participation depends. You will appreciate, therefore, that I could undertake the formation of so unusual an orchestra as is needed for my purpose, only by counting on the most eminent members of those German court orchestras which enjoy lengthy summer holidays . . . which are so well endowed that they pay their members even during the vacation, thus enabling me to take it for granted that it would be a question here of expenses payable for travel and for board and lodging, but not of an actual fee. I assume therefore that you will devote your artistic performances to my work voluntarily and without reimbursement . . . and I offer you a monthly living allowance of 60 thaler, free lodging with a respectable family and a second class rail return ticket. . . . Since this is a formal invitation, I shall refrain from stressing the importance of your highly valued participation in the performances of my work, preferring to reserve my cordial greetings for the hour of our first meeting. But I salute you now, gratefully appreciating your

Adolf Menzel drawing of Wagner rehearsing on the stage at Bayreuth

willingness, so greatly to my honour, to further my undertaking as a true artistic collaborator. (WK 84–7)

On 1 July 1875 Wagner begins his six weeks of rehearsals. In the next year he rehearses from 3 June to 9 August, and on 12 August he opens the Festspielhaus to the world. The young Felix Mottl, future Bayreuth conductor and opera director at Munich, assists on and behind the stage.* He opens his diary for the year 1876 with a credo:

> The Bayreuth year! The most important one in my development as an artist, it decides my fate for the rest of my life. I have been fortunate enough to be allowed personal contact with Richard Wagner for three whole months, and I was able to learn from him whatever an enthusiastic pupil can learn from the greatest of masters. Everything I know I owe to this Bayreuth apprenticeship. (NW 189)

Mottl describes how, assisted by two colleagues, he teaches the Rhinemaidens to swim:

> In 1876 we still had to make do with those clumsy swimming vehicles. The three carts needed two stage hands and one musical assistant each who, unseen by the audience, managed the whole business. Seidl was in charge of Woglinde's cart, while I and Fischer directed Wellgunde's and Flosshilde's vehicles. The precision and meticulousness with which Wagner conducted these rehearsals is indescribable. He was determined that every musical phrase in the orchestra should find its visual equivalent on the stage, so that an attentive student would have understood the principles of Wagnerian performance in the first rehearsals. The action on the stage is always the main thing and determines the manner in which the orchestra accompanies. (*Der Merker*, Vienna, July 1911: p. 9)

Lilli Lehmann sings Woglinde and she does not care at all for the swimming machinery. She remembers:

> When one considers that the Rhinemaidens were shunted around on the tops of specially manufactured swimming machines, squeezed into tight corsets, one might appreciate the physical effort which was

---

* Felix Mottl (1856–1911) conducted at Bayreuth from 1886 to 1906. Later he became opera director at Munich. Also a composer of operas, he made instrumental arrangements of four of the five *Wesendonck Lieder*.

The swimming machines in action

. . . as seen by the audience

required of us, quite apart from our musical performances.

(LL 235)

Richard Fricke, production assistant and maître de ballet, inspects the aquatic paraphernalia and has his doubts. He too keeps a diary:

26. 5.

I must admit I was greatly surprised, and I am not at all sure whether and to what extent the ladies will muster up courage and place themselves in

274

these cradles and – sing. Not that they would be unable to sing half standing, half lying, but they will be too scared to utter a sound. (FW 81)

The three Rhinemaidens view the machinery with dismay:

3.6.

'No,' says Lilli, 'nobody can expect that of me. This is out of the question. I have only just risen from my sick-bed, and I am always liable to get dizzy turns.' The other two kept quiet. 'Fräulein Marie,' I said, 'courage, just try it for once, and I bet your fear will grow less, as your pleasure in swimming increases.' The ladder is put in position, Brandt and I help her into the cradle. We fasten her belts, while she cries and squeaks, and the journey begins, slowly at first. Gradually her anxious expression gives way to smiles, and she says she is beginning to enjoy it. Now Lilli is determined to try, and, would you believe it, in a few seconds she has become quite intrepid. Frl. Lammert follows too, and all three swim and laugh delightedly. Now Wagner appears, and we go through the whole scene, without mishap, while the ladies sing beautifully. (FW 88–9)

Things improve by the hour. Flosshilde jokes, 'Mottl, do keep me steady, or I'll spit on your head.' Fricke reports:

4.6.

Swimming rehearsal half past seven in the evening, this time with the orchestra members watching from the stalls. After a few minutes there was loud applause. Wagner had placed flower bouquets in the swimming cradles. (FW 89–90)

At his rehearsals Wagner demonstrates gestures and movement to his singers. He leaps over cliffs, races up mountain tops and halts inches from a yawning abyss, terrifying soloists and orchestra. 'Do not fear,' he calms them down, 'I am used to standing on the brink of disaster.' Unfortunately, his Alberich, Carl Hill, will not obey instructions. Mottl relates:

Several times Wagner stepped inside the contraption which rushes Alberich at top speed from the summit of the cliff to the depth below, in order to put courage into the nervous Hill. (*Der Merker*, Vienna, July 1911: p. 10)

At last Hill undertakes the trip. He arrives at the bottom, bathed in sweat, where he finds a bottle of champagne which Wagner has placed there. The label reads RHEINGOLD.

*　　　*　　　*

A disturbing feature of Wagner's rehearsals is his unpredictability, as Fricke records:

> 15.6.
> Wagner was in great pain yesterday and was unable to attend the rehearsal. Schnappauf, his barber (who is also a Nibelung), told me that an abscess in Wagner's gums would have to be lanced in the afternoon.

> 17.6.
> The Master arrives, the rehearsals begin, and I knew beforehand what would happen. Wagner forgot his pain, jumped up the rocks and down again and completely changed everything we had arranged at the previous rehearsal. The doctor remarked, 'This will probably do him good. He works up a sweat and prescribes himself a kill-or-cure remedy.'
> (FW 100–2)

Since he is an experienced man of the theatre, he occasionally deletes stage directions which had seemed indispensable at his writing desk. He knows that animals on stage are liable to provoke disasters. Fricke notes:

> 17.6.
> Today the horse Grane joins the cast. Brünnhilde leads it, as directed, slowly along the rocky path. In the third scene (*Walküre*) in which Brünnhilde informs Siegmund that Hunding will kill him, Wagner found that the horse would distract the audience's attention from this highly important and indeed magnificent scene. . . . He says one could not exclude the possibility of an unforeseen incident disconcerting the animal and thus ruining the whole scene. So Brünnhilde enters alone and Grane stays away. (FW 102)

In spite of his painful dental operation Wagner continues cavorting nimbly up and down the stage. Fricke again:

> 17.6.
> It was highly instructive and comical to see what happened when Fräulein Scheffsky did not fling her arms with sufficient ardour round Siegmund's neck. Wagner demonstrated, and promptly the small composer clung to the tall Niemann's neck, almost causing the singer to stagger, with Wagner's feet hardly touching the ground. He sang Siegmund's passage, swung him around and said, 'This is where you

two change positions.' Then he let go, and when he passed me he remarked, 'The ladies don't like being too demonstrative – they think they might not get a husband.' At that moment Hunding launches out with his 'Wehwalt, Wehwalt, be on your guard!' Wagner comments, 'Good God, how that fellow bellows!' It was quite terrifying to witness

Ludwig Bechstein drawing of Wagner rehearsing Albert Niemann as Siegmund

how dynamically he directed the fight up there on the mountain top. Niemann turns away, 'For God's sake, let him come down. If he slips, we can all pack up.' But he did not slip. Like a mountain goat with a swollen face, bandaged in lint and cotton wool, he leapt down into the valley below. (FW 103)

The faithful Felix Mottl collides with Wagner's unpredictability:

On a particularly hot afternoon we rehearsed the first act of *Walküre*. It was my job to give the signal for the door to fly open. I noticed the Master pacing up and down the stage, as though he was looking for something, and I immediately asked him whether I could help him. He answered he would very much like to have a glass of beer. I ran across to the restaurant and soon returned proudly with the tankard in my hands. In the meantime the moment had arrived when the door should have sprung open but did not, since I was not there. When I appeared, the Master thundered, 'Have I engaged you as a waiter? Drink your stupid beer yourself!' (*Der Merker*, Vienna, July 1911: 10–11)

The Festspielhaus is entirely Wagner's conception. He procures the means for building it. He selects his artists and persuades them to serve him. He teaches them how to sing and to play Wagner. He is director, producer, coach, conductor, singer, actor, stage manager, stage hand and prompter. At rehearsals he copes with artistic shortcomings, technical obstacles and human failings by exercising his personal brand of diplomacy, laced with tantrums and flashes of charm. With the first performances of the *Ring* approaching, several of the leading artists, revelling in their indispensability, indulge in prima-donna posturings – petty jealousies, psychological throat conditions. At the beginning of each rehearsal Wagner asks, 'Is nobody leaving today?'

The technical apparatus is overtaxed. Steam is required for the cloud-capped mountains, for the caverns of Nibelheim, for the flying horses, for Mime's smithy, for the dragon, and much of it settles upon the orchestra where it puts the harps out of tune. One swims in the Rhine, one rides through the air, one plunges into the underworld, one turns into a dragon, into a toad, into another person, one becomes invisible. The cast list requires giants, dwarfs, rams, stallions, ravens, woodbirds and a bear. A rainbow bridge is needed, as well as a grand conflagration and a universal flood. All this looked feasible to the poet's imagination, but now it will have to look plausible on stage.

A formidable dragon has been commissioned from a London firm specialising in pantomime beasts. It can shuffle, writhe and rear up, it can roll its eyes and breathe steam and fire. Front, rump with tail, middle section with space for interior personnel, and neck are being transported by Channel steamer. Or should be transported. Shortly before the dress rehearsal Wagner sends a telegram to London, 'Why nowhere dragon? Urgently required!' Separate sections arrive, but several parts are missing. Wagner orders, 'The beast must be hidden in the background, so that the King will not notice that it has no head.' At last the head arrives, but without its neck. Fricke tells his diary:

9.8.

Another piece of the front has come, but I could not make head or tail of it. All I can see is that the 'zierliche Fresse' (its dainty jaws) is still missing. . . . Better that the dragon should stay away. To think it costs 500 pounds sterling! (FW 134–5)

The neck is nowhere to be found. Perhaps it went to Beirut! For the opening performance head and body are hastily stitched together. No wonder the Berlin critic Paul Lindau reports:

It is a huge monster . . . a cross between lizard and porcupine. (LNB 64)

After the first performance Wagner strikes a fatalistic note:

Our dragon was judged a bungled job, and nobody stopped to consider that we were forced to make do with an unfinished product. . . . At the last moment we had to decide to present our monster without its neck, which still lies undiscovered at one of the stations between London and Bayreuth. It certainly did look grotesque, with its head stuck to its enormous body. (GS X 111)

On 13 August Kaiser Wilhelm arrives at Bayreuth and watches the first performances of *Rheingold* and *Walküre*. He meets the composer and confesses to him, 'I did not believe you could achieve all this.' To give the Emperor a special surprise, Wagner asks Karl Runkwitz, who built the Festspielhaus, to illuminate the whole complex. Runkwitz recounts:

A special train brought the German Emperor, together with his daughter, the Grand Duchess of Baden. In honour of our illustrious guests I had arranged for the whole Festspielhaus to be illuminated. I gave instructions for several thousand clay dishes to be placed all along the ridges of the roof. These should have been dabbed with turpentine, in order to effect a swift ignition, but the workmen, meaning well, had soaked the clay dishes with the stuff. When the festivities began, the guests were horrified to witness not an illumination but a conflagration, which became uglier with every moment. Burning turpentine cascaded down the walls, licking flames and fire everywhere, the guests terror-struck, and a panic seemed unavoidable, with everybody about to flee from the festival hill. . . . So I rushed up to the roof, in my evening dress, found the main source of the blaze, and with the help of a few intrepid workmen, succeeded in dislodging the burning dishes from the roof. The disaster was averted in time, but the labour of four long, hard years could easily have gone up in smoke before our very eyes.

(SR 109–10)

By a strange coincidence, an ill-disposed journalist had already envisaged such a conflagration and had wished it, in the spring of 1875, on Wagner's head. Cosima records in her diary her discussion with Wagner of an article which had appeared in a clerical journal and which she now inserts between the pages of her diary:

Adversity which is held by all Christian believers to be the rod of God Almighty, will plague Bavaria, threatening ordeal by fire and water. Hail will destroy the harvest in many parts of the country, while torrential floods of water will lay waste numerous fields and meadows. It is in a town, however, that a dreadful calamity will occur. A huge structure will be erected, and countless onlookers will hurry there from far and wide. Music, song and glittering, vain pomp will beguile the senses of the curious. But one day, through an unfortunate accident, fire will break out at a time when the building is filled with thousands of people. It will spread with lightning speed, and the people will be seized with terror. Where a moment before sinful song and music had rung out, the despairing shrieks of the damned as in Hell will now resound. Hundreds will be trampled to death or burn alive and, picking one's way over the smoking rubble on the next day, each step will encounter charred bodies. The whole world will groan with horror at this frightful calamity which will cause bitter tears in most countries, even across the ocean. But the place where the ill-fated building had stood will serve the sinful indulgences of its voluptuaries no longer. A temple dedicated to God Almighty will be built there, as a memorial to the lost souls.

(CWT I 1230–1: 1.6.1875)

The Bayreuth structure, however, escapes destruction by pen or turpentine, and the sinful indulgences of the voluptuaries will not cease until the end of August 1876. Naturally a few mishaps do occur. Cosima complains in her diary:

13.8.1876

First performance of *Rheingold* under a wholly unlucky star. Betz loses the ring, runs twice into the wings during the curse, a stage hand raises the backdrop too soon at the change from the first to the second scene, and the audience can see men standing about in shirtsleeves and the rear wall of the theatre, all singers embarrassed, etc. etc. (CWT I 998)

By the end of the third cycle the press is on the whole cautious, but the public feel sure that they have witnessed something quite extraordinary. Bruckner, Liszt, Nietzsche and Saint-Saëns are there. So are Levi, Klindworth, Mathilde Maier, Judith Gautier, and Tchaikovsky, who declares:

> I must say that anyone who puts his faith in the civilising power of art, is bound to take away from Bayreuth a very positive impression of this marvellous artistic enterprise which – through its innate value and its effect on us – can be nothing less than a milestone in the history of art. . . . The Bayreuth Festival is also a lesson to those clandestine denigrators of art who so arrogantly believe that progressive people ought to occupy themselves with nothing other than that which is of immediate practical value. True, the Bayreuth Festival will not improve the material welfare of man, but the quest for artistic ideals will have benefited from it quite decisively. . . . That much is certain, that something has taken place at Bayreuth which our grandchildren and their children will still remember. (*Allgemeine Musik-Zeitung*, Berlin: March 1906)

The young Hubert Parry, future director, as Sir Hubert, of the Royal College of Music, visits the Festival, in spite of his teacher's dire warnings. George Alexander Macfarren, principal of the Royal Academy of Music, had tried to dissuade his former pupil:

> I am sorry you are going to Bayreuth, for every presence there gives countenance to the monstrous self-inflation. The principle of the thing is bad, the means for its realisation preposterous. An earthquake would be good that would swallow up the spot and everybody on it, so I wish you were away. (Percy A. Scholes: *The Mirror of Music*, London 1947: I, 254)

At the beginning of September artists and guests depart, and the inevitable anticlimax hits both the composer and his wife. Cosima observes:

> 9.9.1876
>
> In the evening we talk at length about the performances and what they have taught us. R. no longer wants the stalwarts Betz and Niemann. The former, infuriated at not being called before the curtain, made a downright travesty of his assignment! Brandt's achievements far short of what was expected! Richter not sure of a single tempo – all very

depressing experiences! . . . Costumes, scenery, everything must be reconsidered and redesigned for the repeat performances. R. is very sad, says he wants to die. (CWT I 1001–2)

Financially, the Bayreuth Festival is a disaster and, in view of the enormous deficit, a repeat in 1877 is immediately ruled out. A good deal of money, however, pours into the town where astute hoteliers and shopkeepers know how to beguile their customers. At a later festival, for instance, Café Sammet-Angermann offers:

Flosshilde Soup with Alberich Morsels   Wotan Ham à la Walhall
Stuffed breast of Swan à la Lohengrin   Siegmund Asparagus Spears
Nibelungen Dumplings   Siegfried Schnitzel
Rheingold Beer   (Richard-Wagner-Gedenkstätte, Bayreuth)

The firm of Moosdorf & Hochhäusler, bathroom equipment manufacturers, advertises:

'Wagalaweia, waving waters' – how many times have we admired those joyful Rhinemaidens' ditties in Wagner's incomparable *Rheingold*

while, in their natural state, they frolicked in the billowing waters. As for ourselves, we travel to the seaside in summer and let the invigorating spray splash all over us. But to do that we have to leave home and do without our home comforts, in order to enjoy bathing in the foaming waves. All this has now been remedied. A cleverly constructed bathtub provides the bather with the most splendid self-induced cascades of water. With the help of only a few buckets of water you can easily produce the wildest tidal flow, by gripping the upper end of the bathtub and making it rock back and forth. 'Wagalaweia, waving waters' – amidst the rushing and splashing of the water you seem to hear Wagnerian chords. Consider, the complete appliance costs just forty marks. It will not be long before every house has its own WAVEMAKER BATHTUB, when everybody can chant his joyful 'Wagalaweia, waving waters.' Wagalaweia! (*Illustrirte Zeitung*, Leipzig and Berlin: 20.4.1895)

Festival fever, banquets, the general hullabaloo – Friedrich Nietzsche does not like it at all:

My mistake was to come to Bayreuth with an ideal, so the result was bitter disenchantment. . . . It was my lot to see that even those who were intimately involved in the proceedings lost sight of the 'ideal' and regarded extraneous things as more important, more worthy of their fancy. And then that wretched pack of patrons and patronesses, flirtatious, bored to death and as unmusical as an alley cat. . . . All Europe's idle vagabonds were there. (WN 230)

So it is 'with an ideal' that Nietzsche goes to Bayreuth. He intends to get to the bottom of this complex *Ring* tetralogy which seems to be part opera, part drama, part mystery play, part allegorical cosmology. But Nietzsche turns away from Bayreuth and from Wagner, because the trappings – the search for food, the foolish small talk, the women's jewellery, the men's medals – irritate his susceptible nature, foiling his search for the revolutionary aspect of the work.

Revolutionary? Wagner constantly stresses this idea and has built his own stage to realise it. A stage which rejects the kind of entertainment which conservative audiences expect – a stage which offers instead fundamental self-confrontation. Look, says the score of the *Ring*, this is the world, and this is how it all began.

This is you, and this is what you have done to the world, because you did not love your fellow beings. Only the century that saw the splitting of the atom can fully comprehend the events on the stage, can find there its own predicaments. Yet the final holocaust can be avoided. Wotan, hungry for power, and Brünnhilde, all love, both perish in the cosmic catastrophe, yet the tetralogy ends with a theme which transcends the individual claims of both love and power, by symbolising the timeless power of love. Since the days of Aeschylus no artist has dared to unsettle his audience to this degree, to confront it with its aspirations and its transgressions, and at the same time to hold out the possibility of a future which might yet prove to man that the intrinsic perfection of the cosmic design only needs man's co-operation to secure his survival and ultimate happiness.

It takes six years until the Festspielhaus can reopen in the summer of 1882. Wagner has only seven months left, but he lives to see *Parsifal*, his final work. Its conductor, Hermann Levi, writes to his father, chief rabbi in Giessen:

Hermann Levi

12.3.1882

Do not worry about my salary in Bayreuth. It will all work out. Our orchestra members get 250 marks per month, free travel, and board and lodging. I shall ask for 500 marks, for that is all I need, and I do not wish to make a profit out of Bayreuth. (HL 9)

Can a Jew trust Wagner, asks the rabbi. Levi reassures him:

13.4.1882

Wagner is the best and noblest of men. . . . I thank God daily for the privilege to be close to such a man. It is the most beautiful experience of my life. (HL 9)

Levi is deeply moved by *Parsifal*, by Wagner, by the whole Bayreuth atmosphere. He tells his father:

July 1882

The rehearsals are in full swing and promise a stupendous performance. You cannot imagine what I had to go through until the cast had been finalised and until the Meister expressed his satisfaction with me. The orchestra is incredibly beautiful. 32 violins, 12 celli, 12 violas. The chorus, too, is fine. All this week we rehearsed the first act. Tonight is the first full dress rehearsal. The Wagners are so good to me that I am quite touched. I arrived here on June 12th and from that day until July 1st I have lunched and dined every day at Wahnfried. Frequently I called at 12 noon and only left at midnight. Apart from me there were two other daily guests, Joukovsky, a painter who has designed the scenery and who is a great friend of mine, and the young Baron Stein, lecturer in philosophy at Halle. In the evenings the Meister read to us, and we had the most absorbing discussions. Never have I lived through a happier period than those 3 weeks. Now, however, things are rather different. At 9 in the morning I walk to the theatre which is half an hour's walk from the town, and return at 8 in the evening. I lunch at the restaurant which is next to the theatre, then I sleep for an hour, but the rest is work. 3 hours with the orchestra, 3 hours with the singers, and a further 3 hours for meetings and discussions with the technical staff and the chorus master. (HL 9–10)

At the conclusion of a triumphant festival season Levi informs his father:

31.8.1882

After the performance two days ago I collapsed, slept all through the next day and today until one o'clock – really slept, in bed –, have just finished lunch with Wagners and am now feeling myself again. The final performance was magnificent. During the transformation music

*Joukovsky used a squared
pad of Cosima's to do
this sketch of Wagner
on the day before
the composer's death.
It is captioned
'Wagner reading'*

the Meister appeared in the pit, twisted and turned his way up to my desk, took the baton from my hand and conducted the performance to the end. I remained by his side, because I was afraid he might slip up, but my fears were quite groundless – his conducting was so assured that he might have been nothing but a Kapellmeister all his life. At the end the audience burst into applause which defies all description. But the Meister did not show himself and remained with us musicians, cracking feeble jokes. When after 10 minutes the noise in the audience showed no signs of abating, I shouted, 'Quiet! Quiet!', at the top of my voice. This was heard above, they really calmed down, and then the Meister began to speak from the conductor's desk, first to me and to the orchestra, then – with the curtain raised – to the whole cast and the technical staff who were assembled on stage. The Meister spoke with such warmth that everybody was reduced to tears – it was an unforgettable moment! (HL 11)

In the November of that year Levi stays with the Wagner family in Venice and he reports to his father:

It was wonderful in Venice. I went daily to him in the Palazzo Vendramin, arriving at 11 in the morning and leaving at 11 at night, had all meals with them, joined in the gondola outings, and every day we visited a different church. In short, I was intoxicated with sheer joy. Therefore I refuse even to consider whether I deserve an order or any other kind of recognition for *Parsifal*. As for my 'prestige', I have plenty of that and I feel, as I have already mentioned, that I am far too well off as it is. Moreover, I have no idea what award they could give me. The Order of Merit is the appropriate award of the Bavarian crown, but that might be rather awkward, considering my name is Levi. (HL 11)

Wagner dies in Venice on 13 February 1883, and two days later Hermann Levi sends his father a heavy-hearted letter:

Bechstein drawing of Wagner's funeral procession as it passes the old opera house in Bayreuth

287

15.2.1883

In my dreadful, indescribable grief you are in my loving thoughts. Future generations will realise what he was to the world and what the world has lost in him. It was my good fortune to see him 24 hours before his death . . . he was in a most cheerful mood, as we strolled in the procession of masked revellers on the piazza as late as midnight. He led the way with his daughter Isolde, striding with the liveliness of a young man . . . it was a glorious night, and at 1 o'clock we drove home. The following day the Meister complained that he was not feeling well and did not appear at the dinner table, but the day after . . . he was quite well again. . . . On Monday midday I left Venice, the Meister accompanied me to the stairs, kissed me several times – I was much moved – and 24 hours later!! (HL 12–13)

The 1883 Bayreuth Festival takes place without its founder, but his *Parsifal* is in good hands. The Giessen rabbi rejoices in his son's enthusiasm when he reads:

7.8.1883

I do not think I have ever known such happiness. When I look back at this glorious period in my life, I find that from the first hour of the first rehearsal to the dying away of the last note of the final performance my mood has been one of solemn elation. Everything worked out well; I cannot remember even the slightest annoyance; the outward success was in keeping with my own deep satisfaction; my enchantment with this most glorious, most sublime of all works intensified from performance to performance, and so did my pride in being summoned to be its interpreter. (HL 14)

Six years later, at the end of another festival season, Levi's confession to his father echoes the feelings of countless Bayreuth visitors, from that century to ours:

16.8.1889

The Festspiele, alas, are over! It will not be easy to find my way back into the world. (HL 22)

ENVOI

The Prelude to *Tristan und Isolde* reminds me of the old Italian painting of a martyr whose intestines are slowly unwound from his body on a reel.

Eduard Hanslick, 1868

I am a mixture of Hamlet and Don Quixote.

Richard Wagner, 1878

Richard Wagner lives in Zurich, not only in ostentatious luxury, but he also purchases the most valuable articles such as gold watches, at great expense. His apartment is filled with very handsome furniture and carpets, and decorated with silk curtains and fine chandeliers. . . . The public's belief in his music of the future is fading rapidly, while the conviction is growing that his works, though brilliantly orchestrated, are devoid of soul and of melody. What there is of the latter, he is thought to have stolen.

Confidential report on Wagner's
life in Switzerland by the
Vienna Police, 1854

Is Wagner human at all? Is he not rather a disease? Whatever he touches he infects. He has made music sick. . . . Only sick music makes money nowadays. Our big theatres thrive on Wagner.

Friedrich Nietzsche, 1888

I have observed that his [the young Hans von Bülow's] love of art, especially of music, is not a passing whim. It is the result of his great and quite exceptional talent. . . . I am certain that after this testimony you will share your son's desire to devote himself entirely to music. . . . You might object that your son should at least finish his education as a law student, so that he could pursue that career, in case the musical one should prove to be profitless. In this I would recognise your motherly love and care, but I must beg you to let me object that I consider such thinking as injurious for the development of your son's character and career, and for the continuation of a fruitful, secure and loving relationship between son and mother. . . . I am certain that you, too, consider distrust to be the root of all evil. If you were to show your son this lack of confidence now of all times, by insisting on your authority as a mother, that he return to a course of study which he abhors with all his heart, you would destroy his appetite for any kind of study, since a law career finds him totally indifferent, and thus he would never be able to reap the slightest material advantages from it. . . . Please allow your son to stay with me in Zurich for the next six winter months, in order to study conducting under my supervision. . . . So will you gain the satisfaction of seeing your son become a competent and possibly a great artist. You will have given the world a happy, confident individual, and you will have won and continue to retain the precious gift of truly heartfelt filial love!   Wagner to Franziska von Bülow, 1850

Just now I am undecided whether to shoot myself or not. My wife had rather I didn't. . . . In Germany, they give my *Tannhäuser* from time to time. . . . Here, I only give myself, and people don't like *him* very much. Neither do I.   Wagner to Frl. Ritter, 1852

Our impression is that the overture to *Tannhäuser* is one of the most curious pieces of patchwork ever passed off by self-delusion for a complete and significant creation. . . . In London, we repeat, he fails to make any converts; either as a conductor or composer.

Athenaeum, 1855

I do not suffer because my *Tannhäuser* has failed, or because the critics belittle my achievements. Oh no! My agony is of another kind. It is rooted in my own works.   Richard Wagner to King Ludwig, 1865

We cannot refrain from making a protest against the worship of animal passion which is so striking a feature in the later works of Wagner. We grant there is nothing so repulsive in *Tristan* as in *Die Walküre*, but the system is the same. The passion is unholy in itself and its representation is impure, and for those reasons we rejoice in believing that such works will not become popular. If they did we are certain their tendency would be mischievous, and there is, therefore, some cause for congratulation in the fact that Wagner's music, in spite of all its wondrous skill and power, repels a greater number than it fascinates.

The Era, on the first performance in England of *Tristan und Isolde*, at Drury Lane Theatre, 1882

So there I sat in the topmost gallery of the Berlin Opera House, and from the first sound of the cellos my heart contracted spasmodically. . . . Never before had my soul been so deluged with floods of sound and passion, never had my heart been consumed by such yearning and sublime bliss. . . . A new epoch had begun: Wagner was my god, and I wanted to become his prophet.

The young music student Bruno Walter, after hearing his first *Tristan und Isolde*, 1889

I have just conducted my first *Tristan*.
It was the most wonderful day of my life.

Richard Strauss to Cosima Wagner, 1892

Let us not beat about the bush. In *Tristan und Isolde* sensual pleasure is glorified with every kind of titillating device. . . . We think that the stage presentation of the poem *Tristan und Isolde* amounts to an act of indecency. Wagner does not show us the life of the heroes of Nordic sagas which would edify and strengthen the spirit of his German audiences. What he does present is the ruination of the life of heroes through sensuality.

Allgemeine Musikalische Zeitung, 1865

He has used music as a drug, as an intoxicant, as a philosophy of life. This is a phenomenon unknown before his time in the history of music and of culture. Its consequences were fatal.

Hartmut Zelinsky, 1982

This is infamous!

> Schopenhauer, in the margin of his *Walküre* libretto, 1854

A man like you, one who has no peers, who stands apart from the multitude, who belongs to an order different from the common and trivial kind – how could such a man ever have friends? One looks *at* friends, but one looks *up* at you. For instance, I – who consider myself a tolerably decent fellow – would rather be your bootboy or your factotum than be impudent enough to expect you to call me friend.

> Hans von Bülow to Wagner, 1859

There is no need for me to repeat that I have ceased long ago to swear by Wagner's words and to take them for gospel truth. It hurts me to learn that, in addition to his graceless and unfriendly behaviour, he can also play the hypocrite. . . . Wagner must be treated like a great potentate who is somewhat ill and therefore not accountable.

> Hans von Bülow to Franz Liszt, 1859

This century has produced three famous men, Napoleon, Bismarck and Wagner, and none of them should be made answerable for their behaviour, or indeed for anything.

> Hans von Bülow, 1883

Wagner's music awakens the swine rather than the angel. It is the music of a demented eunuch.

> *Figaro*, Paris 1876

His and all other decent and great Germans' way of thinking transcends the purely German, while his art speaks not to nations but to people.

> Friedrich Nietzsche, 1876

After *Lohengrin*, I had a splitting headache, and all night I dreamt about a goose.

> Mily Balakirev, 1868

Truth to tell these old gods and heroes, these giants and dwarfs, were most abominable creatures, and nothing can be more immoral, more repulsive, more absolutely wicked than some of their doings, and not all the artistic skill of Wagner can make them otherwise. When we say that the principal hero is the offspring of an incestuous union with a brother and sister we ask if the modern stage, or indeed the stage at any period, ever witnessed a more horrible and revolting subject; and this is in no way softened down, for the glow and fervour of the music simply intensifies the scenes in which the hero and heroine appear. . . . There is no mistake about it, no excuse that the relationship is unknown, for the hero openly requests Sieglinde to become 'his sister and his bride', which the lady consents to without the slightest hesitation, and the climax of the first act is when the guilty and incestuous pair agree to fly at once; the act closing with a duet, the music of which is evidently written to suggest animal passion in its utmost excess. . . . A composer must have lost all sense of decency and all respect for the dignity of human nature who could thus employ his genius and skill to heighten and render more effective a situation which should never again, if our authorities exert their power, be witnessed upon the English stage.

> *The Era*, reporting on the first *Ring*
> in England, at Her Majesty's Theatre, 1882

I like Wagner's music better than anybody's. It's so loud that one can talk the whole time without other people hearing what one says.

> Oscar Wilde (*The Picture of Dorian Gray*), 1891

Suffering and great as his century, the nineteenth whose perfect manifestation he is, the spirit of Richard Wagner stands before my eyes. . . . Wagner the mythologist, the discoverer of the myth as a basis for his operas, the saviour of opera through the myth. . . . He makes us believe that music is made for nothing else but to be mythology's handmaiden, nor could it ever again have any other purpose.

> Thomas Mann (*Leiden und Grösse*
> *der Meister*), 1935

After ten o'clock they began upon that terrible Wagner music, and for nearly an hour they kept at it with intense effort, till many of the audience, finding Wagner worse than caviar, and as indigestible as lobster salad, left in a gradually increasing stream. If we are permitted to express a plain opinion about Wagner, it is music with a stomach ache. It has knots and cramps and spasms, increasing in violence suddenly and subsiding as quickly, but never quite coming to a state of internal rest. The contortions are simply awful and exhibit all the symptoms of musical colic verging on cholera morbus.

Commercial (Cincinnati), 1880

Of all the bête, clumsy, blundering, boggling, baboon-blooded stuff I ever saw on a human stage . . . and of all the affected, sapless, soulless, beginningless, endless, topless, bottomless, topsiturviest, tongs and boniest doggerel of sounds I ever endured the deadliness of, that eternity of nothing was the deadliest, as far as the sound went. I never was so relieved, so far as I can remember in my life, by the stopping of any sound – not excepting railway whistles – as I was by the cessation of the cobbler's bellowing.

John Ruskin, on *Meistersinger*, 1882

Die Meistersinger is the most German of his music dramas. It is the incarnation of our national tradition pure and simple. It contains everything in which the soul of German culture moves and has its being. It brilliantly combines German sobriety, German romanticism, German pride, German industry and German humour.

Joseph Goebbels, 1933

Wagner is the antidote par excellence for all that is German.

Friedrich Nietzsche, 1888

Wagner begins by praising the last period of Beethoven, and combines this music with the mystical theory of Schopenhauer, which is just as silly as Beethoven's music, and then, in accordance with his theory, he writes his own music, in connection with a still falser system of uniting all the arts. And after Wagner come still newer imitators, departing still further from art – Brahms, Richard Strauss and others.

Leon Tolstoy, 1896

In the final duet between Octavian and Sophie [*Der Rosenkavalier*] you have circumscribed my metrical freedom by prescribing your own metre, though I actually quite like to be tied to a set melody which I find somehow Mozartian and quite different from Wagner's insufferable erotic screaming.

Hugo von Hofmannsthal to
Richard Strauss, 1910

No matter how painstakingly I study the scores of *Tristan* and of *Meistersinger* at home, I always find new aspects in them. As for *Parsifal* and the *Ring*, I must have heard them some fifty times (usually when rehearsing and conducting them myself) . . . yet every time I discover new beauties and new revelations.

Richard Strauss, 1940

This helmet is a very common article in our streets, where it generally takes the form of a tall hat. It makes a man invisible as a shareholder, and changes him into various shapes, such as a pious Christian, a subscriber to hospitals, a benefactor of the poor, a model husband and father, a shrewd, practical, independent Englishman, and what not, when he is really a pitiful parasite on the commonwealth, consuming a great deal, and producing nothing, feeling nothing, knowing nothing, believing nothing, and doing nothing except what all the rest do.

George Bernard Shaw, on the
Tarnhelm, the magic helmet of
invisibility, change of appearance
and instantaneous transportation
(*Rheingold* and *Götterdämmerung*), 1898

The last chords of *Götterdämmerung* coincided with my feeling of liberation from captivity.

Piotr Ilyich Tchaikovsky, 1876

Wagner was not a Schopenhauerite every day in the week, nor even a Wagnerite. His mind changes as often as his mood. . . . Wagner can be quoted against himself almost without limit, much as Beethoven's adagios could be quoted against his scherzos if a dispute arose between two fools as to whether he was a melancholy man or a merry one.

George Bernard Shaw, 1908

I was in Bayreuth for three days to hear *Parsifal* and *Tristan und Isolde*. . . . Sunday *Parsifal*. Began at four o'clock. Cloudburst between three and four, of course. Took a cab for two marks, though I lodge near by. Into the Festspielhaus, trousers tucked into socks, damp and cold, smell of washing on line. Fifteen hundred people inside, house full. I am beginning to feel peculiar. All doors locked. Utter darkness, except dim light through curtain, just as in *Macbeth*, when King Duncan is murdered. But now the tubas begin to blow, as though the Day of Judgement had come. I feel even more peculiar, and at the end of the overture I know – another two minutes and I shall faint or drop dead. I get up. Since I was the last of forty in my row, I have to make my way out the same way. . . . The whole exhausting business has cost me one hundred marks, but I have no regrets. To have seen Bayreuth, its festival season and its Wagner worship has been worth the trouble.

Theodor Fontane to friend, 1889

I have just come out of *Parsifal*. If only you were here, even though we were not able to have this overwhelming experience together. . . . No words can describe the immensely invigorating and at the same time shattering experience this work has made on me. It would be idle to try and tell you of this music. All I can say is that I need you now more than ever, to help me bear this great, this greatest experience. . . . I have now crept back into my room and shall take the *Parsifal* score to bed with me, and continue the hosannas of this day.

Alban Berg to his fiancée, 1909

Wagner's artistic judgement was as sure, as his personal judgement was erratic. Such a confusion between inner and outer reality occurs to all of us, but too much of it leads to the borders of insanity or beyond. Not that Wagner was insane; but there were times when he could hardly have tried his contemporaries more sorely if he had been. His megalomania was a burden to them and still more to himself; but there can be very little doubt that we owe to it Wagner's ability to carry through so prodigious a feat of concentrated insight and creativeness.

Robert Donington (*Wagner's Ring and Its Symbols*), 1963

My dear little Myrrha,
You have sent me a truly wonderful copybook letter. I wish I could write so beautifully, but I fear I am too old for that. Yes, I too wept with you for your dear little brother Guido who died last year. When you visit him and bring him flowers, give him my love. I am very pleased that your youngest brother Karl is growing so well. Don't worry if he does not have Guido's face. Just take him for another Guido all the same. You see, when it comes to really important things like laughing or crying, one face is as good as another. Since you have invited me so prettily to visit you, I really will come soon, and then we can continue discussing these matters. Now promise to work hard at your reading, so that you can make out my untidy writing without help. This way we two can conduct a regular correspondence.

Wagner writes to a child, 1859

I will agree to your decorating the title SYMPHONY IN D MINOR with a few ornamental patterns, but no more. My name is to be left quite plain. . . . But the name [of the dedicatee] RICHARD WAGNER must be illuminated in gold, simple but dignified.

> Anton Bruckner to the designer of
> the title page of his Symphony No. 3, 1872

SIEGFRIED
(*alone in the forest, he has
just learned that Mime is not
his father*)

What was my father like?
I suppose, like myself.
If Mime had sired a son,
Would he not look
Like his father?
Just as gruesome,
Grisly and grey,

Stooping and small,
Hunchbacked, hobbling,
With dangling ears
And drivelling eyes –
Off with the imp!
I've seen the last of him.

I'd love to know
What my mother was like.
Alas, that
Is hard to imagine.
A roe-deer, perhaps,
Lucid and light,
Has such eyes when they sparkle;
Only far fairer.
In bitter fear she bore me;
But why did she have to die?
Must all mothers perish,
That their sons may
Have their lives?
That would be sad indeed.
The son longs to look
On his mother's likeness.
My own mother,
A mortal wife.

Siegfried, Act Two

SOURCES AND ABBREVIATIONS

ASB *Richard Wagner: Ausgewählte Schriften und Briefe* (Selection of Writings and Letters), ed. A. Lorenz, 2 vols, Berlin 1938

BB *Bayreuther Briefe* (Letters from Bayreuth), ed. C. Fr. Glasenapp, Berlin/Leipzig 1907

BMV *Wagner: Dokumentarbiographie* (Documentary Biography), ed. H. Barth, D. Mack, and E. Voss, Vienna 1975

BP *Bayreuth Programmhefte* (Bayreuth Festival Programme Booklets)

BRC *Der Briefwechsel Richard und Cosima Wagner* (Correspondence between Richard and Cosima Wagner), ed. M. Eger, BP *Das Rheingold* and *Die Walküre*, 1979

BWL *Briefwechsel zwischen Wagner und Liszt* (Correspondence between Wagner and Liszt), 2 vols, Leipzig 1900

CWB *Cosima Wagners Briefe an ihre Tochter Daniela von Bülow* (Cosima Wagner's Letters to her Daughter Daniela von Bülow), ed. M. von Waldberg, Stuttgart/Berlin 1933

CWT Cosima Wagner: *Die Tagebücher* (The Diaries), 2 vols, ed. M. Gregor-Dellin and D. Mack, Munich/Zurich 1976–7

CWZ *Cosima Wagner, Das zweite Leben* (Cosima Wagner, The Second Life), 1883 to 1930, ed. D. Mack, Munich/Zurich 1980

DB *Richard Wagner: Das braune Buch* (The Brown Book), ed. J. Bergfeld, Zurich/Freiburg i. Br. 1975

EL Wm. Ashton Ellis: *Life of Richard Wagner*, 6 vols, London 1900–8

EW E. Wille: *15 Briefe von Richard Wagner* (15 Letters of Richard Wagner), Berlin 1894

FB *Familienbriefe von Richard Wagner* (Family Letters of Richard Wagner), ed. C. Fr. Glasenapp, Berlin 1907

FH F. Herzfeld: *Minna Planer*, Leipzig 1938

FW R. Fricke: *Richard Wagner auf der Probe* (Richard Wagner Rehearses), Stuttgart 1983

FZ M. Fehr: *Richard Wagners Schweizer Zeit* (Richard Wagner's Time in Switzerland), 2 vols, Aarau/Leipzig 1934 and Aarau/Frankfurt 1953

GS Richard Wagner: *Gesammelte Schriften und Dichtungen* (Collected Writings and Poems), ed. W. Golther, 10 vols, Berlin/Leipzig/Vienna/Stuttgart n.d.

GW *Gedichte von Richard Wagner* (Poems by Richard Wagner), ed. C. Fr. Glasenapp, Berlin 1905

HB *Hans von Bülow, Neue Briefe* (New Letters), ed. R. Graf Du Moulin Eckart, Munich 1927

HL *Hermann Levi an seinen Vater* (Hermann Levi to his Father), *unveröffentlichte Briefe aus Bayreuth* (unpublished letters from Bayreuth), BP *Parsifal*, Bayreuth 1959

HR *Richard Wagner: Briefe an Hans Richter* (Letters to Hans Richter), ed. L. Karpath, Berlin/Vienna/Leipzig 1924

JD   J. Deathridge: *Wagner und sein erster Lehrmeister* (Wagner and His First Teacher), Bavarian State Opera Programme Booklet: *Die Meistersinger von Nürnberg*, Munich 1979

JG   *Die Briefe Richard Wagners an Judith Gautier* (The Letters of Richard Wagner to Judith Gautier), ed. W. Schuh, Zurich/Leipzig 1936

JR   *Richard Wagner: Briefe an Frau Julie Ritter* (Richard Wagner's letters to Frau Julie Ritter), ed. S. von Hausegger, Munich 1920

KB   L. Karpath: *Zu den Briefen Richard Wagners an eine Putzmacherin* (On Richard Wagner's Letters to a Milliner), n.d. (1906?)

KL   *König Ludwig II und Richard Wagner Briefwechsel* (Correspondence between King Ludwig II and Richard Wagner), ed. O. Strobel, 5 vols, Karlsruhe 1936–9

KM   A. Kohut: *Der Meister von Bayreuth* (The Master of Bayreuth), Berlin 1905

KRW   E. Kretzschmar: *Richard Wagner*, Berlin 1939

KWP   L. Kusche: *Wagner und die Putzmacherin* (Wagner and the Milliner): Wilhelmshaven 1967

LL   Lilly Lehmann: *Mein Weg* (My Way), Leipzig 1913

LNB   P. Lindau: *Nüchterne Briefe aus Bayreuth* (Sober Letters from Bayreuth), Breslau 1876

LS   L. Strecker: *Richard Wagner als Verlagsgefährte* (Richard Wagner's Collaboration with His Publisher), Mainz 1951

LWV   W. Lange: *Richard Wagner und seine Vaterstadt Leipzig* (Richard Wagner and his Home Town Leipzig), Leipzig 1921

MB   Marie von Bülow: *Hans von Bülow*, Stuttgart 1925

MEC   R. Graf Du Moulin Eckart: *Cosima Wagner*, 2 vols, Munich/Berlin, 1929/31

MEH   R. Graf Du Moulin Eckart: *Hans von Bülow*, Munich 1921

ML   Richard Wagner: *Mein Leben* (My Life), 2 vols, ed. M. Gregor-Dellin, Munich 1969

MM   *Richard Wagner an Mathilde Maier* (Richard Wagner to Mathilde Maier), ed. H. Scholz, Leipzig 1930

NW   O. Strobel: *Neue Wagner-Forschungen* (Recent Wagner Research), Karlsruhe 1943

OD   Otto Daube: *Ich schreibe keine Symphonien mehr* (I shall write no more Symphonies), Cologne 1960

OW   *Briefe Richard Wagners an Otto Wesendonck* (Letters of Richard Wagner to Otto Wesendonck), ed. W. Golther, Berlin 1905

PP   D. & M. Petzet: *Die Richard Wagner-Bühne König Ludwigs II* (The Richard Wagner Stage of King Ludwig II), Munich 1970

RD   R. Donington: *Wagner's 'Ring' and Its Symbols*, London 1963

RF   R. Fricke: *Bayreuth vor dreissig Jahren* (Bayreuth Thirty Years Ago), Dresden 1906

RWF   *Richard Wagner an Freunde und Zeitgenossen* (Richard Wagner's Letters to Friends and Acquaintances), ed. E. Kloss, Berlin/Leipzig 1909

RWM   *Richard Wagner an Minna Wagner* (Richard Wagner to Minna Wagner), 2 vols, Berlin/Leipzig 1908

RWW   *Richard Wagner an Mathilde Wesendonck* (Richard Wagner to Mathilde Wesendonck), ed. W. Golther, Berlin 1904

SB   *Die Sammlung Burrell: Richard Wagner Briefe* (The Burrell Collection: Richard Wagner Letters), ed. J. Burk, Frankfurt 1953

SBNF   Robert Schumanns Briefe, Neu Folge, ed. F. G. Jansen, Leipzig 1904

SR   S. Rützow: *Richard Wagner und Bayreuth* (Richard Wagner and Bayreuth), Munich 1943

UFH   *Richard Wagner: Briefe an Theodor Uhlig, Wilhelm Fischer, Ferdinand Heine* (Wagner's Letters to Uhlig, Fischer and Heine), Leipzig 1888

WB   *Richard Wagner Briefe* (Richard Wagner Letters), ed. H. Kesting, Munich/Zurich 1983

WK   *Richard Wagner an seine Künstler* (Richard Wagner to his Artists), ed. E. Kloss, Berlin/Leipzig 1908

WN   F. Würzbach: *Nietzsche*, Munich 1966

WR   W. Reich: *Richard Wagner*, Olten 1948

WSB   *Richard Wagner: Sämtliche Briefe* (Collected Letters), 4 vols at present, ed. G. Strobel and W. Wolf, Leipzig/Mainz 1967–79

ZH   *Zwei unveröffentlichte Briefe an Robert von Hornstein* (Two unpublished Letters to Robert von Hornstein), ed. F. von Hornstein, Munich 1911

INDEX